O D Y S S E Y

VICTIM TO VICTORY

Jennifer Elizabeth Masters

This book is dedicated to those of you
who have spent a lifetime looking outside of yourself for love.
Look no further.
Not only is it within your reach,
but it is that spark of God within you.

Contents

Disclaimer

The author of this book does not presume to offer therapy or advocate the use of any technique for the treatment of specific traumatic psychological conditions or other mental concerns. The intent of the author is to offer her personal perspective and experience for the purpose of assisting you on your journey. This book is provided to offer new ways of seeing and living in the world. If you use any information as a form of therapy, the author and publisher assumes no responsibility for your actions.

Self conquest is the greatest of all victories.

— Plato

Introduction

Some people are born under a lucky star. For reasons unknown to us, their lives appear balanced and in harmony. They seem to live their lives consciously without the pain and suffering others go through. They manage to get through school and land decent jobs. They make money as well as invest and save successfully. They may encounter challenges throughout their lives but for the most part life goes along relatively smoothly accepting their individual responsibility. Their lives are not wrought with struggle, pain and suffering. They meet someone, fall in love in an ever deepening relationship and live an almost fairytale life filled with bliss and joy. They really enjoy each other's company and truly love one another. They treat each other with respect and have a deep sense of commitment to one another. They have issues and problems, but there is an awareness and they are able to talk through their issues calmly. They honor, love and support each other while they are on their journey accepting each other as they are. As alarming as this may seem to the rest of us, to the 2% of the population, this is not a fairytale, this is their life.

Others are not so lucky. In spite of our best intentions, we fall in love with Mr. or Mrs. Right and marry; sometimes for the wrong reasons. We often discover later that there is a side of our partner we did not realize was there. Some saw the signs beforehand but made excuses for the behavior that they witnessed. We chose to ignore the signs thinking that the red warning flags waving in our faces were a parade instead. When the honeymoon is over, we wake up to reality and find what seems like "Mr. or Mrs. Wrong" is lying in bed next to us. We find ourselves in fear and wonder what have I done? Some of us end up feeling like a victim of an abusive or emotionally withholding relationship. Our partners are emotionally unavailable.

We end one relationship waiting years before we find and marry again. Then we find the perfect partner, thinking that surely this must be the one! Only to discover we have replicated our previous relationship. With each successive relationship that challenges us, the stakes seem to be raised higher and higher only this time it is worse in so many ways. The face and name may have changed, however the relationship and abuse remains.

After seeking counseling, therapy and thousands of hours of healing sessions, hypnotherapy, Emotional Freedom Technique (EFT) or Neurolinguistic Programming (NLP) some people have relationship after relationship with the same issues. They marry again and again, only to find out that they have married a gambler, philanderer, an addict, alcoholic or control freak and find themselves being abused all over again. Why do some of us keep attracting the wrong mates, who turn out to be angry and abusive partners? Why is it so difficult to change our patterns and beliefs? How can we ever hope to have a healthy, happy emotionally balanced and supportive relationship?

These are some of the questions that I asked myself for decades. I often felt embarrassment and shame about my life and my relationships. After a lifetime of personal reflection, searching for answers and self-healing, I have found the answers to these questions and many others. From the beginning of my life I felt small, dependent and ugly, less than everyone around me. I was a victim and a people pleaser, a chameleon, like a quick-change artist becoming whomever and whatever you wanted me to be in any given moment. Through the process of my self-discovery of who Jennifer really was, I delved into the depths of darkness and despair uncovering shame and guilt for events I could not possibly be blamed. Layer by layer I discovered my true self and found an inner beauty and Divine being along with inner peace and causeless joy. I found peace and happiness in being alone, without needing a partner to lean on or support me. I became empowered. From poverty to riches and back, to living my Divine Purpose in the flow of the Universe, I give a step-by-step account of my life and the path that brought me to the ultimate place of living in peace, joy, unconditional love, infinite freedom and prosperity.

Due to the content of this book and the very personal issues discussed, I have changed the names of the players to protect those involved. My purpose is to use my life experience to help others who have had similar issues and can't seem to get beyond the pain and suffering. Whether my story is similar to yours, or someone you know, this book will help to bring clarity and understanding as well as healing to you through my experiences. Perhaps you have stood in judgment of another, or you complain, gossip or have married and divorced multiple times. Perhaps you felt there was something seriously wrong with them or you. You may know that something is missing in your life and you wanted more. Maybe you are an employer and you want to have a better understanding of one or more of your employees and why they do the things they do. This book will assist you to come to a place of compassion instead of judgment, joy instead of fear and prosperity instead of lack and limitation.

This book has been encoded with Divine Light and high vibrational frequencies. There is a healing within the pages of this book for anyone who takes the time to read it. Feel free to check out the calibration of my work. The majority of the pages vibrate at 775 or above. I have been told that there is a less than 1% error rate with the help of The Ascended Masters, my angels, guides and loved ones on the other side, and most of all, The Divine. I was called to write this book as a vehicle to be of assistance to others. It is with that Divine purpose that it has been written.

I mention the calibration and use Dr. David Hawkins book *Power vs. Force*, throughout this book to show the vibration of specific emotions or feelings. He has calibrated the energies of various human states of consciousness from the lowest being shame to enlightenment, to that of Jesus, who vibrated at 1,000. I utilize the chart of consciousness levels with his permission.

The level of my consciousness in each stage of my life is shown on the last page of most chapters as well as the level of consciousness I am at now. For this reason I have included the chart for your reference. Raising our consciousness is why we are here. I highly recommend it as a powerful tool to raise awareness of your own state. Once you become aware of something it cannot stay the same. It has to change.

As I became more aware of my own feelings, I would ask myself, "What am I feeling right now?" When you begin to name what it is you are feeling, you become aware of your emotions and level of consciousness. If I felt fear for example, I would look at the chart of consciousness and see that fear registers at 100, anger is 150. I would aim to raise myself above my current state. As I cleared my unconscious mind gradually, and kept my thoughts positive, I began to stay at higher states of consciousness. When your consciousness is higher and you can visualize what you want, you are better able to attract what it is you desire. We want to be in a state of expanded consciousness at radiant love or above whenever possible. When in a state of radiant love you will attract love and synchronicity. Conversely, when in a state of fear you attract that which you fear, usually more negativity. Whatever you focus on expands as illustrated throughout my life story whether positive or negative.

If you have lived with criticism, complaining, guilt, shame or different types of abuse, molestation or even rape, the underlying issues about why those events occurred in your life will be explained and gently uncovered to bring you to a better place of awareness and understanding of yourself and your world. My goal in writing my autobiography, since I am not a celebrated individual, is to assist others with their own evolution and growth. If I have helped one person, my purpose has been fulfilled.

I realize now that although most of my childhood was very difficult, it has led me to be who I am today. Everyone has some sort of difficulties and pain in their childhood. Like so many others, mine was filled with issues and challenges. I do not claim to be special as a result of what I went through. I am not better or worse than anyone else. What I have come to realize is that every experience, however painful and no matter the amount of suffering that is endured, leads us to be who we are today.

I have learned over the years of intense healing and struggle with the pain of my childhood memories that what happened to me during my life was pre-ordained. Contracts were formed before I was born with those I previously considered to be perpetrators or victimizers. They were all for the purpose of evolving my soul for my highest and best good. Had the events not happened in my life as they did, I would be different from who I am today. I love who I have become. I feel that I am beautiful inside instead of feeling the shame, guilt and fear that used to envelop and consume me.

I no longer blame anyone who caused me pain or suffering, as I recognize that each of those players on the stage of my life were doing what we had agreed to do before I was incarnated. This may seem difficult for some to believe, but once you remove the victim, perpetrator and rescuer triangle, you begin to take responsibility for your life. When you take responsibility for yourself and everything that happens to you, you realize that your world is a reflection of you, your thoughts and beliefs. If you are being criticized you are probably being critical. If those around you are angry, it is probably because you have unresolved anger in you. If people are gossiping about you, you are probably talking about things that really don't concern you. The people in your life become the mirror for what is going on inside of you. It becomes so much easier to let go and forgive those who you perceive have hurt you when you recognize that all they did was show you who you are. We sometimes feel hatred and anger toward our partners who have very similar issues to our own. Perhaps the issues manifest differently, or they have a different aspect of our issue, like a cup and saucer are different, but fit together nonetheless. We attract the people we do because they are vibrating at approximately the same level.

It has taken some time, work and energy to get to this place of peace. No longer do I feel like a victim in my own life. Instead I am a victor, empowered and heart centered.

There are no mistakes in life. Whoever we encounter in our life is the "right one." No one comes into our life by chance. Each person that enters our stage of life has something to teach us about ourselves or to improve the current situation. Each relationship we have teaches us more about our issues and ourselves.

There is no point in rehashing events and wishing that we had done things differently because everything happens just as it should. Events unfold as they were meant to be. Each situation that we encounter in life is perfect. However, it may not seem so at the time.

Everything that happens begins at exactly the right moment. Everything is in Divine order and Divine timing. When we are ready for something new to come into our life it appears seemingly out of nowhere and at the right time.

Sadly, relationships end. When something in our lives ends, we grow. The experience that just occurred enriches our lives. The ending gives us pause to look at ourselves and what we could have done differently, or better. What is over is truly over. It is better to just let go.

It may be difficult for some to look at the events that occurred in their lives that were difficult and painful and to accept that they were created exclusively for our soul development. For some the event may be the loss of a child or partner, or the loss at an early age of one or both of your parents. In my case I lost my childhood. It took years before I recognized that I was angry and even full of rage. I blamed boyfriends, my husbands, brothers and my parents. This is the story of my life as Jane Fonda puts it, "so far." Every unbelievable part of it is true. As weird and horrible as it may sound to you, everything I have written about happened. I have written this account of my life truthfully from my heart and the soul of my being. I share with you the spiritual wisdom I received along the way.

Due to the personal experiences that I have had I am a healer, a hypnotherapist, an ordained minister and a life coach. My purpose in life is to help others through my own experience and my humanity. In my astrology chart I am the wounded healer.

I received very strong guidance for well over 10 years to write this book. My personal fear of how others would receive it kept it stifled inside of me until the guidance I got from God, my guides, the Ascended Masters and angels have made it so powerfully strong that I was compelled to write. I have written this book without malice and harm to none.

I have been told that a very special energy has been created within this work to heal and balance those who are open to it. If you have not done any healing work, just allow the tears to flow when you feel them come up, allow any pain that is in your body to surface and allow it to flow out. It will assist you to release old patterns. Drink plenty of water just as you would with any type of healing or massage work. This book is detoxifying. As you read you may feel a connection with the words that allow you to release any pain and suffering you have been through as well. Tears release stress from the body, just let go and allow it to happen.

While I have been writing this book new methods of clearing the body have surfaced for me. While writing some of the chapters that have been very intense for me to experience and live through, I noticed that my spine needed to be adjusted. I found that writing was moving energy in my body, which often got stuck in my vertebrae. It created subluxations in my spinal column. A subluxation is what occurs in the spine when energy gets stuck. Sometimes an automobile accident will create a subluxation. A chiropractor makes an adjustment and the spine cracks, which releases the energy of the block. I could not get to a chiropractor each time, so I had to lie down on the floor to adjust my back many times a day as the energy moved through, up and out of my body. My experience was that energy from a painful experience, even when it is recalled, or re-experienced through thought or writing, brought the energy up to be released. It is essential and vital for vibrant health that emotions and energy are released. Adjusting my back and releasing it from my vibration is what this is all about. Releasing energy is healthy and positive.

It is my heartfelt wish that you will identify with some of these pages, and that you will receive all that you need for your own healing and growth. Whether similar events occurred in your life or not, if reading this book allows you to cry, to mend your broken heart or release your pain, I am grateful for that healing for you. Although this is my autobiography some of this book is channeled material. We will heal through this together you and I.

With deepest and heartfelt love and gratitude for you and where you are on your path.
Jennifer Elizabeth

OMEGA
Chart of Conciousness

GOD CONSCIOUSNESS

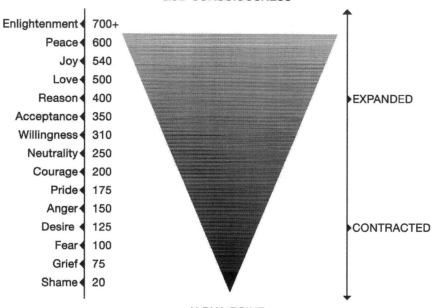

Enlightenment	700+	
Peace	600	
Joy	540	
Love	500	
Reason	400	EXPANDED
Acceptance	350	
Willingness	310	
Neutrality	250	
Courage	200	
Pride	175	
Anger	150	
Desire	125	CONTRACTED
Fear	100	
Grief	75	
Shame	20	

ALPHA POINT
Power vs. Force, Dr. David R. Hawkins - Page 68

CHAPTER ONE

Family of Origin

My mother, Katia, was one of seven children. Her parents were Ukrainian country folk, who immigrated to Manitoba, Alberta from the Ukraine along with my great-grandmother. They lived in the tiny town of Ethelbert in a very small home that they built by hand. After my grandmother's sixth home birth and with no one to assist her, Olivia, my grandmother, died of uremic poisoning on October 6, 1926. The living room in their tiny home was filed with roses, the fragrance etched into Katia's childhood memory, forevermore associating her beloved mother's death with the smell of roses.

Grief-stricken and missing his beautiful wife, my grandfather, Yuri, muddled through his days. Only six months after his wife's death he turned to his oldest daughter, Natalia, for solace. After fumbling with his daughter's breast and a failed attempt at a physical encounter with his daughter he committed suicide April 11, 1927, filled with guilt, shame and grief. His selfish choice left his seven children, including a brand new baby, as orphans. My mother, Katia, was only 5 years old at the time. She was an extremely sensitive and intuitive child. Katia awakened when her father climbed upstairs the night before he died to get stored sugar. Sensing her father's presence, she sat up in bed. Yuri told her to go back to sleep. She was the last to see her father alive. The next day a priest and several nuns came to take the children away. They all scattered like scared chickens in the yard. My mother still remembers the smell of burning cedar stumps that hung in the air on that warm morning as they watched their childhood home and all things familiar fade away.

Katia was the keeper of family secrets. Her ability to comprehend adult situations and remember things that were well beyond her level of understanding and maturity was uncanny. She kept a secret that no one talked about after her mother's death. Olivia, like so many women before her did what she had to do to provide for her family. Since there was no work for her husband locally, he had to find work elsewhere causing him to be away from home for months at a time. Olivia had to fend for herself and her family.

When their winter food supply was depleted with no money to buy anything, she went into town leaving the children in the care of her eldest daughter. No one was sure exactly when she returned, but there was food on the table once again. When a pregnancy resulted no one questioned it. The family had food to eat and the events were soon forgotten. It was part of life. You do what you have to do to feed your family.

Losing a parent can have long-term and permanent effects. Dissociative disorder and brain chemistry changes can occur without the nurturing love, support and guidance of a mother. To lose both parents in less than a year created emotional trauma and damage to all the remaining children.

Feeling desperately sad and alone, the six older children banded together. They conferred with one another and made the joint decision to stay together no matter what, rather than risk being separated by adoption to different families. It was the six of them against the world. This decision made it impossible for them to be adopted. It became clear that their infant brother would easily be adopted while the older children remained in the orphanage, lonely and without parental love, nurturing and support. After what seemed like an eternity to the five sisters and their brother; Maria, Natalia, Anika, Katia, Daisy and Dimitri, forlorn and grief-stricken, were finally released from the desolate orphanage. Their grandmother, the only living relative, finally resigned herself to the idea of having to raise and support her daughter's children. Filled with resentment, she sent for them. She could barely afford to feed herself. She wondered how on earth she would feed six more hungry mouths. Never mind finding a way to put clothes on their backs and shoes on their growing feet. They traveled from Vancouver by railway to the tiny town of Ethelbert to become her wards. To be without both parents at such an early age etched their psyches and left them defensive and shut down emotionally. My mother remembers feeling ill from a migraine headache and vomiting into a white pillowslip as the train conductor held it open for her on the way to Manitoba. To this day migraine headaches plague her and she wonders why.

Her grandmother, Baba, was a tough old bird, small of stature and a force to be reckoned with. She was cold, angry and distant. If her charges failed to use proper manners or etiquette at the table they were whacked on the back of the hand with her trusty wooden spoon. Grandmother always planted a garden and grew enough vegetables to get the family through the winter. The children had many chores to do; gardening was the least of them. Baba loved flowers and grew daisies, California poppies, bachelor buttons and sweet peas. Everyone pulled his or her weight. They chopped wood, worked in the garden, washed dishes and did whatever was needed around the house. The house had no running water, so trudging to the outhouse even in the middle of the Manitoba winter was in order. It was a very hard life for this family and they lived through extremes. In the summer they slept fitfully sweating on the veranda at the front of the house in an attempt to keep cool. In the winter there was so much ice on the windows that they could not see out. The children would put their tongues on the windows to melt the ice to be able to look out through the ice-covered glass. The five girls slept together in one bed, head-to-foot, to keep warm.

Their oldest sister, Natalia, quit school and began working when she was 14 to help feed and clothe the family. After several years of hard work, she began seeing a young man and soon had an excuse to leave her harsh disciplinarian grandmother. She asked permission of her grandmother to get married. Grandmother would have none of it. Soon after Natalia discovered an excuse to get married when she announced that she had become pregnant. She and Mickey were married when Natalia was four months pregnant.

Natalia and Mickey began a life together, building a mud brick home for their family. Very shortly thereafter, Natalia invited her younger sisters to join them in what they thought would be safety and solace from their hard case of a grandmother. Sleeping in one room but separate beds, what began as a haven soon turned into a prison, when the young girls were fondled by their older brother-in-law. While they were snuggled in their bed they were not safe. They could not say anything as they thought rightly that Natalia would never believe them. Thinking them ungrateful she would throw them all out. After they could not take it any longer the girls fled their sister's home for the big city of Toronto and went to finishing school at the tender ages of 14, 16, 18 and 20.

The girls were talented and picked up cooking easily — all of them becoming fabulous cooks and seamstresses. This became a source of pride for them. They were all beautifully attractive, vibrant and intelligent. Each of them had curves in all the right places and soon found husbands when they were in their early 20s.

My dad, Leonard, was born an adventurer. His parents crossed the Atlantic from England on the Queen Mary with the promise of free acreage in northern Ontario to anyone who wanted to homestead there. After creating a life for themselves and building a log home, the black flies nearly drove my city-born grandmother crazy and forced them to flee to more civilized territory. They moved to the city of Toronto. My paternal grandfather was kind to me, but was a tough taskmaster to his children. He frequently used a cane to whip, spank and punish which did not sit well with my father. At the age of seven he hopped a freight train for points west, always wanting to see the city of Vancouver and the Rocky Mountains. He got his wish, if only for a day. The Mounted Police picked him up and shipped him back home to his father on a passenger train, destined for another beating.

My father had difficulty paying attention in school and was frequently beaten by the principal and his teachers for his unruliness. The school frequently contacted his parents regarding his behavior and let my grandfather know that he had received a caning. Once my father arrived home from school his father would take him into the basement and cane him again.

The strict upbringing at home coupled with an equally strict religious education proved too much for this young maverick. The family attended the Gospel Hall, a strict fundamentalist Christian church. "Meetings" were held on Sunday morning and evening, with prayer meetings every evening. My father's family attended every one. The church was my grandmother, Maggie's life. They only associated with people who attended meeting. She was fervently religious, and abided by all the rules of the Gospel Hall. No drinking, no smoking, no dancing, no makeup, no swearing or taking of the Lord's name in vain and certainly no fornication before marriage.

On Sunday morning, the whole family dressed in their Sunday best clothes and stayed in them for the entire day. Sunday was a day to be stiffly dressed and uncomfortable; there was no playing or having fun on The Lord's Day.

By the time Leonard reached the age of 12 he had enough and again jumped on a freight train. It was not long before he was found and sent back C.O.D. to his father's clutches. This time the reprimand was far worse than when he was seven. When Leonard became 16 he lied about his age and escaped on a merchant marine ship living a life of adventure as he traveled the seas.

My mother and father met at the beginning of World War II. My father, a handsome and grounded Taurus, found Katia, the Cancer, extremely good looking. He was madly in love wanting more than Katia was willing to offer outside of marriage. He could not wait any longer. Leonard came home on leave wearing his handsome Air Force uniform and married Katia six months after their first meeting. They were very much in love. When Katia became pregnant, within their first year of marriage, Leonard blamed her for not preventing it. (This is an interesting insight, as years later I was blamed by my second husband for getting pregnant on purpose. This was not the case.) My mother selflessly kept her rations aside and practically starved herself during her pregnancy so that she would have food to feed her new husband whenever he came home on leave.

CHAPTER TWO

Home is Where The Heart Should Be

In 1954, hurricane Hazel ravaged Haiti killing 1,000 before making landfall on United States soil in North Carolina during a full moon. This created the highest tides of the year and a storm surge of 18 feet. Nine states were ravaged leaving the death toll in the United States at 95. The Category 4 hurricane turned northward and tracked into Canada where it merged with a large cold front and became an extra-tropical storm. It stalled over Toronto raising the death toll by a hundred more. The Canadians were ill-prepared for the damaging storm that hit before dawn.

Just outside of Toronto, Ontario the Humber River overflowed its banks due to the torrents of rain; over a foot in less than 24 hours. It was the deadliest and costliest hurricane of the 1954 Atlantic hurricane season.

My mother impatiently waited for her water to break and labor to begin. Shortly after dawn on the heels of the Hurricane of the Century I unwillingly entered this world kicking and screaming. The brisk October morning was peaceful and calm after the fiercest Hurricane in recorded history. My mother frequently referred to me as Hurricane Hazel because of the fury of the storm. Apparently as a child I could empty a dresser faster than any hurricane.

I chose a challenging path from the beginning. Even my birth order was difficult. The third of four children, I was born in Toronto during a Mercury Retrograde on the fourth Wednesday in October four days before Halloween. A Scorpio with five planets in that sign, including my ascendant and moon, ensured my life path was going to be one bumpy ride. My mother was confident she was having a boy and was immediately disappointed when I was not. I would continue to disappoint her as time wore on. Was the storm a fateful omen for my life?

Raised in a suburb of Toronto, Ontario, I was the only daughter in our family of four children. I grew up with my three brothers as a shy, timid and pretty little girl in a house full of testosterone. I was taught to ask my mother first and to never be disrespectful of adults. Our manners were impeccable due to mother's watchful eye. We were taught to defer to adults and be quiet in their presence. Our parents were of European descent and ran the household like a strict military camp. We were kept on a schedule of chores and household duties. Saturdays were workdays at our home and no one was ever allowed to sleep in.

Although an only daughter, I was not spoiled as one might expect. My parents were strict and treated us all equally, relatively speaking. Given that I was born in 1954, I was taught early to perform tasks that were traditionally relegated to women like cooking, cleaning, and ironing. My brothers would help dust, vacuum, sweep and do the dishes, but they did not cook or do the ironing like I did. We all had daily chores and were kept busy most of the time. My father was an avid gardener and usually had work for us to do in our large backyard garden. We griped and grumbled about having to pull weeds and hoe the rows of vegetables, but we learned the skills of gardening in spite of ourselves. Our father's love of nature and the Earth was easily passed onto us. We all learned at an early age to be able to recognize the different species of birds in our yard and even learned to recognize the different birdcalls.

Looking back at my childhood I have some pleasant memories. Although they were intermittent, I remember fondly being followed home from elementary school by stray cats and dogs, always akin to nature and all its creatures. I also had what my parents term an imaginary friend when I was very young. I would spend hours talking to him. He was kind and helpful and helped me when I was afraid. I was always happy to be outside surrounded by our dogs, cats or pet rabbits. I felt comfortable and safe around our animals. They always showed me unconditional love.

Both of my parents believed in corporal punishment due to their own harsh upbringing. It did not happen often but we all received the lashings of my father's belt or my mother's wooden spoon. Sometimes we were beaten with whatever was closest; in my case it was a hairbrush. I still remember the sound of my father unleashing his belt as he unbuckled it and slid it out of his pant loops in one fell swoop. The sound of a man removing his belt from his pants still makes my blood run cold. Trying to escape and get away never helped. I became fearful of both of my parents' wrath. My fear kept me quiet, respectful and the dutiful, helpful little girl my mother wanted. I tried my best to make her happy. I became a people pleaser and extremely codependent. We were taught to hold our tongues and to keep any disrespectful comments to ourselves. When I cried I was told by my mother, "Be quiet or I'll give you something to cry about." I have come to learn through time that not being allowed to cry when you feel sad or upset causes us to shut down and become repressed.

According to Janice Berger in her book, *Emotional Fitness*, "this repression solidifies into an internal defense that prevents us from feeling the impact of neglect and abuse." She goes on to say, "These defenses carried into our adult life damage our relationships and keep us from being emotionally fit. We have been trained to be "nice" and "civilized" that is emotionally dishonest and hidden. Since our defenses are always holding in our feelings we are always running the risk of allowing others to see how we feel. It takes enormous energy to keep these feelings concealed by keeping our defenses in place. We cannot be clear and well defended because when we are defended we do not know ourselves and do not trust ourselves. We cannot relax and be spontaneous and open because we have to watch everything we say and do."

The only ones in our household that were able to express their emotions were my parents. Mostly they expressed anger. The rest of us held ours in. Some of us have been eating our way through our lives to numb our pain. Others in my family have used alcohol, smoking or sex to disconnect.

I became quiet. I held my emotions in and immersed myself in an imaginary world. Animals and my invisible friend were my solace. I wrote letters about them when a pet would die. I talked to myself and played school alone in our furnace room for hours. I was terrified of the dark and what I could not see under my bed and in my closet. I was in constant fear and worry. My vibration was extremely low. No one believed what I had to say, if they listened at all.

My mother would brush my hair every morning before school. It was rarely a pleasant experience. Instead of holding the bottom of my long hair in her hand and brushing a piece at a time, she dug the brush into the crown of my hair dragging and pulling it through the tangles. She did not make an effort to make the experience easier or less painful, instead it seemed she enjoyed hurting me. I was embarrassed when the hair brushing happened right before I had to walk out the door. I was often moved to tears. The neighborhood girls would show up at the door at the same time to walk me to school. They would stand uncomfortably in the front hall shifting from foot-to-foot while I screamed and cried.

My mother was frequently cruel with erratic and unpredictable emotions. She could turn from being pleasant one moment to angry in another. I was careful not to upset her and tried desperately to please her and win her love and approval. If I behaved myself and did everything I was told, I was rewarded. Mother was kind and pleasant. If I misbehaved especially in public I would be immediately humiliated. None of us had the audacity to misbehave in public. We dare not.

Mother suffered from migraines. She never seemed to associate emotional upsets with them but we did. When she got them on some occasions her eyesight was affected. She would spend hours throwing up and passing out on the bathroom floor. Light bothered her then and she could not eat for fear of vomiting. My father got to the point that he did everything he could to avoid upsetting her so she would not get a migraine. She knew she was in control as long as she had this mighty weapon to wield.

My mother rarely drank, and got tipsy from the smallest amount of wine. The threat of these terribly debilitating headaches kept her alcohol consumption to a minimum. In later years, my mother would get upset if our family gatherings would become rowdy when we were drinking wine together. My father would have so much fun with us; letting down his emotional barriers and laughing with us until the tears would flow. That was usually when my mother would tell us "that's enough" and take the wine away.

My mother stayed home until I was 14, while my father worked as a stationary engineer at an aircraft manufacturer near the airport. She was a great cook and made fabulous roasts, desserts, cookies and cakes. She was famous for her baking. We only had one family car, which was normal for that time. Although my father's income was not huge, we always ate well, but extras like soda pop and ice cream were reserved for very special occasions and candy was rarely, if ever, in our home. We had very little freedom and rarely went on outings with other children or friends. We were seen and not heard. At gatherings my mother was very proud of the fact that other guests would notice our good manners. One woman remarked with surprise that she had never seen a child so obedient as when she offered me a plate of cookies. I immediately glanced over at my mother to see if she would give her permission for me to accept one. When I met my mother's eye, she gave me an affirmative nod and then I said timidly, "Yes, please."

I was obedient, quiet and mouse-like. Due to my strict rearing, I did not possess the ability to speak up for myself. I could easily be controlled and manipulated by fear, especially by my elders. I was a perfect target for a friend of the family. I usually walked home from school with our next-door neighbor. On rare occasions, I made the walk alone. One fateful day I walked home from first grade by myself. Mr. Burton, a man in his late 50s, was outside working in his front yard. His little wrinkly pug dog was with him. I was a magnet for animals and this little dog was no exception. Mr. Burton walked over to talk to me as I walked down the street and neared the middle of their yard. He was balding and had a gray mustache. I bent down to pet his little dog and he asked me if I would like some candy. Mr. Burton knew my parents well. His twin daughters Marie and Carolyn babysat my older brothers years before. Our family attended his daughters' weddings and I had recently been Carolyn's flower girl at her wedding.

I was five years old and very timid and shy when I was asked to be a flower girl. My mother made a beautiful white dress for me made of embroidered white flowers on a beautiful organza fabric, which matched Carolyn's wedding dress. The dress showcased my mother's talent as a seamstress. I looked beautiful and demure. I remember my mother making the dress and how stressed she was to have it be absolutely perfect. I also remember how pretty and excited I felt all at the same time, to be a flower girl. It was every little girl's dream. I remember standing before the double doors preparing to enter the sanctuary. Being as shy as I was, the anxiety and nervousness that I experienced to walk down the aisle in front of everyone was overwhelming. The wedding ceremony itself was a blur. Carolyn was very sweet and kind to me. She had photographs taken of us in her parents' living room before we went to the church.

There had been an incident at Carolyn's wedding that I had kept secret. Secrets were a way of life for my family. At the reception following the wedding I was standing outside the large group of adults who were dancing. Almost everyone was in a big circle in the reception hall. I seemed left out and unsure of how to join in. I wanted to, but did not feel confident enough to find a way to be a part of the revelry. Several times I felt Mr. Burton looking at me. He held out his hand offering to let me join in, but I felt oddly uncomfortable. I shook my head wanting to join in, but not feeling at ease. I could not explain the sick feeling I had in my stomach. I would talk to my invisible friend about it later.

Shortly after the wedding I found myself with the same uncomfortable feeling in my stomach while Mr. Burton waited for my answer about the candy. I wanted some candy, but I did not want to go inside Mr. Burton's house where he said the candy was. I could feel in the pit of my stomach the fear welling up in me. What would I tell my mother? Would it be okay with her? Should I go home and tell her first? I knew I could not bring myself to tell Mr. Burton I could not go in his house with him. I was frozen silent with fear. I had been taught that adults were never to be disrespected. I nodded numbly and walked woodenly behind him through his backyard gate and into his back door. Once inside the house, he went over to a washtub in his laundry room and washed his hands and arms with Comet cleanser. To this day the smell of Comet cleanser brings a rush of memories from this moment crashing back to me. This memory had become indelibly imprinted in my mind.

I knew my mother expected me at home by a certain time after school. She knew how long it took to walk home. I was becoming increasingly nervous and my stomach tightened. Mr. Burton walked around past the cabinet in the dining room where I knew the candy was housed. He moved to the front door and locked it. He walked to the side and back doors and locked them. I asked him about the candy, the reason he invited me in. He put me off by saying he would get it in a minute. Then he pulled the curtains closed in the dining room and living room. The delay in getting to the candy was obvious to me, something bad was about to happen and I felt very ill. I knew something was not right. Mrs. Burton was at work and their daughters, who were more than 15 years older than me, were no longer at home. He lay down on his living room sofa and asked me to come over to him. He unzipped his pants and pulled his flaccid penis out and asked if I had ever seen anything like it before. I had not. I did not want to look. I felt confused and like a caged animal, I wanted out. How could I get out? The doors were locked and I knew I could not get passed him and out the door. I hopped around the floor pretending to be a bunny rabbit. I knew this was not right. I did not feel right. I had to get home to my mother. I wanted to cry. I wanted to throw up. That familiar feeling was in my stomach. I was terribly afraid.

I was lucky. After telling me vehemently that if I ever told anyone anything about what had happened he would hurt both my parents badly. He also said he would deny it ever happened and they would not believe me. Then he let me go home.

Once out of Mr. Burton's house I hurried down his driveway and to the street. We lived only four doors away, but at the far end of the street. I walked home as if in a dream and my mother asked me why I was so late. I told her I stopped to talk to Mr. Burton. I did not say anything else about the incident to my mother. I was very afraid that I would be in big trouble for having candy at Mr. Burton's house before dinner. I was also very afraid that Mr. Burton would make good on his threat to hurt my parents whom I loved very much. It was not until sometime later when Mrs. Burton called to invite me to join them for dinner at their home, my mother covered the black mouthpiece and asked if I would like to go. I shook my head vehemently. It was Mr. Burton's way of checking to see if I had told. I did not want to go and I squirmed. My mother politely declined. Once off the phone she asked me why I did not want to go to their home for dinner. I told her that Mr. Burton touched my bottom and very shyly explained in a condensed version what happened. My mother never mentioned it again and being the polite neighbor she was, never mentioned it to either Mr. or Mrs. Burton. My secret remained safe with my mother.

This was how confrontations were handled in our family. The big items were swept under the rug. The thought was that they would never surface again. We would need a much bigger rug.

Not long after the incident with Mr. Burton, I was molested again, only this time by someone closer. It went on for 7 years without anyone caring enough to do anything about it. My cries for help went unnoticed. Even when I wet the bed, no one paid attention. When my mother was about to leave me with my babysitter, I would plead with her, "Please don't leave me! Please mommy, please!" I would grab onto her skirt as she was walking out the door. She would peel my hands off of her and tell me not to be such a big baby. I learned that the people you loved hurt you and did not protect you. I learned that the people that loved you wanted sex from you. The word "NO" did not mean no for me. Several people I trusted crossed my boundaries. I was no longer safe sleeping alone in my own bed. It became utterly useless to call attention to something that no one wanted to see. I became fear-filled and anxious. I had no sense of security. I hid myself in a world of fantasy; playing with my animals and speaking to my imaginary friend. I found out many years later that my brother was also molested but never told a soul. It would not surprise me at all if others were molested as well. During the summer of my 56th year I had flashbacks of events of molestation beginning when I was eighteen months old.

Although I did not have any physical scarring, the shame and guilt that I carried into my adulthood was very evident in my lack of self-esteem and confidence. I was popular and well liked at school, but plagued by self-loathing and fears. Due to the sexual abuse, I confused sex with love. The people I loved crossed my boundaries and touched me in inappropriate ways. I did not develop healthy boundaries as a teenager. When I started to become interested in boys and men, I found it very difficult to say no, because there were no healthy boundaries at home. I was not allowed to say no at home. I had no one to reinforce what was right and wrong since my family taught me that there was no wrong.

Making decisions was not something I was allowed to do often. I attended a church fundraising bazaar with my mother with a few dollars to spend. I was told it was my money and I could spend it however I wanted. I spotted a little concertina or squeezebox instrument for sale. I was so excited and wanted to buy it. When I went back with my mother who held my allowance money, she questioned me, "Are you sure you want to spend your money on that?" Rather than let me buy the instrument and feel my own feelings about getting what I wanted, she made me feel guilty for wanting it. She must know better than me, I thought and we walked away. I felt manipulated and guilty for not buying it. I felt small for not being able to do what I wanted. I left the church that day wanting that concertina and wishing I had the guts to stand up to my mother. I wished I had bought it and to heck with what my mother thought. I was a timid little girl, who was controlled by what my mother said; even her looks could stop me from doing something. I was afraid of her wrath. I did not want to displease her and I did everything I could not to.

My mother babysat children in our home for extra money. The cruel side of her was sometimes exhibited in her care of these children also. My favorite aunt, a retired medical doctor, confided

10

in me later that my mother should never have had children. She felt her childhood left her ill-equipped to be a loving and caring mother.

The treatment I received by my parents left me feeling unvalued and unimportant. My feelings were emitted unconsciously to others through my vibration. On Friday afternoon after most of the children in my mother's care had been picked up by their parents, my mother sent me down the street to collect payment for one little girl's babysitting. I was told not to leave until I got the money. My mother was annoyed with the woman because she regularly wiggled out of paying at the end of the week. When I arrived at her bungalow I knocked timidly at the door and was invited in. The woman asked me to wait while she got a check for me. After waiting alone at the front door for well over ten minutes, I wondered if she had forgotten about me. I smelled cigarette smoke. I called to her with no response. I walked down the hall to see where she had gone. I was not a rude child, so walking into someone's house was not taken lightly. I called out to her softly wondering where she had gone. I looked into the living room and kitchen and called her name again. No one responded. I walked down the hall and started into her bedroom where she was standing in a darkened room. As my eyes adjusted to the dim light I realized that she was absolutely stark naked. I never saw my own mother naked. This was a shock to me. She was angry that I wandered into her room and I was extremely embarrassed and ashamed. I knew what she did was wrong, but somehow she blamed me for seeing her naked.

The fact that I was sent on an adult errand by my mother was inappropriate. My mother avoided dealing with an issue by having me (a child) intervene. I was not equipped to handle the disrespect and rudeness of yet another adult in my life. This incident caused additional repression of my feelings and emotions, which created deeper blocks for me later in life.

School became a respite and a comfort. It gave me a chance to have a little peace and kindness in my life. Strangely, when a close elementary school friend was moving, her mother invited me to lunch. I was to walk home with her to have lunch, and return to school in the afternoon with my friend. Instead of going home with my friend to eat I became so upset that I would not see my mother at lunchtime. I went home instead. I was terribly tormented about the thought of missing the lunch with my friend. On the other hand, I was very enmeshed and codependent with my mother. I experienced anguish over the thought of not being near her at lunchtime. My mother made almost all of my decisions for me. I had little self-empowerment whatsoever. When it came time to be without her, even though she was abusive and cruel, I could not.

My mother had a softer side as well. When she was happy and not angry or upset she could be sweet and caring. The problem was that we never knew which part of her would show up, walking on eggshells with both of my parents' anger and moods became a way of life.

In 5th grade I was invited to go away for a weekend with a fellow classmate, Pamela Bangle and two of our physical education teachers, to visit Miss Sparrow. She had left the school to teach at the Belleville School for the Deaf. Miss Sparrow, our favorite teacher, was very sweet, kind and soft spoken. The weekend was very exciting for both Pamela and me. I could barely imagine a special weekend away with three teachers and just the two of us. The weekend should have been a wonderful experience. A pall was cast over the entire weekend. It was not by anything that was done to me, but of my own creation.

Every time Miss Sparrow bent over to put something in or take something out of the oven I smacked her across her backside. I was unable to stop myself. I was alert enough to notice that the teachers exchanged odd glances after it happened the third or fourth time. They may even have taken me aside to ask me to stop doing it. The bottom line was this was behavior I had seen my father exhibit with my mother. I knew he loved my mother. I loved Miss Sparrow. I was surrounded with inappropriate behavior at home and did not know how to act when my parents were not around. I felt so guilty and ashamed by my unexplainable automatic and inappropriate behavior that I pretended to sleep the entire drive home.

One summer while making the three-hour drive to our lakeside cottage we got a flat tire. My father was so enraged that he had to stop and fix a tire. My mother told us to stay in the car and be quiet. The four of us sat quietly not moving an inch while my father jacked up the car and changed the tire. We were silent for the entire time it took him to cool down afterwards as well. The tension in the car was palpable by the youngest of us. I call this walking on eggshells.

Most summers we spent at the cottage that my father built. It took us three hours to drive to Lake of Bays in Muskoka.

We made the trek to the cottage sometimes on weekends, but mostly at the beginning of the summer. I loved being at the lake because I had much more freedom there. We had a canoe, and two boats my dad built in our backyard back in the city. He purchased plans and manufactured the boats covered with fiberglass. He was talented and creative, making everything "built to last." The motorboat was very heavy and lumbered in the water. I was allowed to use it, because both my parents knew I could not go very fast. While at the cottage I spent almost every minute I could swimming, canoeing or waterskiing with friends. I remember fondly the day my father taught me how to swim. He stood on a stump that was submerged under the water and backed up having me swim towards him. He kept moving backwards further and further until I realized I was swimming all by myself.

We still had chores at the cottage, but there was no garden. Once our chores were completed we ran off through the woods to meet our friends. The kids we hung around with were from well-to-do families with nicer cottages and certainly more streamlined and beautiful boats. We skied and swam with them all summer. We got together and with my creative mind planned regattas. We had crazy pajama races from the dock that my father built to the raft, which he also built. The most fun was our crazy canoe race where we had to use our hands instead of the wooden paddles. By the time we got to our destination the canoe was filled with water and we were laughing and sinking all at the same time.

My aunt and uncle rented our cottage a couple of weeks every year, until they decided they enjoyed it enough to buy their own place. After that time I spent many fun days with my favorite cousins swimming and racing with them. The fondest memories of my childhood were the times we spent there. I loved the woods and being near the cool, clear water of the lake. I challenged myself while I was there. When I became a teenager we began an annual swim of about 2 miles to the Portage store. It was an exhilarating challenge to my little brother and me. We did this several times with our friends, laughing and talking while we swam the distance. We always had an adult in a boat nearby, just in case, and there were never any mishaps.

There was an odd thing about the cottage that others commented about to me. My mother did not want me doing anything with boys, sexually. She warned me constantly about boys and men only wanting "one thing." Because of the location of our cottage at the top of a steep hill and overlooking the lake, the sound from approaching boats carried. We could always see when someone was coming to visit and hear the engine noise clearly. It was one of those days that my mother yelled to me, "Jennifer, the boys are coming over. Put on your bikini!" My sister-in-law thought that this was very peculiar since my mother was constantly trying to keep me chaste and pure.

There was a constant underlying competition between my mother and me. Not that I competed with her, but she did with me. I could not understand why she would feel jealous or competitive with her daughter. She was a very attractive woman. My mother was always concerned about appearances and dressed nicely. Considering my father's income and the babysitting she did, my mother always had quite the wardrobe. She sewed and fashioned clothes from things others gave her. She was very talented and creative.

I was a cheerleader in high school and well liked by my teachers. I participated in almost every sport offered. Although not a stellar athlete I was adequate and loved to compete. I swam competitively with my high school swim team and participated in track and field in the spring. I ran with the popular crowd but felt inferior. I was allowed to participate in any sport I wanted to but if I asked my mother to do something with friends over the weekend, the answer was always, "No." After asking over and over, I gave up. I knew if I had to ask, it was pointless to even bother. I became nervous and afraid to ask for anything. On weekends we were kept busy with household chores and rarely had a Saturday off. My mother would not let me go to the mall or a movie with girlfriends. I was relegated to visiting my friend Dini a few houses away. That was as far as I could go until my senior year. When I wanted to attend a dance away from school my brother had to accompany me.

My mother was extremely controlling and manipulative. She was adept at dishing out dinner with large helpings of guilt. I remember one particular incident that haunted me as much as it humiliated me. I was asked to clean my room and the bathroom off the living room as my mother was having a group of her lady friends over for a Tupperware party or some such event. I went to throw the contents of the bathroom trash into the kitchen garbage can. She stopped me and instructed me to put the bathroom trash into the fireplace instead so she could burn it.

I protested, "But mom!" She would not let me finish. "Do what I ask and don't have so much to say about it!" I did as she requested, feeling that this was going to blow up in my face somehow. That evening her lady friends sat in the living room carrying on, when all of a sudden I looked up and saw my mother's disgusted and angry face. She was looking angrily at me. I followed her gaze to the fireplace where my Kotex pad was laying there now open for the world to see. When the ladies left she screamed at me. "How could you do something like that? I was mortified and embarrassed in front of my friends!" She screamed at me for doing what she had told me to do. I could not win with her. There was no point in trying.

My father was often in his own world, talking at the dinner table of the latest book he was reading or current events. My mother was largely the disciplinarian unless some jarring event occurred with one of us, and then he would jump on the bandwagon. Mostly he was not even aware of what was going on in our lives. When I was a teen I felt he rarely noticed what I was wearing or me. My mother had recently berated me in my father's presence for wearing too much make-up. Soon after I remember sitting at the dinner table one evening. He looked over at me and said, "You're wearing too much make-up." "But Dad," I said vehemently, "I don't have any on." "Don't give me that! Go and get me a flannel!" I dutifully got a wet washcloth and handed it to him. I stood silently next to the captain's chair at his end of the table, while he scrubbed my eyes vigorously. "Hold still!" All the while he continued his vendetta against the scourge of youth, make-up. I could feel my brothers squirming uncomfortably trying to finish their dinner in silence. I was left crying with red skin around my eyes where he had rubbed my lids raw. It was a humiliating experience. He refused to believe he could somehow have been wrong. The skin on my face is very thin, and my veins showed through my eyelid making my eyes look naturally purple.

My parents played cards with their best friends once a month or so. They played for quarters putting money in a bowl or as they called it a "kitty." When they had enough money the four would use this money to go out for dinner. This worked really well for them, which gave mom a brilliant idea. She found a way to use a kitty for her own family, offering us more dinners out.

My mother was always looking for ways to "improve" us. She thought it would be a great idea to put a wooden bowl in the center of the table at dinnertime. Each time someone made a grammatical mistake, they had to "put a penny in the pot." It began as a game, offering us much enjoyment when we could tell each other, "Oh that's not the right use of that word," or "that's grammatically incorrect." One thing our family was really good at was pointing out someone else's shortcomings. We became very competitive with one another. We fought to be the first to make the correction and say, "put a penny in a pot, you just said gonna!" We especially loved pointing out our father's grammatical mistakes.

My father was an earthy, casual man. He really did not care what other's thought of him. He made conjunctions and grammatical errors my mother did not like. I think she felt he did not measure up to her in some ways. He was not the gentry man she felt she deserved. He regularly used conjunctions and other words incorrectly. Mother loved to point this out to him and we quickly followed suit. Both my parents were critical but mother was nitpicky. She passed her critical nature on to all of her children. As we witnessed this behavior in our parents, we constantly criticized each other as well as our friends. It was one of the first things that outsiders noticed about our family. We would often excitedly point out well over ten errors for dad in one dinner. He would count his change into the bowl. Instead of being his talkative self at mealtime, he governed himself and sometimes became completely silent and brooding. One day, after months of playing the game, someone excitedly pointed out, "Dad, put a penny in the pot!" My father hit the rage button and said, "I have had just about enough of this! Take that damn thing off the table right now!" My mother bristled in response but dutifully removed the bowl. Her little game was over. Once dad declared something was over, there was no turning back and certainly no questioning his decision. His word was final.

I took home economics classes in junior high and high school. I enjoyed our teacher and the classes very much. Sewing was not my favorite part, cooking was. In ninth grade, when I was 14, I managed to create a cute little mini skirt out of a cotton print. I was really pleased that it had turned out so well, even with the complicated waste band and zipper. I happily donned it one morning to wear to school. My father was standing in the kitchen talking with my mother as I prepared to leave the house. My dad took one look at me in my fabulous skirt and said, "That skirt is way too short!" "But Dad!" I cried. "I made it myself!" "I don't care who made it. Bend over and we'll see if it is too short." I was horrified. "You're expecting me to bend over in front of you? No one bends over in a mini skirt, ladies squat." "Bend over or you are not going to wear it at all!" My mother stayed out of our encounter, focusing on the porridge on the stove. I dutifully bent over, feeling humiliated, my face burning. "That skirt is too short. I can see your whiskers!" he said. I stormed out of the kitchen to change my clothes not looking back. I was horrified. My brand new skirt that I was so proud of was not to be worn. I felt crushed, beaten and reduced to tears.

I wanted to go to veterinarian school. My father felt I would never amount to much and would not allow me to go. He told me that because I was a girl, I would only want to get married and have babies. He did not want to waste a college education on a girl. So I was required to take secretarial classes instead. He felt that was all I was capable of achieving. It could be argued that if I had enough drive, I could have achieved much without my father's support. However, when you are programmed to have low self esteem you grow up believing what you are told by those you love and trust. What your parents believe is true is what you begin to accept as fact. It became my belief that I would never amount to much. I would get married and have babies. I was forced to take shorthand and typing in high school. I continued to be angry every time I had to sit in my secretarial classes. It did not matter that having typing was a good skill that I could use and continue to use to this day. The fact that I was forced against my will to do something continued to perpetuate the undercurrent that my desires did not matter. My will was being diminished. It did not matter what I wanted. I had to do what the men around me wanted me to do.

My parent's relationship ran the gamut from happy go lucky to nagging, turmoil and drama. We could hit all four seasons in one day. It could be frosty in the morning and warm and friendly the same night. My mother was a really good scorekeeper. She did a great deal for my Dad and expected to be remembered. One year my father forgot her birthday. I thought the world was going to end that day. I had never seen my mother so upset. She told my little brother and me that we were going out to our favorite restaurant. This restaurant was a favorite of ours because they had a fabulous buffet with lobster and standing ribs of beef. My brothers, who ate like horses, were able to eat as much as they wanted. The restaurant always lost money the nights that our family showed up. They would go up to the buffet at least four or five times each. On the day that my older brothers and my father forgot her birthday, we got really dressed up and went out to eat without my father. I thought she was going to leave him. My father never forgot her birthday again.

I remember one two-week period when my parents did not speak to each other at all. My mother would say, "Tell your father dinner is ready." My dad would say to us, "Tell your mother I'm not hungry." We were caught in the cross fire and used as go-betweens. My little brother and I seemed to be more involved in the covert operations than the older two. When they were able they borrowed the family car and went out.

My father made wine in our basement. When my parents fought my dad spent his evenings filtering his wine and bottling. My dad became quite the winemaker over the years. He learned a lot about the art, but moreover it was an escape for him. He would come up from the basement with a red nose and a rosy face carrying his glass.

We always had animals around our home. The dogs stayed in our backyard and came into the basement at night. We always had one. My father was the kind of person that believed in tying up dogs in the backyard. Years later they moved into the country where they had room to let a dog run. When my younger brother, Paul, and I came home from school after having to put our dog to sleep for biting a neighborhood kid, my dad brought a little black dog home and gave it to my brother. He instantly fell in love with the little puppy and named him Shadow. Paul grew attached to the little black dog and hurried to get home from school and play with him. One day after about a month or so, we got home and there was no dog. I raced to find my mother and thought it odd later that she did not say anything to either of us. I asked where Shadow was. She said that dad had taken the dog back to the man he got the puppy from. He was upset he was not going to be a big dog. Apparently it was a case of misrepresentation and my father was angry. Paul ran to his room and closed the door. He was in there for a long, long time. I went to check on him. I found him sitting at his desk quietly crying. He never said a word about it to my dad. It was as if it never happened.

The winter I was 14, my mother nagged my father about not treating my brothers equally. He seemed to favor my second brother. My mother complained that the rules were not the same for both boys. Mac was able to use the car and did not have to fill up the tank when he returned it. It seemed when Tim borrowed the family car not only did he have to put gas in it; he did not get the car whenever he asked. When Mac asked my dad, he seemed to have free reign. Mom had a knack for needling my father and twisting the needle once she hit a nerve. On one such occasion she continued to nag my father about the inequality of his relationship with his sons and the return of the car without fuel. I could see the signs of rage building within my father's face. I would have dropped the subject long before, but my mother nattered on and on.

The nagging was wearing him down. As she poured scalding hot tea from the teapot my father hit at her arm. As my mother's armed waved back and forth from the assault, the hot tea flew all over my father's chest. My father's boiling point was reached in a flash and was something to behold. I was absolutely frozen, my shoulders tingled and my face felt like I could not move it if I tried. The scene unfolded in front of me in slow motion with the yelling and screaming in words I could not discern. My mother ended up on the floor as I watched my father going after her, attempting to kick her while she lay on the floor. We all were standing up at the dining room table with our chairs pushed back like gunslingers readying for a gunfight. I screamed at my father to stop — again I screamed. It seemed enough. He was burned badly and extremely angry. He grabbed his coat and keys and was out the door. That was the way we resolved a family crisis, we ran away.

After the tea party incident my mother asked me to set the table with my father opposite her instead of beside her at mealtime. For years after this event I found myself having to run away to calm down when I was angry. Driving seemed to be what I needed to quiet my mind and get the space I needed. I finished doing the dishes and grabbed my coat and left after I knew my mother was okay. I was the only one that had the balls to say anything. My brothers all stood there dumbfounded. This was not even about me. I would not be old enough to drive for another two years.

The imprint of this event was indelibly recorded in my DNA, my unconscious and in my body. Any time I had a loud disagreement, my unconscious mind swept back to this point in time where I went into fear, my adrenaline kicking in. I equated men with abuse. There seemed to be no way around it. Although my mother had no intention of ever letting me drive the family car.

I eventually won the attention of a sweet natured and very good-looking senior, named Rob Gardner. He was radically different from what my parents wanted for me. He was tall, handsome and sweet. He had long, curly blonde hair and ran with a very different crowd than the goody-goody cheerleaders and jocks at my school. He seemed like a bad boy and that was what attracted me. What was not immediately apparent to me was that his low self-esteem matched mine. His father ran around on his mother. His mother was an alcoholic. He was a perfect energetic match for me. My parents were horrified.

One evening after Rob and I dated my parents were playing cards with their best friends. Rob and I walked into the house and my mother called us in to speak to them. She asked her friends, "Doesn't he look like a girl?" It was 1970 and long hair was "in." My mother did not like anything that was different or out of the ordinary. My father was clean cut, my parents expected me to date someone like them. This upset her world. Rob clearly did. When she was upset about something she would let my father know. When my mother was upset, my father lost out. He took me aside and told me, "In order to keep peace in the family, you will not be allowed to date that boy." "But Dad," I replied, "He's a nice guy." My father was backed into a corner, "You know your mother. We can't have her upset."

When someone told me I could not do something it ignited a fire within me. I got angry. It did not matter if I felt it was a bad idea, I would do it anyway. No one was going to tell me I could not date him! I was beside myself. Their restriction of me pushed us closer together. It felt like the Capulets and the Montagues. I felt like I was Juliet and he was my Romeo. I found ways around the restriction. I had to walk everywhere I went. Even in the winter in Ontario I would go roller-skating. It was a great way to get out of the house and away from my parents.

My mother became suspicious of my activities and felt she had the right to read my personal diary. Shamed and invaded by my mother's inappropriate behavior I made preparations to move out of the house. Fearing the worst, my mother dragged me to her Catholic gynecologist. Dr. Howell was a woman and the most offensive of gynecologists. She seemed to hate the fact that I was having sex before marriage and clearly exhibited her feelings when she gave me my very first internal examination. Checking to see if I was pregnant against my will, it was the most painful examination I ever had. This equated to more abuse and intense humiliation. After asking the doctor if indeed I was no longer a virgin, my mother complained to my father until he did something about it. He forbade me to see Rob. His exact words were, "to keep peace in the family, you can no longer date that boy."

I snuck out as long as I could to see him at the local skating rink or at friends' houses. Eventually, on a snowy winter night, I made my departure for the roller skating rink. Unbeknownst to me my father followed me in the family car and caught me headed in the opposite direction towards Rob's house. He had a terrible temper and my behavior really riled him. From that point forward my parents became so suspicious it became impossible to see Rob even secretly, all roads out of the house were blocked. I knew what I had to do. Having my parents tell me I could no longer see Rob to keep peace in the family only made us want to be together more. We plotted together to unite against them.

I have five planets in Scorpio, which made me a headstrong, stubborn girl. The years of control and repression took their toll on me. My anger was building inside along with my raging hormones. I challenged my mother, not caring about the ramifications. One day while on my hands and knees washing the floor, I became angry at my mother's punishment for something I had done. I wanted to go somewhere with friends. Since this was a request of mine, the answer was again no. The anger welled up inside me and I could not keep my silence any longer. I blurted out, "Why do you have to be such a bitch?" I instantly regretted my words. I was in for it now! She flew across the room reaching me in a flash and began beating me across my shoulders and back with a flat open hand as I continued to hunch over the checkerboard kitchen floor, rag in hand. She continued to hit me with all her might for what seemed like an eternity, until I screamed at her, "That's enough! Stop!" I continued to pay for my words for several weeks. Any freedoms I had were removed. Whether my words were warranted or not did not matter. My father would hear about this as well and there would be hell to pay.

The tension in our household continued to build with no end in sight. My mother seemed to hate me and was jealous of me all at the same time. I was pretty, popular and good at sports. I should be grateful after all for the years and years of piano lessons that I had been given with my mother's hard earned babysitting money, even if I did not want to play the piano. My mother was living vicariously through me. I had to practice an hour every morning before school. I would play the piano in the basement, practicing scales and arpeggios while my mother went about her business of cleaning stopping only to yell, "No!" every time I played a wrong note. The fact that I did not want to play in the first place coupled with her constant criticism of everything wrong I did was becoming too much to bare. I hated every minute of it. I played the piano for eight years frequently being put on the spot for my mother's entertainment when she demanded that I play for her friends. I never was very good at it. Playing for others made me feel even smaller and more insecure. It highlighted my faults for all to see. My mother felt justified showing me off; after all she paid for the lessons.

The summer of my 15th year my parents sent me to California to visit a girlfriend that had moved there. When I got off the plane they did not recognize me. I had lost so much weight and become so thin and anxious I did not look like the same person. That summer away did so much good for me. I was able to see what loving, compassionate parents were like. It did not matter what Leslie did or didn't do her parents loved her anyway. Their love was not conditional upon her behavior. This was a striking contrast for me with my family. When I returned to Toronto after my trip I knew something had to change.

I was a nervous wreck my senior year of high school. Living at home under my parent's strict control and supervision was too much for me. With the assistance of the guidance department, I found out about a financial aid program that could assist teens to live on their own when there were intense family situations. I qualified for assistance, however my parents needed to give their permission. I had to jump through the government hoops and allow the team of social workers to interview our family, including my dad. I was absolutely terrified. My dad would be furious to have our family's dirty laundry hung out for the world to see.

I tried every way possible to circumvent this incredibly terrifying step. I knew I would be safe from harm until the team left our home. After that it would be bad. There was no way around it. I informed my parents of the meeting and that they both had to be present at home for it. My father was furious. To have strangers in our home getting private information about us was more than he could stand. He never trusted strangers. Having people he did not know asking questions about the rearing of his own children was none of their business. He was angry. When the interview began and the personal questions were asked about whether he ever hit me with a belt or not, that was it. He blew up in the meeting. Everyone had the opportunity to see my father's rage. The interview was not completed before he told everyone they had to leave. The social workers had all the information they needed and my financial aid was granted.

My first job was at the nearby Woolco department store in the candy department. I had gotten the job with my mother's help at the age of 15, a year before I legally was able to work. With the little money I made at the store and the financial aid I moved into a basement apartment with a girl I barely knew who was in her first year of University. Her father had just had a heart attack and had to quit his job. She had to move out of her parents' home because she could not study and focus on school with three little sisters living in a small apartment. Susan would be my first roommate.

I finished grade 13 living on my own. Without all the stress of living with my parents my grades were better. After graduating from high school I applied to Air Canada to be a flight attendant. I was told it might be six months or more before I received word about my dream job. I had wanted to be a flight attendant and travel since I could remember. In the meantime I was hired by the prestigious Hyatt Regency hotel in Toronto as a receptionist in the catering department.

Before my 18th birthday, I announced that Rob and I were getting married. Neither of my parents were excited about the prospect of me getting married so young. My father said, "Well I suppose I should say congratulations" as his voice trailed off. Words of congratulations never came. My parents paid for our wedding and my Dad actually walked me down the aisle. He even cried a little. However, they made their wishes known. My father called Rob a "weak sister." They were not happy about this marriage.

Three weeks before our October wedding date I realized that I was making a huge mistake and I was getting married for the wrong reasons. I nervously talked with my mother. I told her I did not want to marry Rob after all. With our trousseau tea party just one week away, my mother did not want to suffer the embarrassment of me calling off my wedding. She told me it would be easier for me to get a divorce down the road than to call off the wedding at this point. Needless to say, my mother got her wish; the wedding went on as planned. Heaven forbid that someone should make her look bad. We honeymooned in Hawaii. Not a bad honeymoon for a couple of kids.

Soon after we were married, I manifested the job of my dreams and became a flight attendant for Air Canada. I left Toronto to attend the three months of training in Montreal. Our marriage never stood a chance. Besides being too young and marrying for all the wrong reasons, I was about to embark on the most exciting five years of my life, traveling the world without my new husband by my side. Unfortunately for Rob he was not the bad boy I thought he was. He never mistreated or abused me, and I was not used to this. I was out of my comfort zone. I had an affair with a male flight attendant who mistreated me. Rob and I were divorced before I turned 21.

The years of sexual abuse had robbed me of my self-respect. I was filled with contempt and shame. I had extreme boundary issues and could not recognize when I was being abused or disrespected. I felt broken and incomplete; this to some extent began my journey towards healing. I enrolled in counseling with a psychiatrist and began therapy.

My first therapist was from Iceland. Strange that I should find someone from that country in Toronto, I thought. She did not want to talk about my sexual abuse and shunned talk about my parents. I could not believe that a therapist would not want to get to the root of the problem that I knew it to be. It was about this time that I found alcohol and my therapy ended. I began going to clubs to dance and drink the night away with friends. It helped to subdue the ache in my heart and eventually I forgot about being in so much pain.

I was young and divorced without responsibilities. I drank with my girlfriends and drank on layovers. I slept with pilots and other male flight attendants. After five years of flying I developed intense fears and had panic attacks on layovers. I had experienced a few emergencies mid-air and an emergency landing. I knew by the law of averages, if I continued to fly the risk of death became higher and higher. I became a white-knuckle flyer. Take offs and landings were the worst. I prayed fervently during those times. It never got any easier. After five years of being on-call as a flight attendant, I gave up my dream job for something where I would use my brain a little more. I found it difficult to leave my cat for five or six days at a time, never knowing when I would return.

I never had difficulty getting a job, keeping it was another thing. I got bored easily and tried various professions, from selling temporary help and dictation equipment to being a trainer for data processing installations. Nothing really thrilled me or kept my attention for long.

I also attracted people that would not respect me, as I had no respect for myself. Although not apparent upon first meeting me, I was filled with shame and guilt. I was plagued with fear and had terrible nightmares.

I had a difficult time staying out late at night and getting up for my sales job in the morning. I changed jobs fairly quickly and spent money like a drunken sailor. I had no anchor, no grounding in the spiritual. I was totally unbalanced and irresponsible. I had an affair with a handsome Italian married man with a really great ass that I dubbed, "J. Buns," which was short-lived. I recognized my error in judgment, believing that he was really going to leave his wife, and that he actually slept on the couch like he told me he did.

I was too young to know what marriage was about, I got my dream job with Air Canada, as a flight attendant when I was 19. Not long after that our marriage ended with me being the unfaithful party. It was sad; he was a really nice boy.

LESSONS LEARNED

I recognize that I am not alone and that many children are molested and unprotected. My mother continued to ignore my cries and the other signs of molestation. Her disconnection with herself as well as what I perceived as callousness and cruelty left me feeling unloved and unwanted. The fact that she bestowed jealousy as the icing on the cake and disallowed any kind of normal relationship with my father further cut me off from any kind of love. Because she felt unloved as a child, she was not able to love her own children beyond a cursory and caretaking capacity. She had her own feelings of unworthiness as well as the underlying feeling of being unlovable.

My codependency and people pleasing were created at a tender age. My parent's criticism of Rob and my father calling him a weak sister created doubt in my mind. They felt he was not good enough and never accepted him. When I became an adult they criticized my decisions. They felt that I couldn't make a good decision if my life depended on it. I came to believe I could not make good decisions and second-guessed myself. Why couldn't I be more like them? Their criticism of my partners continued into my fifties.

Due to the patterns set up within my family I confused sex with love and became promiscuous in my twenties. I found that my encounters left me increasingly empty, feeling guilty and ashamed. I had no discernible boundaries because of the early on molestation and abuse. My boundary issues continued to create issues in my life with my partners and as I attempted to raise my children. Because my parents and other perpetrators treated me with disrespect as a child I had no respect for myself. It was not until I was in my fifties that I was able to recognize these issues and do something about them.

All the events that occurred in my childhood served as a catalyst to evolve my soul. Had these events not occurred I would not be who I am now. I would not have had the burning desire inside me to get to the bottom of my pain and unworthiness. I do not blame my parents or those who molested me as they all fulfilled their contract with me, as Judas did with Jesus. I am sure their part was not played with ease. I have forgiven all the people who appeared to have hurt me as well as myself for feeling so lowly and unworthy for so long. I feel gratitude for all who played their part in my life so well.

Vibration: Between 100 Fear and 150 Anger

Life Force At Age 21: 65%

Mom And Dad

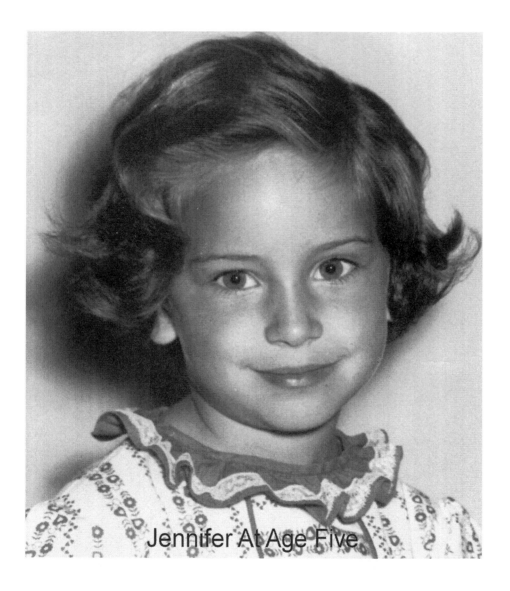

Jennifer At Age Five

Jennifer as a Teenager

CHAPTER THREE

Renaissance Man

It is said that if we have issues with money, we have issues with our fathers.

My father passed away after a long, difficult battle with leukemia. He died surrounded by almost all of his family at home in my parents' family room. He had been confined to a hospital bed for the final year of his life. My mother took care of him; barely leaving his side and only for groceries or a newspaper during that difficult final year. My father did not want to be left alone. He had become totally dependent on my mother at the end of his life. It was exhausting for her and very difficult to watch. This strong virile man reduced to 90 pounds at death did not feel like my father. He was not the man he used to be. He clung to life long after a rational mind would have. The morphine caused him to be in a dreamlike state for the last several months. The morphine drip did not eliminate the pain.

Although he was raised in a strict Gospel Hall Brethren household as a child, he turned away from his faith and organized religion. He felt that the main reason churches were created was for control and money. These beliefs made him question other things about Christianity. He felt that the birth of Christ was not actually on December 25th. He had read that scientists tracked the Christmas star to substantiate Jesus' birth and to verify the date. They found scientific proof that Jesus had been born on June 17th and not as we have been led to believe. Apparently shepherds did not sleep in the fields in the Palestine winters; it was far too cold. He also said that many of the Christian holidays originated from pagan celebrations and over time had become Christian holidays. The fact that Christians now looked down on pagans seemed ludicrous to him. Not that my father was a pagan, if he was anything he was agnostic. Dinner table discussions with my father frequently involved the most recent book he was reading. I was raised not to trust what I heard, or what I read. "Take it with a grain of salt," my father would say and "check it out for yourself."

He questioned everything. He felt that man had altered the Bible. He was not certain about where we go when we die because he had more questions than he had answers. Believing there was no afterlife and wondering about the existence of God was okay until it came time to die. This was the case with my father. He seemed fearless until he knew he was going to die. Then he really wondered what would happen to him upon his death. Where would he go? Would this be the end? Would he go to heaven or hell? Was there even a heaven or hell to go to? Most of all, he did not want to leave my mother.

Knowing now how our thoughts and words create our reality and that whatever you focus on you attract I remember hearing my dad talk about the latest discovery of cancer causing foods almost every night at the dinner table. After reading the newspaper at work, he would recount the latest cancer-causing discovery while we sat together munching on our cancer-causing bacon, or cancer-causing roast beef at the dinner table. It is not surprising that in the end, my father died of his own creation, myelodysplastic leukemia.

He was a stubborn man and wanted to make sure he exhausted every possibility for his survival. Going against his doctors' wishes he opted to have chemotherapy. His doctor told him it would not increase his chances for survival. In reality it most likely reduced his life. It weakened his constitution and made him very sick. Two of my brothers were policemen and had guns. He requested that my oldest brother buy him a gun so that he could kill himself. It was a selfish request, one that would have ended up with my father dead and my mother having to find him. He did not want to continue to experience the pain and suffering that became his life. My brother told him flatly that he could never do that to mom. Tim suggested that he take extra pills instead. My father said he had tried but could not keep them down. I can't imagine the pain he was in to ask my brother to do that.

I was not aware that my brothers had the inclination to talk to my dad about spiritual matters. I told him that it did not matter whether he believed in God or not, his soul would live on. His body would not be a part of him any longer but his soul would continue on. He argued with me while lying in the hospital bed my mother had purchased to make him more comfortable. Instead of having my father upstairs away from everyone and everything, mom opted to put the bed in the family room of their home in rural Ontario.

Dad did not believe in life after death. He clutched at life not wanting to leave my mother who had been his wife for 49 years. Thinking there was nothing after life made him afraid to let go. This man, who in his vibrant health seemed totally fearless, did not believe there was a soft place to land on the other side. It made him afraid of what was ahead of him. He questioned his beliefs. He wanted to believe in life after death.

The family room was a lovely place; sunny and warm in the winter and even sunnier and warmer in the short Ontario summer. From my father's bed he could see the pond and watch the birds flit in and out of the red current bush on the hillside and at the neighbor's hay field. He was no longer able to focus enough to read; the pain in his body was too great. He was loaded up with his morphine pump. There was too much of the mind-numbing stuff running through his veins for his brain and body to really function, but not enough morphine to kill the pain. He faded in and out of sleep while lying there.

As the Ontario summer faded, I visited my parents and saw my father one last time. My mother had her hands full taking care of dad. I decided to help mom out and mow their three acres of lawn with their John Deere ride-on tractor. It was cumbersome to me, the turning radius too large to really maneuver quickly, but the best one they ever had. Their ten acres were lovely with a barn dad had built in the back with a workshop and a pool between it and the house. Dad had created a solar water heater for the pool that looked really tacky, but did the trick. It allowed them to heat the pool cheaply without having to use oil.

As I moved to the last section of grass mowing where my dad could see me, I rounded the area near the pond. After a couple of passes near the fence and around the trees I moved toward the bank at the edge of the pond. I will never forget his booming voice yelling at me over the sound of the John Deere engine, "For goodness sakes don't mow so close to the pond! You're going to fall in with that blessed mower!" How he managed to summon the strength to yell loud enough for me to hear him all the way from the house, I will never know, but that was dad. He died September 22, 1993. He had tried desperately to hang on until my sons and I arrived from Atlanta. We sat helplessly in our seats on a Lockheed aircraft watching the minutes tick by, stuck, as luck would have it on an airplane on the Cleveland tarmac due to a mechanical problem. We never had the chance to hug him one last time or to tell him how much we loved him or even say good-bye.

I never expected the onslaught of emotion that spewed forth from me after his death. Knowing he was dying gave me many chances to visit him and speak with him before he crossed over. I knew that it was more than many people get. I was appreciative of that. His form of cancer killed him slowly and we watched his body deteriorate during the last four years of his life.

I worked as an executive secretary at GTE in Atlanta. I remember sitting at my desk the day my mother phoned me at work and said, "It's time. You better come now!" I knew what that meant. You never are really prepared emotionally. I could barely function enough to make the travel arrangements before I left work. I picked up Adam and Matthew from school and we all hastily threw some clothes in our suitcases.

We were out the door on our way to the airport within hours. I could not bare the thought of not seeing him one more time. The hour drive to my parents' house from the airport seemed interminable. I was tense and anxious. My youngest brother was standing outside the house my dad had built as we turned into the tree-lined, gravel driveway. The walnut and locust trees my father had planted over 20 years ago had grown so large. Evidence of my father's life was all around. I knew as my heart sank in my chest that in his weakened state he could not wait any longer and had finally succumbed to the strong pull of death.

I was grief stricken and emotional. I felt it was important for my boys to see their grandfather one last time. I made my youngest son go into the room where my dad lay. He was almost unrecognizable, thin, frail and small. Matthew was very sensitive and did not want to go in. He was so afraid as he had never seen a dead person before. I had no idea the trauma that seeing his grandfather so tiny and withered would have on him. I felt intense guilt afterwards for making him do something he was so adamantly opposed to. Death makes people do strange things. We deal with it so rarely and the finality of the physical is overwhelming. Looking back now I know I would have done things differently.

My Aunt Daisy and Uncle Will were visiting from Detroit. They were with my mother and father at the time of my dad's passing. They were a huge support for my mother and the rest of the family as well. The day after we arrived, we were all sitting in the kitchen drinking tea. The kettle was plugged in and starting to boil. All at once the power went out, lights and all. We all looked at each other and said, "It's Dad!" We all laughed. It was not a scary thing. My oldest brother Tim had jokingly said to my dad some months before, "Hey Dad, when you are here after you kick the bucket, do something to let us know you're visiting us, like turn the lights off, or something." Tim never minced words. No one questioned the validity of the statement; we all just knew. He was letting us know he had arrived!

Three months after my father's passing, I had a very intense and colorful dream of my father. We walked together along a beautiful, tree-lined pathway. As we walked side by side with the warmth of a lifetime between us we communicated without speaking, and walked up a steep incline. The terrain became steeper and steeper and abruptly ended. The ground fell away at the edge of an abyss. My father continued walking through the air suspended above the chasm as if supported by an invisible bridge. I stood at the edge of the cliff crying out to him, "Dad! Dad!" He turned and said, "I have to go, Chicken." He had always called me "Chicken" as a term of endearment. I knew he had to go, but I had such an upwelling of emotion I longed to join him. "Dad, I want to go with you!" I felt such a pull from my heart. He turned his head to look at me and told me lovingly but firmly, "You can't come with me now, you have to stay here." He continued walking away from me through the air as if he had a schedule to keep. In a flash he was gone. He had disappeared. I woke up feeling intense emotion and in tears. In my adult life I had never had such an intensely emotional dream, nor had I awakened crying. I knew he had visited me. It was too real to just be a dream. I felt as though I had been in my father's presence. After my dream he visited me at times during my waking state. I could feel his presence for a fleeting moment as I would have a thought about him. It was like a quick hello and then he was gone again.

After this dream experience, I noticed that my father would energetically "stop by" when I was gardening. I would be pruning my rose bushes or weeding in my flowerbeds, lost in my gardening, my mind in neutral then suddenly I would have a thought about my dad. I would not see him, but I certainly felt him. It took me three years to process his death and what it meant to me. My father had been a powerful figure in my life. He was the one that interested me in learning about metaphysics, meditation, Eric Von Daniken and Edgar Cayce. He had been an avid reader and a seeker.

I blamed him for my stubbornness. I could really be pigheaded, just like my dad. He would argue till he was blue in the face even when you proved him wrong. He never admitted defeat and never, ever apologized. He was also the biggest reason for imprinting me with the program that I was less than a man. He also felt I needed to have a man in my life to support me. He said he would always worry about me when I was single. Little did he know that my single days were the safest times in my life. These were unconscious thoughts, but formed a foundational part of my psyche.

My father was a formidable presence physically and energetically in our family. When I was in high school he had pushed me in the direction of secretarial work. I had a love for animals from the day I was born. When I wanted to be a veterinarian, he made it known he would not "waste" his money on a college education for his daughter when he knew she would grow up, and just get married and have babies. I was spitting angry with him and his beliefs about women for a very long time. It was as if he had cursed me with his words. I always felt that men were better than me and that they disrespected me and did not treat me as equals. What I was unaware of at the time was how long this issue would haunt and challenge me. The strange thing about this situation was that my father thought of me as strong even though I felt weak and fearful. When he spoke of his children to his friends he expressed that he had three sons, but his daughter had the biggest balls of all of them.

I had issues making money, keeping money and I spent all I made. I couldn't save it for the life of me. My parents could not understand it when they had been so frugal. I was raised in a family where food was doled out, counted and carefully measured. No one was to have more than another. We rarely had leftovers. When we did, they were surely eaten the next day. My parents went through a depression and a war. We heard frequently about how poor they were and that they knew what it was like to go hungry. My mother recounted stories of her childhood in the orphanage and later with her grandmother where she would play with fish and dress them up as dolls because they were so poor. Stories about rationing during the war were repeated over and over. I could recount the details of my mother saving her rations so my father would have food to eat when home on leave, while practically starving herself when she was pregnant with her first child. Its no wonder my oldest brother was a low birth weight baby. Years later he continues to battle overeating and being overweight. Is it because he was starved in utero? My parents continued to harp on frugality and not wasting anything throughout our childhood.

After my father's death I was hit very hard by all that my father was. My dad was a "larger than life" kind of person. He was the kind of man that lived life to the fullest, with gusto. I remember him well into his seventies during some of our summertime family gatherings with all of us siblings roughhousing around the pool, playing our version of volleyball tag. He found ways of beaning us as hard as he could with the ball just as we were coming up out of the water for a breath of air. Before we even had a chance to wipe the water out of our eyes or gasp for air - whammo! Mercy was not in his vocabulary. The volleyball would hit our heads so hard it would ricochet out of the pool and bounce over the fence. Sometimes it left large round red marks on the middle of our foreheads or shoulder. He would laugh so hard tears would roll down his face. This was not a sport for the faint of heart. There was always a gallery of women and small children sitting with my mother under the large umbrella, sipping iced tea and being entertained by the game. Watching the rivalry and ruckus was always entertaining and not always safe. The game often ended up on the pool deck with splashing and pushing into the pool. My father took great joy in embracing my mother and hugging her to him while he was soaking wet. He pretended to jump in with her while she screamed. He would laugh uproariously while my mother, the fair maiden, protested.

Swimming was my sport and I was in there with the men playing as hard as I could. My dad was certainly a physical man. He would often terrify my mother by jumping off the roof of the change house into the deep end of the pool. He was a vigorous man; fit and handsome into his seventies. He never lost his hair or his sense of humor.

The flip side of dad was his anger, criticism and his judgment of me. He was a bigot, raised by a bigot. He felt women should do women's duties as well as men's. My mother was a strong woman and a hard worker. He expected me to be the same. I had been terrified of my father, but now he was gone.

Thinking about how my father judged me reminded me of the last visit that my parents made to Georgia. Sitting at my kitchen table we got into an argument because he had taken my brother's word for something just because he was a guy. He figured I would not know anything about buying a gun and the laws related to it. My brother was a Canadian policeman, so my dad assumed he must know about things related to guns in Georgia! My brother told my father that since I was Canadian that I would not be able to purchase a handgun in Georgia. I handed my father the bottle of "Know It All" pills that Mike Crofton had recently given me. The apple did not fall far from the tree that was for sure. We were both stubborn and pigheaded, but he was worse. At least I would admit when I was wrong and say I am sorry, when I needed to. When I called a gun shop in Smyrna confirming what I believed, he changed the subject, never apologizing nor admitting he was wrong.

My father's anger could be seething and uncomfortable to be around. He could stay angry for days, even weeks. I did not understand the point of this. Where did that kind of anger get you? It certainly doesn't get you any love. My mother told me that he would be angry with her during the day and then expect some loving at night. Without eating crow or an apology he would storm about slamming things or go off in a huff in the car.

I grieved longer than I expected. His death affected my life profoundly for over two years. I found myself contemplating him and what he taught me. I thought about how his presence in my life affected my interests and even the joys in my life. I found myself pruning my roses and feeling my father's presence. I had a very strong feeling of him standing there beside me, only for a moment, but I felt him and I heard his voice saying to me in his loud booming way, "For goodness sakes change your oil!" He had always stressed how important it was to change your oil if you wanted your vehicle to last a long time. He said to me when he was alive, if there was only one thing I did to maintain the life of my vehicle, it was to change my oil. My dad never took his vehicle to a mechanic to have his own oil changed. He did it himself. He had little time for people who were not handy and do-it-yourselfers. He was self-made and expected the people in his world to be like him.

My dad influenced the fact that I enjoyed being outside and gardening, weeding or mowing my lawn. My father read constantly when he was alive. I adopted his crazy style of reading several books at one time. I liked to be challenged and learn new things. My father rarely went to doctors, and took responsibility for his own health until he got leukemia. Prior to that time, when he had an ache or pain, instead of reaching for a pill to relieve it, he would research what caused it and remove the food or drink from his diet. He had gout and after the diagnosis instead of going on medication, he used his diet to control it. He quit drinking alcohol because he found that it made his gout worse. When he realized that cheese caused his joints to ache and swell he cut that out too. Through process of elimination he changed his diet to heal his body. This was a great lesson for me.

I took my personal health into my own hands. In contrast with where I had been in the past, when I lived in constant fear and worry, I was visiting doctors often and frequently ill. I was now healthy and getting healthier all the time. I was still working at GTE and had medical insurance, so I went to doctors when a problem arose. However, I was finding that the healthier I ate, the better I felt and the less I got sick. I was very interested in natural health and healing. I found a fabulous book one day in a health food store, *Prescription for Nutritional Healing* by Phyllis Balch and James Balch. I used this book like a Bible, reading it cover to cover several times. Every time a problem arose with my boys or me, from a simple cold sore to a rash, the flu or acne, I looked it up myself and used herbs, vitamins and food to heal. I took responsibility for my own health and that of my children. I taught myself all about foods, herbs and healing the body naturally. I became an avid reader and usually read one or two books a week. I heard about a book by Florence Schovel Shinn, *The Game of Life and How to Play It*. I used this book also to manifest what I wanted in my life.

My father had influenced so much of what I was doing. He was a self-made man. He had varied interests from astrology and trance healer Edgar Cayce to conspiracy theories, alternate realities and the lost continents of Mu and Atlantis. He taught himself carpentry, plumbing and wood-working skills. He took art courses and painted in his spare time. He was a Renaissance man without being aware of it. I was fast becoming a Renaissance woman. I was educating myself, and learning constantly. On top of all the learning I wrote in my journal every night.

LESSONS LEARNED

My father's feelings about women plagued me until my mid fifties. My belief that I was subservient to men created internal conflict for me. I continued to perform household tasks that fell to women. I felt angry about having to do these chores while the men in my life did not participate. My belief that I had to work hard for my money was passed on by both of my parents.

My father's anger was something that impacted my relationships with men. I continued to attract men with anger issues that abused me. My relationships mirrored that of my parents, which is not surprising since they were my role models. The problems that my father had with communication and rage became my issues also. Instead of being able to communicate with the men in my life I tended to run away when there was conflict. I often got into my vehicle and left as my father did with my mother.

My father's continuing interest in learning about spiritual matters like Edgar Cayce, the lost continent of Mu and Atlantis became the cornerstone for my interest in metaphysics later on. I also picked up on his love of gardening, later owning my own landscaping business. My father discovered how foods affected his health by removing dairy from his diet. He taught me an increased awareness in my own health, later causing me to take responsibility for my own.

Vibration at my father's death: 75 – 100

Life Force at my father's death: 55%

Children Learn What They Live
If a child lives with criticism, they learn to condemn.
If a child lives with hostility, they learn to fight.
If children live with fear, they learn to be apprehensive,
If children live with pity, they learn to feel sorry for themselves,
If a child lives with ridicule, he learns to be shy.

But do not despair. . .

If a child lives with tolerance, they learn to be patient.
If a child lives with encouragement, they learn confidence.
If a child lives with praise, they learn to appreciate.
If a child lives with fairness, they live with justice.
If a child lives with security, they live to have faith.
If a child lives with approval, they learn to like themselves.
If a child lives with acceptance and friendship,
they learn to find love in the world.

Dorothy Law Nolte

CHAPTER FOUR

Queen of Spades

When Phil and I visited my mother we drove from Maryland up through Pennsylvania with the boys. The drive took us a full twelve hours. Sometimes we spent the night along the way. Usually we did it in one fell swoop. By the time we arrived we were all exhausted and it took several days of just lying around by the pool and doing nothing to recover.

Phil and I had just returned from England and Matthew was very excited to see his grandmother. Matthew was a sweet little two year old. He hit people he loved when he became excited. He just could not contain his joy and that was how he expressed himself. We always corrected him gently and explained to others that this was how Matthew was when he could not contain his joy and excitement. After all, he was only two. Fortunately he passed through this phase quickly.

My parents' house had a few strange quirks in its construction. My father built it himself and since he was not a contractor he missed a few crucial areas. He paid a grading contractor to cut out the basement. I cannot remember if he misread the plan or if the plan was incorrect but the end result was that the basement had a step down to a second level and was not cut deep enough, and there were two areas on the main level where there were two steps down.

We had just arrived from Maryland the day before. Phil and I had taken the boys out to give them a little break and had returned to my parents' home. As we all came into the house my mother stood at the top of the two steps. We walked up to the living room towards her. Matthew began hitting his grandmother on her backside with his two little hands open with great excitement. My mother grabbed one of his little wrists in her hand. While holding on tightly she paddled his backside, all the while saying, "Don't hit me!" She hit him three times before I had time to grab his other little wrist to prevent him from lurching down the two steps and falling face first on the tile floor.

It was very rare that I would speak out directly to my mother. She was the matriarch of our family and everyone deferred to her. She was also very defensive. We all were trained to keep our mouths shut where our mother was concerned. It was a very rare occurrence for me to say anything at all. However, this was my child, my sweet little Matthew, who would not hurt a fly!

To top it off he was a skinny little two year old! It was unlikely he weighed more than eighteen pounds.

I gave my mother a fierce look and said, "How could you tell Matthew not to hit you and then, as an adult who is supposed to be setting the example, hit him? What kind of example are you showing him especially when I am standing right here?" I went on to say that it was one thing for her to discipline my children when I was not around, and a completely different issue when I was standing right there. My mother's response was, "Well you would not do anything!" I told her, "You never even gave me a chance. Your response was so automatic I had no time to respond." Phil and I looked at each other. I said, "Let's go," as I grabbed our car keys and scooped Matthew up. Phil and Adam followed us out the door quickly. We could not exit fast enough. We quickly piled into the BMW and drove off. I was so upset my face was on fire. I knew we could not let this event go. We decided to go to the closest fast food restaurant. We sat there quietly discussing what we needed to do. Phil said we had to leave. After just making the drive the day before, neither of us really wanted to go, but we knew we had to. We returned to my parents' home and packed our belongings into the car and told my parents we were leaving. I remember my father expressing his regret at our decision. I said under the circumstances we had to leave. I expressed to him that this was not the first time that mom had taken the discipline of our children into her own hands without consulting us. My mother overstepped her bounds. She did not see that she did anything wrong. To stay was to agree with her.

We returned home from the long trip exhausted and emotionally spent. As the boys slept, Phil and I talked about what had happened and all the history of my mother and disciplining our children. She felt that she had every right to discipline anyone's children anywhere. She corrected their manners at the table, she told them which hand to eat with, she felt she had the market cornered on etiquette and felt compelled to correct everyone. I had grown up with my mother correcting my friends if they ate at our house. Some would never return because of it. My parents were quite a team. All my father had to do to scare someone was stand there; my mother only had to speak.

I decided to write my parents a letter. I addressed it to both of them. I wrote it evenly and sternly, like I really meant it. It is one thing for someone to hurt me, a completely different thing when you attack an innocent child. I could not allow this to continue. I made it clear that my mother had no right to discipline our children if we were present. If she witnessed something happening when I was not in the room or the house, she was to tell me, unless it was a matter of life or death. I went on to explain that they had their children, it was our turn to raise our children as Phil and I saw fit. They may not agree with the way we raised them, but they needed to keep their hands off from now on.

It was over a year before we had another visit with my parents. I had not phoned them during this time either. I felt that enough time had passed that both of them knew that I was serious. Neither of us wanted this to occur again. They still felt that they were within their right and no apology or assurances were ever given. I was the stubborn, angry one; the unspoken undercurrent was they blamed me. They felt if I raised my children properly, like they did, this kind of thing would never happen. My father supported my mother's choices. Even if he did not agree he backed her up.

Rebuilding our relationship was a gradual process. I had severed all ties with my parents before. I had left home at sixteen when I did not agree with their punishment and control of me. Now there were two more grandchildren in the mix.

I was not unique when it came to my beliefs and feelings about mother interfering in our lives and that of our children. Visits with the grandchildren were strained because Grandma expected perfect manners and behavior. It was not the easy, loving kind of relationship I see with other families. Our kids felt the tension when we visited. There were certain children that were favorites and then there were the "others." Adam was one of the others. Everything he did rubbed my mother the wrong way. He bullied his little brother and my mother constantly took up for Matthew. Spending time around the pool helped to ease the tension because the children could act as children. In the house however, they were expected to behave like adults — quiet and reserved.

My mother felt that she could say what she wanted whenever she wanted. She was not concerned with tact or diplomacy. People's feelings were hurt when she unleashed her judgment or criticism. It was nothing for my mother to tell people in her church that they should not wear certain colors or plaids because they made them look fat, or something of that nature. For me, as a child, my grades were never good enough. I did not practice hard enough; my room wasn't clean enough. Why did I want to look like everybody else? Why couldn't I have my own style? There was no acceptance for who I was, even though I didn't know who that was.

I had long beautiful hair. I raised my voice and cried too many times as she violently brushed it she had it cut off when I was about ten. I hated it. I came home from the hairdresser with a short haircut that was not flattering to me. She got her way. I walked in the door and angrily said to both my parents, "There! I hope you're happy! Now you have four boys!" My mother still tells people that story thinking that it is funny. She did not realize how she destroyed what little self-esteem I had by systematically breaking me down.

When it came time for me to date, my mother expressed her opinion loudly. If I had a boy over we had to sit in the living room uncomfortably and talk while she rushed about the house doing things in the next room and making her presence known. When she wanted him to leave at the end of the night, instead of asking politely, she would stand in the front hall winding an alarm clock. She would say in her domineering and controlling way, "When my grandmother wanted someone to leave she would wind her alarm clock." She was as subtle as a ton of bricks on a windy day.

I was embarrassed to bring friends home because of how strict my parents were. My father scared the crap out of everyone except my friend, Dini. Her father was Macedonian and was just like mine, angry. My dad had a loud booming voice because of the machinery that he worked around. She was not bothered by either of my parents at all. In fact, she liked my mother. My mother liked Dini also and encouraged our friendship.

My father really loved my mother. He was not a romantic type that brought home flowers or presents. He did show he cared on occasion. My mother had migraines ever since I could remember. Sometimes she would be down for days where she could not even see. She would vomit and pass out from the pain in the bathroom. On one occasion I visited my parents and found her lying in bed and repeating the same thing over and over again. She kept asking me, "What time is it?" I would tell her the time and she would ask me again. A few moments later she asked me again. After two hours of keeping an eye on her, her right arm shook uncontrollably. I wondered if she had a stroke. I told my father we needed to get her to the hospital. When we arrived at the hospital they did not believe she was having a migraine. At first they thought that my mother was drunk. After realizing there was no alcohol on her breath they took a different approach. They wanted to do tests to see if she was having an epileptic seizure, or a stroke. After over two hours of observation they believed us and gave her a shot of demoral for pain. My mother finally slept after that, but it took another four days before she was really functional. The aftermath of one of her migraine episodes could last a week or more where my mother was still feeling the effects of a migraine and on edge. Usually an emotional upset would set her off. When I was a teenager my father rode us all pretty hard to make sure we did not upset her to keep her from getting "sick." This was a very powerful tool for my mother and she wielded it like a weapon.

My mother was very worried about what the neighbors thought about us. My boyfriend, Rob's, long hair embarrassed her. To her it was different and she did not like that. She was used to men and boys with short, neat haircuts. The fact that Rob's parents did not make him get a haircut really bothered her. She could not understand why anyone would want to have hair like that. When my mother did not want me dating Rob she let my dad know how upset she was. He had to make a judgment call. It did not matter that I thought I was in love with him. My behavior was upsetting his kingdom. I had to be the one to sacrifice.

When Rob and I were dating we talked about wanting to go to the cottage as my older brothers had done with their wives and children. I loved the lake and swimming and looked forward to being able to have a romantic weekend with Rob. Even though we were engaged at the time my mother told me in no uncertain terms we were not going to use it until we were married. By the time we were married my mother had convinced my father that they needed to sell the cottage because no one was helping them take care of the place. Everyone wanted to use it but no one wanted to do any work. Before we had a chance to have our weekend it was sold. It felt as if any joy I had my mother had to take away.

My mother regularly expressed to me what I should or should not be doing with my children. I would never measure up as a parent in her eyes. I wasn't firm enough with my children she would say. When I talked to her of not feeling good abut myself she would say exasperatedly,

"Nonsense! You are strong! There is nothing wrong with your self-esteem!" There was little validation for my feelings.

We had a relationship that could be really wonderful with us sharing jokes and stories either on the phone or during a visit and laughing together and enjoying each other. The first two or three days of a visit with my mother went fairly smoothly. She would cook my favorite foods and even buy avocados for me, knowing how much I like them. We both loved to shop years ago and enjoyed going shopping together. After three days the newness of being together would wear off and so would my mother's best behavior. The gloves came off and my mother expressed her disdain for my viewpoint or the way I lived my life. She told me point blank that I should be more like her. It could be something as simple as telling me how to prepare some food item that I had made for years. I felt that she was treating me as a child and I would be taken back to my younger years. I heard in between her words that she did not love and accept me as I was and I would want to leave.

Over the past ten years or so I visited my mother with my daughter Ana. While I was talking to my mom about flights and the cost, she offered the suggestion that I should leave Ana with her father and come alone. Ana wanted to travel with me, as most children do. Ana never got to meet her grandfather but did get to see the house that he built for them. While we visited, my mother offered to brush Ana's hair. I told my mother that Ana was quite capable of brushing her own hair. As usual, mom thought she could do better. I did not think she would want her to do that. Ana, like me, did not know how to say "No!" to my mother. She said a meek, "Sure, Grandma." I gave her a knowing look that said to beware. It was not long before mother was yanking my daughter's hair and causing her pain. Ana was not like I was as a child and pulled away. As she did so my mother yanked her hair and pulled her back towards her. When she expressed that my mother was hurting her she told her granddaughter in a harsh tone, "Oh, Ana, you are such a brat."

During the same visit, the summer that Ana was ten, my mother asked her if she needed to go to the bathroom before we left the house to visit my brother's farm. As far as social graces, Ana was quite mature. She was tall and looked much older than ten. I did not ask her those kinds of questions giving her the benefit of the doubt. Ana looked embarrassed at the question and said, "No I don't have to go." My mother pulled the door closed and locked it preparing to get into her car. Once outside the door we all stood there for a moment and Ana said, "You know I guess I do have to go." My mother said harshly, "Oh, Ana, you are such a pain in the ass!" I was absolutely dumbfounded. It was so cruel and lacking any compassion at all.

I wondered why I continued to spend money on plane tickets and take the time to come and visit when she was so cruel to my daughter and so disrespectful to me. She was clearly jealous of anyone who took time and attention away from her. I doted on Ana, she was my long awaited and late-in-life little girl. I was so delighted to have her in my life and found her to be such an incredible gift. She was constantly a source of light and joy to me and that I revered her bothered my mother terribly. She thought that I acted like the sun rose and set over Ana. She once told me exasperatedly, "For goodness sakes, Jennifer, you treat her like she's something special!" My mother had a low opinion of children. She did not revere them at all. It should definitely be the other way around in her opinion. A grandmother that felt children were a bother raised her. Children raised my mother's dander and made her uncomfortable. My mother expressed it to me when I was a child and now to my children.

During the same visit, Alan, my sister-in-law's brother from England, was in Canada and wanted to spend time with Ana and me. He rented a car so we could tour around a little together. My mother was resentful that I wanted to spend some time with him away from her. She invited Alan to dinner one evening. It was clear she wished she had not been so open with the invitation when she yelled at Ana during dinner for doing something she did not approve of. Ana looked at Alan with embarrassment. When my mother saw Ana look at Alan for support she became incendiary. "What are you looking at HIM for? He's not your father, he doesn't mean ANYTHING to you!" I could not believe that she could be so overtly cruel, rude and disrespectful to a guest at her dinner table. I sat at the table with my mouth hanging open. Alan stood up pushing his chair away from the table, leaving his dinner barely touched and commented that he felt that he was in a stage play and it felt surreal. He did not return to my mother's home for a long time after this incident. Not that I blamed him at all. My mother was jealous of him and the fact that his presence meant she would have less time with me.

Where most people would be polite to a guest that they did not like my mother would sooner invite someone to dinner and then crucify them over dessert. The manipulation and control that she powerfully exercised continued to be evident throughout my life. She did not like the fact that Alan loved me.

When I visited my mother's home, I felt like a captive. I could not leave or visit my other family without my mother insisting on coming with me. It was as if I had never left home and I was still a child.

When I talked about how intuitive Ana was and that she was gifted my mother got extremely exasperated with me, "She's just a child!" she would say. We had a very big difference of opinion on most things, but especially children. I came to learn that my children taught me many things. Ana spoke to her angels and frequently had very insightful comments about what I was doing in my life. They constantly showed me things about myself that I did to notice on my own until I became completely conscious and awake.

The best thing I ever did for my soul was to move out of Canada far enough that I could not return home in a moment's notice. This space allowed me to change and grow becoming new and improved, different from anyone else in my family. My youngest brother did something similar. He and his family moved out of the area and keep to themselves. He visits Mother rarely and for short periods of time.

I know that my mother did not have the burning desire to evolve her soul and heal like I did. It was too painful for her. She did not want to dredge up the past and look at all that happened to her from a deep level. Shortly after a particularly bad migraine her neurologist suggested that she go to therapy. She felt the source of her migraines was emotional. My father and I went with her for her first appointment. I will never forget my father and I sitting in their car in the doctor's parking lot waiting for mom to return. Mother walked woodenly out of the building and got into the front seat. As she sat down we both looked at her expectantly wondering how her first session went. She was extremely upset. We wondered what on Earth had happened. She said emotionally, "I will never go back there ever again! She made me talk about my family and the past and I started to cry. I will never go back." She did not want to look at the issues. She continued to suffer in constant pain because of her past. She never resolved her childhood in her mind. My mother constantly felt victimized because she lost her parents when she was so young. When an event occurred that was upsetting to her she was emotionally overloaded; hence the migraine. It was interesting that she told me "Get over it, Jennifer!" when I talked about the effect that being molested had on me as an adult.

There were many years that I wished that things were different. I wished that my mother had an easy manner with her grandchildren and could enjoy them in a relaxed way. Her own childhood had set deep grooves in her brain that she did not know how to get past.

For years I railed against being like my mother at all. After years of resisting I have learned how what you resist persists. I stopped resisting. I have heard the adage "the apple does not fall too far from the tree" more times than I care to remember. I have come to realize things about myself and the way I was with my own children. I was extremely critical and judgmental when Adam was young. Because my own parents spanked and hit us with belts, spoons and hairbrushes, it was commonplace until Adam was 14 for me to do the same on occasion. I hated myself afterward and knew there was a better way. Between the harsh guidance of Mitch and my mother about how I should handle my oldest son, I vacillated from one extreme to the other. Sometimes I would lecture him endlessly and he would tune me out. When he swore at me one day coupled with the pressure that Mitch was putting on me to get Adam under control, I cracked a wooden spoon over his backside and went into my room and wept afterward. I was angry with Adam, but also myself for listening to others about how I needed to get Adam to listen to me. This was the last time I laid a hand on him. Afterward I still let cruel words slip before I became conscious of how negatively they impacted my children. I called Adam an idiot the day he arrived from Colorado for a visit after he opened the garage door to see the dogs and they ran away. I felt horrible guilt when I saw Adam's face.

I grew up with criticism and inherited my mother's tendency to criticize my children and the gifts that they gave me. It was a pattern that my mother had. I am not sure if it came from never getting what she wanted as a child, or not being able to ask for what she wanted. I grew up being ever so careful to buy personal items for my mother instead of anything pertaining to the house. We all learned the harsh reality of giving mother an item that had anything to do with cooking or cleaning. It was never well received. I found it interesting when the people at the library she volunteered at surprised her with a homemade carrot cake for her eighty-eighth birthday. She told them that she hated carrot cake. It is sad that she fails to see that people love her and she cannot receive love graciously. Instead she has to push it away. One of my favorite cousins takes the time to bring a poinsettia to my mother every Christmas since his mother passed away. It takes him over two hours round trip plus the time to visit with my mother. Sadly my mother wants to tell him that she hates poinsettias.

Over the years I have come to an understanding of my mother. Through understanding my mother I have learned to understand myself. I hoped that she would change. Instead I have changed. Accepting others as they are is unconditional love. Once we come to accept ourselves as we are, we have compassion for others and love them where they are. When your formative years are indelibly imprinted with pain, the discomfort of the pain is what you live with every day. It becomes your reality. The discomfort has to be so bad that you want to make a change for your perspective to be different. My mother continued to perpetuate her past by talking about it and never letting it go. She could not get beyond the paradigm of being an orphan. Even at eighty-eight years old it is the excuse for everything in her life that does not go well. She over-spends on clothes and her teeth because she had nothing as a child because she was an orphan.

Perspective is an interesting thing. If you continue to focus on your anger it is impossible to forgive anyone for anything. Anger gives us an out; it makes us feel that we are right. Righteousness is the fastest way to self-destruction. Anger also makes the issue we are dealing with seem larger as it blows things out of proportion. We make up stories that vindicate ourselves and keep us apart from those we love and are in relationships with. Once you release the anger you realize that under it is a hurt little child that just wants to be loved. Being able to express the pain that our inner child feels allows us to move forward. We think that the pain is too difficult to experience. We will do anything to avoid it including drinking, smoking or eating our drug of choice; in my case it was chocolate. Allowing ourselves to really experience all of the emotions fully releases the charge of the original event and allows forward motion in our lives.

When you let go of the anger you are able to touch and feel into the pain that is underneath. What I have found through my own journey is that the experience of suffering with the pain is far greater in intensity and discomfort than just feeling the pain. Suffering is what happens when we resist. I have realized that we often miss out on events, dates, relationships and joy because we are so busy feeling angry and filled with righteous indignation.

Letting go of anger first allows us to move through to forgiveness. Forgiveness is what happens when you let go of the anger and resentment. Forgiving is freeing for the person doing the forgiving. The process of forgiving someone is for us, not the person we are forgiving. It removes the focus from the person we are upset and angry with and allows us to move on with our lives. My mother never let go of being angry with her mother for leaving her. She remains resentful about her life to this day. Which means that for eighty-three years my mother brooded and resented her life because she focused on what she did not have, instead of what she did have.

My mother called me recently and asked what I was up to. I told her I was finishing my book. She told me that she was reading Jane Fonda's memoir and found it interesting. As she was getting ready to hang up she told me that I had to write the good, the bad and the ugly. She said, "You have to write about it all." A week later she realized what that meant and told me if I chose to write about my childhood she would never forgive me. I considered letting it go but realized that I have graduated. I no longer keep my truth hidden just to keep the peace and her life from shattering. I replied honestly, "Mother I am writing about my childhood. As you said, the good, the bad and the ugly. It is the cornerstone of my life and I will write about it." The following week she called to tell me she had decided that she did not want me to be one of the executors in her estate after all. She said it was because I lived so far away. Instead she chose to have all three of my brothers. I was the only one left out.

When you have issues with your mother you have issues with relationships. It does not take a rocket scientist to see that is the case with me. I have spent the past fifty years unraveling the effects of my childhood through the journey that is my life. I love both of my parents. My relationship with my mother has been rough and rocky as well as loving and fun. As I have become more honest with my mother there have been moments of raucous laughter as I spoke what was on my mind. My honesty has also stirred my mother's anger when I spoke my truth about some comment she made about my daughter or my life. She has taught me so much about myself. I understand my frailties and hear the stubbornness in my own voice when I hear my mother respond to some suggestion that I make to her about a dietary change that would assist a current health issue. She resists anything I suggest just as I resist her suggestions for my life. It is laughable that we both react to a recommendation that either of us makes with such resistance, mirroring each other.

We had periods of closeness and tenderness that last many months. Bliss ends when I don't agree wholeheartedly with her direction for my life, or when I make a suggestion for hers. I love my mother. She has given me an inner strength to survive no matter what. My vibrant health and good looks I have her to thank for as well. My mother was and is a beautiful woman. She is talented and intelligent and most of all eighty-eight and healthy. She was an integral part of making me who I am today. When we had little money she managed to re-design clothes for me out of dresses people gave her. I was always well dressed going to school. She gave me piano lessons for eight years rather than taking them herself. I have her to thank for being a fabulous cook. I have passed my confidence in the kitchen onto my own daughter as well as both of my sons.

My boys got her drunk at my wedding in 2009. I find it peculiar that the two men in my life she liked the most were both alcoholics. She really liked Jesse. She said she had never seen two people so completely in love. She was so happy that I had found the happiness I had been searching for with him for so long. Too bad it was so short-lived. What I noticed that day was a softness and raw quality to her emotion. Our wedding touched a place in her soul that had been asleep for a long time. She accessed a very deep part of herself that day. We all enjoyed her. Adam and Matthew still talk about handing my mother one margarita after another and laughing with her at the table when she could barely stand up. It was very unusual for my mother to really let her guard down and she did that day. It was really sweet to see. I wish she could do it more often, I think she would be so much happier if she could. After drinking and eating my mother tirelessly worked in the kitchen acting like a far younger woman than her eighty-eight years. Her sense of self worth comes from working hard.

I love my mother. I see the parts of her in me; like fine bone china strong yet fragile at the same time.

LESSONS LEARNED

From the time of my conception I was programmed to be in fear about not having enough money. My mother was worried how they would feed another child when they were already struggling. Once I was born, I became an instant disappointment when I was not born a boy.

Being pretty became a curse for me as my mother became jealous of the way I looked. My father was not allowed to get too close to me, as my mother would intervene. It was one of those things that made me go hmmmm.

My mother was the matriarch of our family. Although my father was the boss, she ruled the roost. My efforts to please her early became a constant running behind me, where I could never be fast enough, pretty enough, smart enough or thin enough. My belief became, "I am not worthy." This belief ruled my life.

The fact that she lost her mother at the age of five and her father six months later colored the landscape of her life. It shaded everything for her. She missed out on the love and nurturing of her parents. As a result of her childhood she was shut down and disconnected from her true self and her heart. She did not have the benefit of the self-healing that I had. She was defended and resisted events in her life. She strove to be the perfect homemaker, decorator and cook. Our home was always tidy and clean. Food was carefully measured and doled out, creating a feeling of lack that we all carried with us into our adult lives. My parents were careful with their money and managed to save a substantial amount considering my father's income. Our family was well thought of in our community. However, the secrets that we all kept ate us alive. We always looked nice, neat and tidy — the perfect family.

I love my mother, but it has not been easy. Mom had difficulty treating her children as adults even when we had our own households and families. She did her very best to love us. Children were not a source of joy for her.

An interesting caveat; while writing this book and speaking with the Ascended Masters I was given a series of clues to my identity. I had difficulty giving birth normally. I was afraid I would die in childbirth. Several different people had told me that I died in my past life from complications from childbirth. My favorite flowers are roses, like my grandmother. I have confirmed with the Ascended Masters, I am the reincarnation of my mother's mother. I am my own grandmother!

Isn't creation wonderful!

CHAPTER FIVE

Material Man, Material Woman

By the time I was 26, I began working at the Constellation Hotel on the airport strip in Toronto. I worked as a waitress during lunch, around the pool in the summer and as a hostess in the lounge overlooking the runway at night. It was a pretty classy place, attracting travelers from all over the world. It was here that I met Phil Yates. I knew when I saw him across the lounge that I was going to marry him. I even said to our bartender, Bobby, "Now that is the kind of guy I could marry." Phil was a very handsome and equally intelligent man originally from Westchester, New York who had moved to Maryland. He had a good job with a large company and I knew just by looking at him he was going places. What I did not know was that he was being drawn to me like a magnet. I had attracted another man who was vibrating at the same rate and level as I was. He had similar issues as I did and was also a Scorpio. It was no surprise to me that he chose a table in my section.

Our connection was instantaneous. Phil was three years older than I, beautifully dressed and handsome. I would have been attracted to him without the beard, but to me that was the icing on the cake. It was obvious he felt the same way about me. Before he left the lounge we made a date. We spent as much time together as we could before his return to Maryland.

We dated long distance for a while. Before long, he broke up with his current girlfriend and I was moving to Maryland to live with him, leaving my roommate, Janie, responsible for the entire rent of the house we had been sharing as well as my cat, Lydia.

My parents were not happy about our live-in arrangement at all. Since the only way my parents expressed themselves was in anger my father did not possess the ability to communicate his sadness about his only daughter moving so far away. I did not realize his unhappiness until much later. In retrospect we often have flashes of insight and that was certainly the case with me.

My mother flew to Maryland ostensibly for my birthday a month later. In reality her mission was the express purpose of talking us into getting married. She did not want me to be living in sin with a man because someone in the family might find out and we could not have that. Before we knew it we were getting married. My mother's philosophy was: "It is just as easy to get divorced if it doesn't work out."

Within months of our meeting we had a small ceremony in Phil's townhouse in Gaithersburg with close friends and family. Those in attendance were a few friends and his Golden Retriever, Brandy. Since both of us had been married once before, neither of us was interested in a large celebration.

Since I was Canadian and did not have my green card yet, I babysat for the family that lived right next door. I was welcomed into the small Jewish community that had formed around us. She worked at Bloomingdale's and he worked at her father's car wash. Working for the Baumer family gave me some spending money and I contributed what I could to the financial pot.

Having Brandy in the house helped me to miss home less. I had reluctantly left my own dog, Jasmine, with my parents. They attempted breeding German Shepherds for a while and had several dogs. My father had suggested I take one of their females, Cleo, with me when my friend Janie and I rented a house in Mississauga. My dad felt she would offer us both some protection. I instantly bonded with Cleo and trained her daily. I changed her name to Jasmine and really grew to love her.

A few months later when it came time to move to Maryland my father suggested that I give Cleo back to him. Phil already had a dog; it would be best. I really wanted to take her, but he was adamant, the answer was "No!" He said he wanted to breed her. When my father was angry he had an intense and wild-eyed look on his face. When he was in this state we knew not to cross him. It did not matter how long we were away from home or how old we were we did not argue.

I was away from my family and friends for the longest period in my life. I lived in Montreal for three months when I was first stationed there with Air Canada, but flew home frequently to visit. However strange it seemed, I still missed my family and wrote my mother to save money on phone calls.

Six months after our wedding I received a letter from my mother. I sat at the kitchen table opening it as I sat down to read it. I read the opening line and picked up on the tension of her words, when all at once I cried. I felt a cascade of emotion that I could not contain. I was overwhelmed with a feeling of please tell me this is not happening! I reread the words on the page a second time to see if I read it correctly. When I realized I had the damn broke. I started to wail. Tears flowed down my cheeks and onto my mother's letter landing in puddles on the ink. "I can't believe he would do such a thing! Why did he not let me take her with me?" Phil came rushing in and asked me what was wrong. By this time I was sobbing and unable to respond. I could not even speak to explain what I had read. Continuing to weep, Phil picked up my mother's letter that had fallen onto the kitchen floor. This is approximately how it read:

"Dear Jennifer,

We have been having quite a time here lately. I have been terribly sick with a migraine for almost two weeks. This is the best I have felt since that time. The weather has gotten warmer and the snow is gone. The grass is beginning to green up and we are seeing lots of birds around the pond. We had let the dogs out for a while after lunch, as it was a nice warm day. Your father and I had just had coffee on the back porch. I returned to do my laundry when I heard a gunshot. Then I heard another one. My first thought was it was your dad! I went running outside to see your father walking with his rifle in his hands. Then I saw Cleo lying in the field next door. Your father shot Cleo. I was so upset that I collapsed right on the spot. She had been chasing cows in the field next door. You know that farmers have the right to shoot a dog when it is chasing their cows. She has done this a couple of times, so your father shot her. She has done this before and he must have felt it would continue to be a problem. I am sorry but I felt you needed to know and I felt that a phone call was not the best way."

I recognized my mother's avoidance in her letter. The fact that she could not call me to tell me put distance between her and the news she had to give me. I knew she was in fear of my father. If he could shoot a dog, what would prevent him from shooting her.

She continued with the rest of her letter about news of other things. Trying to downplay the news. I knew she was terribly upset. I have never known my mother to pass out from anything but a terrible migraine. This marked the beginning of a very trying time for my mother that I would be made aware of later. My father had retired. I was sure he was not an easy man to live with. Neither was she.

I was extremely upset and instantly asked anyone who would listen, "Why oh why did you not let me take her?" He transferred his anger about me leaving Canada onto my dog. It was the way he operated. I recognized from my father's actions that he was in pain about me leaving Canada and moving so far away. He did not have me to argue with anymore. I know he missed that. We had many heated discussions about world issues and metaphysical subjects. I was the only one that would go toe-to-toe with him in a discussion. I was just as stubborn as he was. He had taught me to think for myself even if I did not share all my thoughts. I did not realize how angry he was about my moving until this horrible event occurred with my sweet dog. I know that my mother was having serious concerns about him and wrote a letter to him about being so angry and still expecting her to be warm towards him in bed. He was retired and he still expected her to do everything she had ever done without any help from him. She felt like a servant rather than a partner and definitely not appreciated for all she did. I could only imagine what else was happening back at home.

It took me a long time before I was able to let go of the irrational decision that my father made to kill my dog. I did not speak to him for over a year after this event. I did not realize then that control or the lack of it was at the bottom of my father's irrationality.

Having Brandy, Phil's Golden Retriever, was a comfort to me. I grew up with animals all around me and usually had several at one time. I loved Phil's dog and we became steadfast friends. I would get my clothes out before I took my shower, laying my underwear on our bed. When I got out of the shower my underwear was nowhere to be found. Brandy had taken them off somewhere. It meant he accepted me and was being playful. I belonged to him. Everyone around us loved Brandy. He was unruly on the leash and bolted out the door whenever it was opened. I walked Brandy several times a day usually by the lake in our subdivision. The funny thing about him was that he did not know how to swim. I had never met a dog that could not swim before. With more frequent walks and attention during the day Brandy became more relaxed and calm.

My mother liked Phil but she felt he did not treat me well. She was critical of all her children's choices for mates thinking that no one we picked was good enough. Phil was nicer to me in public than in person and attempted to keep my friends and family at bay. Knowing how critical my parents were was one of the excuses he used. He tended to act grandiose in public and wanted to be the center of attention. In public he acted like he was the most adoring of husbands. Behind closed doors that was not always the case.

My family was very judgmental and critical. Rather than leave our marriages alone they thought they had the right to make comments. They tended to be controlling, manipulating or interfering much of the time. I could understand why he tried to keep my family at arm's length. I felt that Phil was trying to protect me.

Within a year of our marriage I was pregnant. I knew the rhythm method was not very effective. Apparently my cycle was off by two weeks, just enough for a direct hit. Phil was not happy. He had not accomplished all that he wanted to before we started a family. He had hoped to save enough to move into a larger home and to have more of a nest egg. He suggested that we postpone having our first child to a later date. I was adamant that this was meant to be. It was the first of many arguments. He wanted to win every time. Our passion in the bedroom also meant impassioned arguments. We were both strong and determined people when we disagreed, it was a challenge to move forward. I began seeing a counselor before we had been married a year.

Phil was a very good provider for our family. He worked hard at his profession and moved up in his company quickly. Since I ended up quitting my job as a secretary after our first son, Adam, was born he felt the home was my domain and left me to it. Adam was born after a very difficult, thirty-six hour labor by Caesarian section. He looked like a prizefighter all battered and bruised and swollen from his challenging beginning. I could not believe how much I loved him and became very fearful of something happening to him while he slept. I enjoyed the bonding that breastfeeding allowed and grew to enjoy motherhood tremendously. I felt becoming a mother was the best thing that ever happened to me. He was a handsome and bright child and very active. Adam and I attended two playgroups and I developed a strong bond with several of the women in the group. One woman, named Jean, and I got along well and got together outside of the group setting as our two growing boys enjoyed each other's company as well. She was a very strong woman whom I admired. Her husband was almost 20 years her senior and adored her. She and I talked about our husbands and families. I was a little taken back about how she talked about her sex life. Her family was much more open than mine about sex. The relationship she had with her husband seemed warmer and closer than ours.

Although Phil said he loved us, he was disinterested in our children when they were young and was emotionally unavailable and distant. Over time I also recognized that he was obsessive and controlling and when he could not control me he had the propensity to throw his limited weight around. I admit I pushed his buttons regularly. I was in pain, although I did not know it and felt badly about myself. I felt lonely even when he was around. I felt like I raised Adam all by myself. He traveled a great deal, and worked long hours but provided well for our family. After a long week of having Adam to myself it bothered me that Phil would go off and spend half the weekend playing golf with friends.

Phil got promoted and we were able to move to a larger place close to my friend Jean. We had five acres of land with a pond. The house was big with a great place for Adam to play with his friends. I loved the kitchen and having more room outside. Being able to spend more time with Jean and her two boys was a bonus. I visited Jean and her newborn redheaded little boy. I remembered how much I enjoyed Adam when he was an infant. I wondered if that would bring Phil and I closer together.

After nearly three years of our marriage I felt that we needed to do something. We seemed to just be going through the motions of life. I felt disconnected from my husband. I felt that maybe another baby would do the trick. We talked about it and planned our next child. I got pregnant on the first try. I had a wonderful pregnancy with our first, I was sure our second would be just as easy. Jean and I spent several days a week together. We would take turns spending the day at each other's home. Jean was a great cook and loved to make fancy lunches and I loved consuming them. I was getting larger every day. Our oldest boys became best friends and Phil resented it. Jean called sometimes before he left for work and this bothered him. He wanted me all to himself without any interference from anyone else. He felt that she had too strong an influence on me.

Phil had some difficulties with his superiors and moved through several different departments looking for the right fit. Before long I was presented with two alternatives as places to live, Saddlebrook, New Jersey or London, England. Both were difficult choices to make. My aunt Maggie lived in Brighton, England. At least I would have one family member in England if we moved there. I was pregnant and loved my doctor. Jean and I looked forward to having all four of our children play together and now had to face the rest of my pregnancy without her to support me. I would be a long way from friends and family with a new baby. It was a difficult choice. Phil's family came for our first and last Christmas in our new house. Right after Christmas the moving company came and packed everything we owned onto a container to be shipped overseas. Brandy had to go into quarantine for six months. We vowed to visit him as often as we could. We found a beautiful, large home on a private estate called Tyrrells Wood southwest of London in Leatherhead, Surrey.

My choice was to live in the American community of Cobham, near the American school where I would be able to make friends and have the support of other women like me. Cobham offered shopping as well as a train station nearby. Instead, Phil wanted to live in a lavish and elite area, away from the hustle and bustle and the American community. As usual Phil got what he wanted.

I found a very good preparatory school for Adam and enrolled him. He loved school and his teachers loved him. Before long he was coming home with an English accent. He was well liked at school and did very well. He made friends with another child in our estate that we carpooled with. The women helped me out since I did not have a car to drive. A beautiful Irish woman named Anne helped me get acquainted with the customs and helped me find a babysitter. She also lived in the same private estate and shared some of the best-kept secrets with me. Anne shared her babysitter, Mrs. Petterman, with me. Mrs. Petterman was a sweet and kind woman who always brought her handbag loaded with "sweeties." Adam would instantly run to her bag and help himself after gaining permission. He loved to see her. She was a godsend to me and helped me tremendously at the end of my pregnancy as well as afterward.

My last months of pregnancy were very challenging. I had severe sciatica and was only able to move around for the first two hours of the day. After ten o'clock I could not lift my feet to even walk. I had to shuffle my feet to get anywhere. Getting up the stairs to bed was an enormous challenge. I gained weight, which I covered up with a few lovely maternity dresses. I was very lonely and becoming more unhappy by the day. I enjoyed the rich milk and cream in England and had our milk delivered every day to our front door. I loved the sound of the tinkling of the milk bottles as the little electric delivery truck pulled up our drive.

I found a private doctor as suggested by several Americans who had babies born abroad. If I went the public route I would have been subjected to a maternity ward with eight to twelve beds per room. Since I was having a planned Caesarian section, I found an excellent doctor in the center of London. As time progressed and I had to make biweekly visits it became increasingly difficult for me to maneuver. From our home I had to take three-year-old Adam with me in a taxi to the train station in Cobham, a train to Victoria station as well as a subway. After leaving the underground I had to walk three blocks and up a flight of stairs. By the time I got to the doctor's office I could barely move. I had shooting pains all the way up my right leg and a backache as well. After my checkup I had to do it all over again to get home. Phil did not want to buy me a car, as the exchange rate of the U.S. dollar was low. He was very good with money and saving was more important than my health and well-being.

My Air Canada flight attendant friends often flew in for a weekend or an overnight layover. I was very excited to have their company and news from home. I loved those visits, and included Adam in our time together. Phil did not like the fact that my friends came to visit so frequently. He felt that they were taking advantage and mooching from us. I explained that they had a paid hotel as well as their meals. They wanted to visit with Adam and me and that was why they were staying with us.

My dear friend, Janie, flew in from Toronto to visit and was appalled at all I had to do at the end of my pregnancy term with a three year old and no car. If I wanted to have a vehicle for the day, I had to get up early, drive to Kingston, which was forty-five minutes away, with Phil and drive back home in rush hour traffic. By the time I got home I was exhausted. I could barely lift my feet to use the gas and brake pedal with the sciatica. Janie went with me to one of my last appointments and had to pull me by hand down the sidewalk to get back to the train station to return home.

Phil was in an international arena and traveled several times a month. He expected me to drive him to Heathrow airport each time he went out of town as well as pick him up when he returned. He liked the excitement of having us meet him at the airport and send him off each time. I protested that it was too much for me especially after Matthew was born and with a breast-feeding schedule. I really needed a car of my own. Phil's response was that the dollar was still too low and we could spend another $1,200 on the vehicle he was purchasing through his company if we did not wait. We were living in an exclusive part of Surrey with all our expenses paid. Phil was getting a bonus for being there as well as a sign-on bonus. His salary had doubled just by living out of the country. We had more money than we knew what to do with during our time overseas. I became angry, resentful and I knew could not continue living like this much longer. I was in as much physical pain as I was emotional. I wondered if Phil was having an affair. I was becoming increasingly lonely and depressed. He traveled overseas frequently and certainly had the opportunity.

Waiting for a baby to arrive can be stressful. Phil's company was attempting to exert pressure on him to visit offices in the Far East. His position required him to travel to Saudi Arabia, India, China, Hong Kong and Thailand. He was adamant. He made it a point to be present for our baby's birth. We had a scheduled Caesarian, just to be sure Phil stayed in England until the big day.

Matthew was born on a crisp spring day in March with yellow daffodils blooming all around. We had a private room in prestigious Hammersmith Hospital, where Princess Diana gave birth to Prince William. I cried when I saw him. He was beautiful and perfect with fuzz for hair when he was born. Within months, Matthew was a beautiful boy with a round head and gorgeous blonde curls. I had hoped for a girl and left his hair long until he was two. People would stop us on the street to look at him, telling his brother what a gorgeous little sister he had. Adam became increasingly indignant after this happened over and over. He responded angrily, "He's not a sister, he's my brother!" When Matthew was two I reluctantly and under much pressure got his hair cut. Matthew pouted as his blonde curls fell to the floor at the barbershop.

Phil had postponed his business travel until after Matthew was born. After he knew our nanny was taking care of business he left for six weeks. Phil traveled to Hong Kong, Thailand, India, Australia and Japan. He purchased twelve handmade suits and twenty-five handmade dress shirts. He also bought a beautiful Asian room divider with carved soap stone on one side and hand painted on the other. He handpicked pearls for me with a beautiful diamond clasp. On top of all of that he brought back two Japanese robes for the two of us. The boys got two crocheted panda bears that fell apart almost as soon as they touched them.

We visited Brandy religiously. Sitting on the concrete floor breast-feeding Matthew I thought, "I am a long way from being the flight attendant in Toronto."

Three months after Matthew was born, Phil's parents and sister visited us for a month. Phil had just purchased a brand new, shiny red 5 series BMW. I drove a loner from his company until he purchased me a 3 series used automatic BMW. We were one big happy BMW family. I could think of lots of expletives but they all ended in K. He was proud of his new car and wanted to show it off to his family. Phil planned a nine country European tour by car. I was not happy with a five-seater car and seven people. I had one or two children on my lap for the entire week as we toured country by country. I never got the opportunity to drive. By the time the week was done I was ready to kill somebody. I had to breast-feed with his family in the backseat for the entire trip. If Matthew wasn't hungry he was crying because he was hot. It was the longest, most uncomfortable European vacation. I could not wait for it to end. Phil was oblivious to the children's and my discomfort. Adam squirmed from the heat and threw up several times from being carsick. The children's schedules were completely disrupted and Adam was eating junk food to keep him quiet on our long drive through the European countryside. I was furious with Phil for not wanting to stop when Adam vomited in the back seat of his brand new BMW because of all the junk he had consumed.

I was exhausted with the drive and trying to keep both the children quiet and happy for hours in a cramped car. When we got to Paris I had hoped that Phil and I would have a night out alone. I thought it would be wonderful if I could have a break from the children. Once we were stationed in our hotel rooms and he announced that he and his sister were going to dinner and a club, I hit the roof. He did not understand what I was upset about. He suggested I order room service for Adam and me and off he went anyway.

Seven months after Matthew's birth, I turned 30. I had worked diligently with the help of my friends to lose the baby weight I had gained. I had become very thin and fit enough to purchase some beautiful new clothes.

Phil suggested I purchase some diamond earrings for myself like Anne who lived down the street owned. Hers were huge, beautiful stones that glistened in the sunlight. I visited her jeweler in London and brought them home. When Phil first saw them he expressed his disappointment. He sent me back to get larger ones, as these did not depict the statement he wanted to make. He was very concerned about the impression he made on other people. On the evening of my birthday he told me to get dressed; he was taking me out to dinner. The doorbell rang, I answered the door and was greeted by a driver, complete with cap and uniform. "Good evening, ma'am, your car awaits." I looked into the expansive driveway to see the Daimler limousine gleaming in the front garden. We took photographs with the driver before we left. It certainly was a treat. I felt like royalty.

I had recently had my hair cut short; it was easier for me with a new baby. While driving through London our driver explained I was mistaken for Princess Diana as we went to dinner and the club. People on the street were waving at me, so I of course waved back. I felt like a fairy princess. It was one of the best nights of my life. While dancing at the nightclub I felt awkward and uncomfortable. I could not put my finger on it. All the trappings were there. My underlying sadness plagued me and I could not figure out why.

I was becoming restless and increasingly lonely. I wanted Phil to be more involved with our two boys. He was a workaholic and would leave for work before 6:00 a.m. and come home most nights after our children were in bed. Most nights he would look at them while they slept and kiss them good night. Then the cycle would repeat itself.

Phil loved to shop and went to Harrods annual sale our first year in England. He purchased a beautiful twelve place settings of silver flatware, which included a foul and meat carving knife and fork as well as a separate fish service. The silver set was housed in a gorgeous inlaid chest, which was a piece of furniture in itself. There was no doubt he had fabulous taste. We also purchased four sets of china which included an everyday set of Evesham, an oven to tableware set that Princess Diana had, a set of fine bone china as well as a white set for every day use.

We gave wonderful gourmet dinner parties. I cooked and baked like a crazy woman and played the dutiful hostess. We found some wonderful wine selections for next to nothing consuming vast quantities of it. We were spending money traveling, drinking and dining out. We were hanging with a wealthy crowd. We traveled to Spain with our neighbors staying on the Costa del Sol for a week during spring break. I was taken aback to find our friends sunbathing topless next to us on the beach. I got the nerve up to do the same — when in Spain do as they do. We were way out of our league. These people were multimillionaires living off their investments. We found we spent far more than we intended to vacation with them. It was a very different life than we had in Maryland.

After our holiday in Spain, Phil returned from a business trip stateside. He seemed uncomfortable when he discussed the news of his sister, Babbie's, upcoming wedding. I was excited that we would be going home for a visit. That was before his sister called to speak to me. She explained she understood that with two little children I would not attend her wedding and that was fine with her. She knew it was a long flight to make with two small children not to mention the expense. It was very clear that she did not want me at her wedding. I got off the phone feeling dumbfounded. I wanted to go. I could not understand it. I asked Phil questions about the wedding plans. "Who is going to be Babbie's maid of honor?" He looked at the floor and said he was not sure. I knew he was lying. He was very adept at it but I could sense he was hiding something big from me. I pushed for the answers. I threatened to call Babbie back and ask her directly. He did not want me calling his sister for this information. Phil's ex-wife Marian was asked to stand up for Babbie and be her matron of honor. They had, after all, been friends since Phil dated her in college. It was no big deal.

I had been aware from the beginning of our relationship that Phil's parents and family wished I was different. I was not Catholic like they were. I never felt accepted by them. Phil's first wife, Marian, was still very close with his family. She was Catholic. It was very clear that they still adored her and wished Phil and she were still married. They exchanged Christmas gifts with each other every year. When it came time to name our second child, I chose the name Matthew. Phil's mother told me I could not name him that because Marian's son was named Matthew. Not only that, I was not the mother they wished I was to Adam. I was on him constantly correcting him. I was too critical and they did not agree with some of the things I did. Now to hear that they were trying to keep the fact that Babbie had chosen Phil's ex-wife, Marian, as a matron of honor made me livid.

I called Babbie back and let her know we would love to attend her wedding. As soon as I could I went shopping in London and picked out an outfit with a hat and shoes to match fit for Princess Di. I was very upset about the lengths that Babbie had gone to so that I was not at her wedding. I had to make up for the way I was feeling by looking fabulous at the wedding. Phil's mother commented that I did not need to wear a hat. I thanked her for her comment and was as pleasant as I could be with everyone.

This was like an act of high treason! I could not trust Phil to have my back and be on my side. I became increasingly argumentative and less inclined to keep peace. The rift that had begun to grow became a chasm with the wedding and his effort to keep it all a secret. I felt betrayed. What else had he been lying about? He traveled a great deal, and I really wondered.

I had lost interest in sex. I knew part of the reason was postpartum depression but not all. When we made love, it felt like I was not there and it didn't matter if I was or not. It felt to me that I could have been a hole in the wall for the lack of connection there was between us. I worked out hard. I was in a Jazzercise class and lost all my pregnancy weight. I still did not like the way I looked. I told Phil I wanted breast implants and he supported my decision wholeheartedly. I was doing this for me. After breastfeeding two children I was very unhappy with the aftermath. I had never been really vain, but every time I looked at my breasts when I was naked I wanted to cry. After two years in England I told Phil I missed the states and wanted to move back. I missed my family and friends. I was so lonely. All the beautiful things we had did not fill the emptiness I felt inside.

I consulted a barrister in London regarding divorce. He informed me that I would be subject to the laws in England, which would not be very beneficial to me in the long run. He felt it would be best if I waited until I returned to the states to pursue this any further.

We traveled a great deal while we were in England, seeing much of the countryside and Europe. During the week I would take the boys to visit my aunt on the coast. It was good to see family once in a while. I enjoyed the beauty of the country and visited many castles and bought antiques with friends. Phil and I had a wonderful time spending; at least we still had that in common.

Phil liked to cut excursions to the airport short. He did not like to sit and wait on his flights. On one such trip to Switzerland we parked our car and had to run the entire length of Heathrow airport with bags and children in tow, clearing customs and immigration as fast as we could.

Running in heels carrying two children was too much stress for me. We barely made our flight and were quickly ushered to our seats before the aircraft door closed. My soft silk, periwinkle blouse was wrinkled and wet from sweat. I cried.

Phil was not a bad guy. He thought that he was doing what was best for our family. He worked hard to make a living for a better life for us. It probably would not have mattered what he did, I would have found fault with it because I was not happy with me. He was very good with money and taught himself the art of investment. A highly intelligent man, he was able to do almost anything he set his mind to. On the other hand, Phil had an inflated ego and was extremely narcissistic. He rarely thought about how his actions impacted others. I was very jealous of his gifts and the fact that he had a profession. Staying at home with the children no longer was a challenge to me. I needed more. My disappointment with my life was evident. Phil pointed out how reactive I was. I did not understand what he was saying to me at the time. I was increasingly critical, negative and blamed others for everything.

After two years abroad, we moved back to the states. Phil did it for me. He would have been very happy staying in England for another four years. The move probably was one of the biggest faux pas of his career. It cost his company millions and we did not stay long enough to make it worth their while. I felt guilty about it, but I was so miserable I felt like I would die if I stayed there.

We purchased a beautiful traditional home from an executive that had been transferred. The setting was really beautiful with a two-acre lot. We had a beautiful screened in porch on the back. My parents were excited to have us back on U.S. soil; at least it was within driving distance. While they visited, Phil and my father built a climbing frame for the boys. They loved it and wanted to sleep outside on one of the platforms.

Once back in the U.S. Phil had difficulty hitting his stride. He moved from department to department working for different people and finally was let go for insubordination. He refused to fire a friend of his. He was a loyal friend. I panicked with him while he was out of work. After six months of unemployment and with the help of a headhunter, Phil was hired as a vice president of BellSouth and we moved to Atlanta, Georgia.

Once in Atlanta, our relationship became extremely competitive. We both tried to outdo each other as parents. We competed for our children's love and attention. I eased my internal pain by spending Phil's hard earned money and by volunteering. I threw myself into our neighborhood social committee and was elected to the executive board for the boys' PTA. I also cochaired the swim team and hired a new swim coach from a local private school. I had the school lunches improved and really made a difference to the swim team. I did not drink much at all, but I had become a shopaholic. On one occasion over 20 years ago I spent $3,000 on one shopping spree and purchased clothes, shoes and purses for myself. One addiction had been replaced with another. I carefully secreted my purchases away and hid them in the closet taking them out one piece at a time. After that, I was not allowed to spend money without getting permission, and before long I no longer had the checkbook. Money was only doled out to me for food.

While we lived in this beautiful East Cobb affluent neighborhood, we watched as several of our friends' marriages fell apart. It seemed having lots of money created other issues and complicated lives.

I became increasingly unhappy with my own marriage. Even shopping lost its luster and excitement for me. I secretly put myself into counseling. As my family taught me, I kept secrets too. I felt that if Phil knew I was getting counseling he would be angry with me. We could not admit to having any problems. After several weeks of working with my therapist he refused to see me any longer without me telling Phil. When I finally got the courage to tell Phil about it, he refused to go with me. He did not feel that we had problems. I gave up on the private counseling. I was depressed and constantly focused on what ifs. What would it be like if I divorced Phil? Could I support the kids on my own? What would life be like for me? Would I ever get married again? Would I be happy on my own? I saw psychics and astrologers for guidance on a regular basis. Another secret I had from Phil. He did not like that at all.

Phil and I had not gone to church at the beginning of our marriage. It was not important to us at that time. Later on, I found myself wanting to be fed spiritually. I began attending a United Methodist church. I got the boys up every Sunday and made sure everyone was dressed neatly and fed before we left the house. Phil was not interested in attending and stayed home usually sleeping late. Since I was not baptized at birth, the boys and I were baptized together when I was 32, Adam was five and Matthew was two. I invited my in-laws to attend their grandson's baptism. They were not pleased that the boys were baptized in my church. My mother-in-law said, "You know they could have been baptized Catholic." I replied, "Yes they could have if Phil had bothered to get himself and the kids up and take them to church every Sunday. He had the opportunity and I gave him that option, but he chose not to." They never showed up for this wonderful occasion.

Right before a trip to New York for Phil's parents' 50th anniversary, Adam, our oldest son, noticed Brandy, our Golden Retriever, was "shaking." He began convulsing and we found he had an inoperable brain tumor. After being shipped overseas and being in a quarantine for six months, it was a sad day when we realized our dear friend had to be put to sleep.

I went to a group therapy session for abused women on a weekly basis at a local psychiatric hospital. The group was very good for me as I met other women that had been sexually abused with similar stories, some much worse than mine. I was able to hear about what others had gone through and could relate to the problems in their lives. We all had difficulties with boundaries, relationships and men. I attended these weekly sessions for almost a year when the group was disbanded.

On Thanksgiving Day six months after Brandy died, a strange dog showed up in our driveway. He seemed to be homeless, so we took him in. He was a large Weimaraner with an undocked tail. He became a wonderful replacement for Brandy as we all had big holes in our hearts. We name him Beau. He was a big friendly dog, but rather rambunctious. He knocked Matthew over in the driveway causing him to hit his head really hard while Phil was out of town. He had really clobbered his head and I kept a close eye on him afterward. About two hours later I noticed that Matthews' eyes were wobbling all around in his head. He looked like a cartoon character. I felt sure he had a concussion. I consulted my neighbor next door who was a nurse. She looked at him and assured me he was fine; there was nothing to worry about. I continued to feel something was not right, but felt she must know better than me. After all, she was a nurse. I continued to watch him carefully and woke him every hour. Around eleven o'clock I checked Matthew again. I knew something was not right. I called my neighbor and she drove us to the hospital. As Matthew got into her van he threw up macaroni and cheese everywhere. It seemed fitting since she was convinced nothing was wrong.

Matthew indeed had a concussion and had to stay in the hospital overnight. I needed to go with my instinct and not defer to others that I felt knew more than I did. This was a huge lesson for me and I continued to have issues with it. I argued with my own guidance and deferred to others constantly. Every time that something important happened Phil was out of town. He had missed almost every Halloween night preferring to be in San Francisco or anywhere else but home.

When I was in high school on my way to an early morning swim practice, I slipped and fell down a long set of icy wooden stairs bumping all the way to the bottom on my coccyx. I damaged my tailbone and had to undergo physical therapy for several months so that I could sit down comfortably. Twenty years later, I had a recurring pain in the same area after we moved to Atlanta. I ignored it until I realized that a lump had formed there. After receiving test results I was scheduled to have surgery at Piedmont Hospital. Immediately prior to surgery a myelogram was performed. The spinal fluid was tested and I was told that the tumor I had on my spine was benign. I was relieved. The surgery was performed successfully and my parents drove down to help me with Adam and Matthew while I recovered.

Phil picked me up at the hospital the day I was discharged. Once we were home he packed his golf clubs and a suitcase to attend a 5-day golf tournament. He had really been looking forward to this getaway. We had discussed this trip when my surgery was scheduled. I asked him to stay home with me after my surgery. He did not want to miss his tournament. After all I had my parents with me to take care of everything. He grabbed his bags, loaded them into his BMW, and kissed me good-bye and left. There was no doubt where Phil's priorities were. As long as he was happy nothing else mattered.

I could not understand how he could be so heartless. He had no guilt whatsoever in leaving his wife who had been released from the hospital that day. My parents did not have to say anything to me. I could tell by their faces they wanted to strangle him. As my mother brought me my dinner that night and I sat up in bed, a shooting pain shot into my head that was so intense it was unbearable. The pain made me cry. Crying made it hurt even more. I had to lie back down. Once the pain subsided enough that I could eat, my mother fed me dinner while I lay flat in bed. It was obvious I could not sit up. I thought it would get better in a day or two. Three days later, the pain was excruciating. I called my doctor and was told I needed a blood patch. Why it was not done at the time of my myelogram, I will never know. I had to bring myself into the hospital where they would draw blood out of my arm and inject it into the site between my vertebrae where the myelogram needle withdrew my spinal fluid at the time of the test. Apparently this was a common problem. I lost three days having to stay prone and could not be with my children. It made me realize how much I needed to extricate myself from my marriage to Phil. I did not want to stay in a loveless marriage any longer.

The old song by Peggy Lee kept playing in my head, *Is That All There Is?* I sat on the landing of our two-story foyer many nights when I could not sleep. I had everything material I could ever want. We had a beautiful house in a prestigious neighborhood, a Volkswagen and a BMW that were paid for, four sets of china and a gorgeous silver set. I had been given carte blanche and decorated the whole house myself. The house was filled with beautiful things. I had beautiful clothes and the kids had everything they could possibly want. Yet at the same time I had never felt so utterly alone and empty in my entire life.

It was the contrast between the opulence of the outer versus a poverty of the inner. The one thing that was missing was love. It took me five years from the time I saw the attorney in London to finally file for divorce. I did not enter into my new life lightly. I was concerned about the impact of a divorce on our two boys. I felt like our family was out of balance. Our focus was primarily on how we looked to others. We had a shell of a marriage with no foundation. We were cold and distant to one another. Since both of us were Scorpios we were too much alike.

After two years at BellSouth Phil lost his job. I met with an attorney and filed for divorce. When Phil realized what I had done he cleaned out all the bank accounts. I could not take Matthew to the doctor when he was sick because I had no money to do so. I blamed him for my unhappiness. I blamed him for everything. I worried constantly about money and worked part-time. After nine years of being a volunteer and stay-at-home mom, with the help of a neighbor I was hired by a division of GTE and worked as an executive secretary. Not my dream job, but it seemed all I was qualified for. I gladly accepted the job and dressed for success. I became well respected in my company working for the director of data processing.

Our divorce was like the movie *The War of The Roses*. It was horrible. We acted like we hated each other. We continued to live separately but in the same house. After putting over $40,000 into our basement renovation we sold our house at a $60,000 loss. We had bought at the top end of the market and had to sell low. My divorce cost me $32,000. We argued over everything including who got which CD. We focused our attention on the material things and this was what our marriage came down to, dollars and cents. My spending spree was over. I became a single mom.

My parting shot over the bow, which angered Phil, was my affair with someone I worked with. I felt so alone and wanted someone to actually care for me. I rationalized he would never find out and our marriage was over. I knew it hurt Phil nonetheless. He became increasingly angry that he knew I was immovable and would not attempt to repair our marriage. I felt that there was no possible way. I was so angry with him for so many things I could not even consider it. Looking back now, I wish we had separated and taken our time considering our two sons more. I recognized it was my choice to end it. I was responsible for the long-term pain that Adam and Matthew would endure. I just did not know how much.

Moving out of the house was volatile. Phil became combative and physically abusive. I knew he wanted to hang on and couldn't understand why I was throwing in the towel. He called me a quitter, which was something that stuck with me to this day. His father and sister spent hours on the phone with me, trying to talk some sense into me. My mind was made up. I was a stubborn Scorpio. When I say its over, its over.

The boys and our Weimaraner moved into a three-bedroom apartment that kept them in the same school district. They were not happy. After living in a large home in an upscale subdivision with a swim team and all sorts of parties, this was a departure from the lifestyle we had lived with their dad. I felt angry, guilty, sad and depressed all at the same time.

LESSONS LEARNED

My marriage to Phil was the most lavish and materially wealthy time in my life. From the moment I saw him I knew he was going places. I wanted material wealth and got it. I experienced tremendous contrast having everything I ever wanted materially versus the emptiness and loneliness I felt within my marriage. I did not love and accept myself nor did I have a connection with God. I was attending church and enjoying the experience, but the relationship with God was missing. I lacked a deep faith. I blamed my pain and suffering on Phil, because he was the closest one to me at the time. I did not know any better. It was not his fault. He did not do anything to me.

I felt that Phil was unavailable emotionally. What I did not realize at the time was that I was also. He was mirroring what I was projecting.

Phil has come a long way since those days. He has deepened his connection with God and made a commitment to his sons to be present in their lives. I have come to a place of love, acceptance and compassion with Phil. We have both long since forgiven each other for the real and perceived hurts. He has since remarried his first wife and we all came together joyfully as a family and shared the experience of Matthew and Andrea's wedding this past October.

Vibration after the divorce with Phil: 200 Courage

Vibration after moving out of the house with Phil: 150 Fear

CHAPTER SIX

It's Five o'Clock Somewhere

My attorney tried to date me once my divorce was final. I guess I still had it. I thanked him but felt I was not ready for any dating. I did not feel that dating him was a good idea. I was flattered though. I was an attractive, fit, 35-year-old woman with two boys. My priorities shifted. Instead of my focus being family I now had to focus on providing for my family.

Working and managing a household with two young boys became a challenge. Sometimes my days were long and I had to work late. I lived almost an hour away from work and on rainy days it took me more than that to travel back and forth. The boys stayed at the after school program as long as I could keep them there and spent their summers at the YMCA camp. They hated it. They went from having a stay-at-home mom and everything they ever wanted to limited resources and an apartment. It took two months to realize we could not continue to keep Beau, our Weimaraner. He needed space and a place to run outside which I could not give him with my work schedule and an apartment. I could not get home from work early enough and had no one that could stop by and let him out midday. I realized how unfair it was to keep him in an apartment. I talked with the boys and explained why we could not keep him. We were all sad, but everyone wanted the best for the dog.

I advertised and found a very nice couple that owned a store in Roswell. After interviewing several people on the phone, I knew they were perfect for this active dog. I promised the boys that I would get them a cat to replace Beau. We had never been without a pet and they were sad with all the changes in their young lives. I found a wonderful woman who did animal rescue. She told me of a Siamese mother cat that came with a kitten. She had been bred and somehow had her litter of cats outside. By the time they were captured only one was left.

We visited her home and found rows and rows of cages with dogs and cats of various sizes and breeds. Betty was a warm, earthy woman who doubled as a real estate agent when she was not finding homes for endless numbers of cats and dogs. She told us that the cat and kitten were loose in her bedroom. The kitten was skittish; feral she said. We fell in love with them both immediately. After Betty showed us all the other animals she had available, just in case we might want a dog later, we paid our fee and left. The boys were thrilled. The cats fit into our household very well. We named the mother May Ling and the kitten Lo Fu (little tiger).

I did my best to keep our lives as normal as I could for the boys. Rather than enroll Adam and Matthew in the YMCA camp for the summer, a friend from our old subdivision referred me to a nanny. The great thing about a nanny is that she lives in. I did not have to drag the boys out of bed in the morning and take them anywhere. Zia was highly recommended and a fairly mature 21 year old.

Things worked out for the most part until Zia modified the boy's Kraft dinner with broccoli and other green vegetables and baked it. They felt that was sacrilegious. A few things were broken. There was a crystal bowl she poured boiling liquid into. I felt that the first summer after the divorce and the move went pretty smoothly for the most part.

Summer was ending and Zia was getting ready to return to Germany. Adam complained about not going anywhere all summer and asked if they could do something with Zia, before her return to Germany. Adam, my oldest and ever the negotiator, begged me to leave her my car so that they could go somewhere before she left. I felt guilt-ridden about the divorce. I knew that the boys had given up a great deal because of my choice to divorce their father. However, every time I thought about leaving the 21-year-old my car, I got a sinking feeling in my stomach. I knew the boys would have fun on their outing and they really deserved to do something enjoyable. Both the boys expressed that they really wanted to do something. I ignored my misgivings and made plans to be picked up by a coworker and driven to work. I left some money for them and my three-year-old, fully paid for Volkswagen Golf for Zia to drive. She asked if she could invite her friend. I wanted to say no. I hated making unpopular decisions even with my children. I wanted everyone to like me. I told her she could go but she needed to really pay attention while driving. She promised to be careful. They planned to go to MacDonald's for lunch and Sparkles to roller skate. Since I had just started my job, I could not take any time off and had to work all summer. My guilt got the better of me.

The following day I left for work early while the boys remained sleeping. Around lunchtime I was called into one of the manager's office. The Marietta fire department was on the phone for me. I walked quickly to the phone, curious about what they would be calling me about. All at once I realized what it was about when they asked me to confirm who I was. They told me they had my boys and they were in a car accident. They told me they were okay, but Matthew had an apple-sized swelling on his cheek and Adam seemed to have whiplash. Just to be on the safe side they were being transported on backboards to Scottish Rite Children's Hospital. The feelings I had about letting Zia drive my car came flooding back to me. I asked if the driver and her friend were okay too? They told me where the accident happened and that it seemed the driver was not paying attention, talking to the person seated next to her. When she turned back to the road ahead the person in front of her was stopped at a red light. There was no time to downshift and stop the car. Zia had rear-ended the driver in front of her.

I was in no state to drive. Then a coworker offered to take me to the hospital. I wisely accepted. I was distraught, anxious and began to shake. Once at the hospital I assessed the situation. Everyone was okay; banged up but alive. When I realized what could have happened I burst into tears. All my anxiety and fear that had built up was released in a minute. My boys were safe. Zia was safe, and so was her friend. Zia felt terrible and apologized to me. This was like a warning shot over my bow. I needed to pay attention when I got that feeling of dread in my gut.

This was a valuable lesson for me. I was given guidance. My gut instinct was to say no. Furthermore I felt I should not let Zia's friend go because she would be a distraction and detract from her job of keeping my boys safe. Yet I allowed it all to happen. I did not protect my children nor did I use my gift of intuition. I did not want to disappoint my kids and Zia. My little navy blue Golf that was supposed to get me through the next 10 years was totaled. I was grateful that the car was the only one that paid with its life.

We said teary good-byes to Zia as she went back to Germany. Next summer whether the boys wanted to or not, they were going to the YMCA camp.

The boy's father and I were still at odds. We had an antagonistic relationship. He did his best to call the shots whenever he could. We remained angry and resentful of each other for years. Neither of us knew how to get beyond that place of blame, resentment and self-pity. After a few emotional months and weekend visits with the boys, he found a job in Virginia and reluctantly moved out of state. Phil was very good at providing. He paid a healthy amount of child support every month, even while he was not working. Had it not been for the constant financial assistance from him I don't know how I would have made it.

I felt deep and overwhelming sadness. I had begun to read about the effects of depression and recognized that I had many of the symptoms. I could fall asleep at night, but woke up around 2:30 a.m. or 3:00 a.m. It was like clockwork. Once I was awake I wrote letters, read, whatever I could do to try to get back to sleep, but mostly I worried. I would lay awake in the dark and think. My thoughts were obsessive. I ran issues over and over that were going on at work through my mind. I worried about money and whether there would be enough to pay my expenses when they came in.

I had purchased new clothes when I went back to work, as I did not have anything appropriate to wear. I had been spoiled by my years of living in England with my ex and his ample salary. I had champagne taste but a beer budget. I had applied for credit cards and had several. I used the credit as though I made more money. It was a dangerous situation. My income was fixed, but my spending was not. I dressed smartly in Jones of New York suits and designer shoes. I had not managed to settle in to spending less than what I made. I had gotten back into shopping when I felt depressed. Nothing picked up my spirits like a whirlwind shopping spree and a new wardrobe.

About six months or so after my divorce, while delivering documents in another department, I caught the eye of a tall, blonde, handsome Southern gentleman. We did not speak to one another at first, but even across the office the sparks flew. I could see his blue eyes across the room and my interest was piqued. I asked our receptionist who he was and got the low down. He was divorced and was in the office speaking to one of the managers about software. I saw him in the office a few more times before he got the nerve to ask me out for a drink.

Mike and I slowly began to date. He was raised in South Georgia by a big, lovely black woman who cooked, cleaned and took care of Mike while both his parents worked in their shoe store. We met after work once or twice a week for about an hour before I had to rush off and make dinner for my boys. I enjoyed his company and had strong feelings for him. After our third date, over a margarita, I saw a pattern. Every one of our dates involved alcohol. I got that familiar feeling in the pit of my stomach like a warning sign. Was he an alcoholic? I thought about what I was feeling for a while before I brought my misgivings up and discussed it with him. He explained it this way: he liked to have fun. It did not have to involve drinking; he just felt it always made everything more enjoyable. His words sounded hollow. However, he was strikingly handsome and I liked him. He dressed nicely and was well bred. He was nicer than some of the guys that had expressed an interest in me. Besides, he was really good looking. I pushed down the misgivings and continued to date him, becoming absolutely crazy in love with him.

I was very attracted to him. He treated me like a lady and bought me lovely things. We actually went out on dates, to dinner by ourselves and out with friends. I really enjoyed his company. The boys liked him also. He had one son, in his early 20s. He was a polite young man attending college.

I had a good sum of money from the sale of our house and my part of the divorce proceedings. When I tried to purchase a house after our divorce I was told I could not. I had been married eleven years and according to the banks I did not have any credit. They considered all the credit history I had built during my marriage as my ex-husband's. Although I had lost the Volkswagen, it turned out to be a gift in disguise, as I had to purchase a vehicle to establish a credit history.

Mike rented a house in a large subdivision in Cherokee county, north of the city. The appealing thing about this subdivision was that it had large homes as well as smaller, lower-priced homes. The amenities were fabulous for children and families. They had their own golf course and three swimming pools. We loved to visit Mike there and frequently drove around looking at houses.

Mike purchased a lot in Eagle Watch and began building his own home a couple of streets away from where he was renting. He asked me to help him design it. We were seeing each other exclusively and I assumed that I would end up living in this house with him once we were married. We spent most of our time off together. I spent many weekends driving around with him looking at house after house for the perfect plan for him to build. I helped him pick out everything including paint colors, plumbing, cabinets, windows and all of his building materials. I even chose the color of the stucco for the outside of his house. One day while we were driving around the subdivision I noticed a cute house in a semi cul-de-sac. I loved it. As we were passing I said out loud, "That is exactly the house I want. Why can't that house be for sale?" The really interesting thing was that a week after I noticed the house and affirmed that was the one I wanted, a for sale sign appeared in front of it. I immediately called the agent and made an appointment to see it. The timing could not be more perfect. The owners moved out as school was ending making the perfect transition for the boys and school.

We continued to date each other, eating dinner several times a week at Mike's house. The boys would do their homework at his house and watch television afterward. The only thing that really bothered them about Mike was that he asked them to wash their hands after everything they ate. It made them feel like they were babies.

Once Mike moved into his house we were invited to stay overnight. The boys loved his big house; it was more like what they had been used to. He had a big screen television and always cooked delicious meals for us. The relationship had a family feel. What became evident was an underlying insecurity in Mike. He asked me constantly if I wanted to go back with my ex. He suggested it frequently saying that it would be better for the kids if we did. I did not feel that Phil loved me. He said he did, but I did not feel it. It did not feel like his heart was in it as much as his mind when he said it. I also had gotten the feeling with Phil that he was very detached when he made love. It felt to me that it did not matter who I was. It felt as if I was just a receptacle and I had told him so.

Our relationship was addictive. Mike was very insecure and worried constantly about me fooling around on him. He met me for lunch several times a week, which seemed really nice at first. Then he talked me into getting a cell phone. I did not feel I needed one, but he convinced me that with my long commute to and from work it was safer. He called me three times a day, just to say hello. What I came to realize was that he wanted to be able to check up on me at lunch to see whom I was going out with. When he found out I was dining out with a male coworker he flipped out, asking me all kinds of questions and fought with me on my cell phone. I was embarrassed to have this kind of conversation in front of a coworker. I answered all his questions defensively. My lunch was totally innocent, but he felt threatened. His fear of me having an affair was so great a week did not go by without him making some comment about whom I had been with. The strangest thing was that it never entered my mind. Our sexual relationship was exciting and wonderful. I did not feel that there was any lack there at all.

After a year of making regular payments on my car loan I was able to buy that cute little house in Mike's subdivision just north of the city. The commute to work would be longer, but I was able to get more house for less money. We were all very excited about our move. The boys settled into their new school quickly. I was ecstatic. My lovely furniture fit perfectly and we effortlessly made our house a home. This was a far better situation than the apartment. We were all much happier.

Mike and I dated over a period of three years. He took the boys and me to University of Georgia football games and to visit his parents in Warner Robbins. His parents smoked and drank. However, they were kind to the boys and me. The writing was on the wall but it was as if it was in another language. I couldn't seem to grasp it. He never spent one night in my home, offering his instead. We kept having the same arguments over and over. I was upset about him not staying at my house. I carted all our belongings over including our dog Gunner for a spend-the-night for the boys and me and frequently ended up having such a fight that I had to pack us all up again and leave. He felt threatened that I would have an affair. He called me constantly on my cell phone, which created a hardship for me. He was afraid of losing me and I was afraid of losing him. We had no idea how addictive our relationship was.

The awareness that I had early on and denied as the truth was that Mike was an alcoholic. He only drank a couple of beers each night but he drank every night. I was in denial. I made excuse after excuse for him and his behavior. He was verbally abusive. He often made disparaging remarks about me following up his comments with, "I was just kidding." We would drive to Warner Robbins with my two boys in the back seat with Mike's beer cooler between them. He would ask the boys to pass him a beer on the ride. I did not want to lose him and I was too afraid to say anything about his behavior on our trips or even before because he would become so angry and rationalize that he wasn't drunk and it was no big deal, everybody did it.

The boys became quite independent travelers visiting their dad each Christmas break and for two weeks in the summer. I loved my children and did my best to help them keep up with their schoolwork as well as to keep them active in karate and baseball. I signed up for both of the boys' classrooms as a story mom. Even with my workplace being almost 30 miles away from the school, I was involved and there for them whenever I could. I missed them when they were away, but made good use of my time by working late or gardening.

Once we were settled into our house I made good on my promise to get the boys a dog. Betty and I kept in touch after we adopted the cats. She told me about the dogs that she had and then added that she had one dog that she was keeping; he was very special. Gunner was a beautiful Golden Retriever who had been arrested for wandering out of his yard too many times. Betty wanted to keep him. When she mentioned him, I knew he was our dog. Betty laughed on the phone and said if anyone could have him it was us. We went as a family to see Gunner after school. When the boys saw him in the backyard they both said they were sure it was Brandy reincarnated. Gunner was one of the handsomest Goldens I had ever seen. He was also the sweetest.

Gunner was well behaved in the house and great with the boys. We brought him everywhere with us. I even traded in our Volkswagen Passat and bought a Ford Explorer just for Gunner. He loved riding in the back and it was easy for him to get in and out. He loved everyone. Soon after we brought Gunner home Betty asked us to pet sit for her. She brought over a Bearded Collie and a Himalayan cat named Trouble. We had seen both of them when we rescued Gunner. The cat was absolutely the most beautiful cat I had ever seen. He walked like he owned the place. She had named him because he was always in trouble. Gunner saw Trouble and the two were like the characters from the Disney movie *Homeward Bound*. It made me cry to see how glad they were to see each other again. Trouble walked right up to Gunner, placing a paw on either side of his face. He licked and licked Gunner and then rubbed his face all over him. They had been kennel mates at Betty's house. It was obvious that Trouble was staying. The cat and dog loved each other. We loved him as much as we loved Gunner. Betty was not the least surprised when she came to pick up the Bearded Collie that Trouble, now named Katmandu, was staying with us.

I had a strong affinity with animals. They were constant and greeted me happily when I got home. They loved me unconditionally and I felt happy having them around.

I had my astrological chart read once a year. Sherry Henderson had been reading my chart and tarot cards over the years and was very accurate. Mike did not like me going and said that anything like that was from the devil. Even though he did not go to church his Baptist upbringing colored his beliefs. Mike had been raised by a woman of color and used the "n" word whenever he talked about people of color. This went against the grain for me and I always asked him not to use that word. I did not feel he set a very good example for the boys when he did. I found it odd that he felt calling someone the "n" word was okay but getting my cards or chart read was from the devil.

The longer we dated the more obvious it was that Mike was not going to change. He did his best to govern the clothes I wore, buying me many beautiful things. I regularly was given make up gifts after he said something incredibly hurtful or upsetting. We could have a beautiful morning but get into a fight by the end of the day. The up and down of the relationship was very hard to take, but I felt like I could not live without him. I realized that his self-esteem was very low, as was mine. He was not going to quit drinking and he was not ever going to accept me going to astrologers or readers. This was becoming an important part of my life and I would not give it up for him. I saw spirits and felt them; he did not even believe in them. He did not feel comfortable in my house; it was almost like I had the cooties or something. I could never put my finger on what it was and why he never liked to stay long. If he came over for dinner, he would eat and then leave immediately afterward.

We were all invited to a pre-wedding party for a couple of Mike's friends. Usually a gathering that included other people would end up with us fighting. He was insanely jealous for no reason. The men sat with their drinks at one table and all the women were seated at another. We were all excited to hear about Sarah's wedding dress. It sounded lovely and I asked where she bought it. She responded, "at the mall." I replied I would never buy my wedding dress at a mall. I did not think anything of what I had said until much later. My comment eventually made it back to Mike. He gave me such a dressing down about what I said and how I hurt Sarah. However hurtful Mike's words were they were absolutely true. I had not realized how negative, critical and judgmental I was. I was raised with critical parents, as was he. This became a huge turning point for me. I realized that the less I liked myself, the less I liked others and the more critical of others I was. I felt apart from the group as if I was not accepted. Perhaps I did not accept myself.

I nagged my children. Telling them the same thing over and over. Giving them repercussions for negative behavior was not something I knew how to do. If I asked the boys to do something and they did not do it, I would ask again and again until I would end up getting angry and yelling at them. They were crying out for me to set stronger boundaries for them. It was not possible with my frame of reference and childhood history. My boundaries were nonexistent from my own being crossed over and over again as a child. The things that were natural and second nature to most people were not for me. I realized that I had disconnected from myself. Even in the act of lovemaking I would find myself there and into it and then boom I was cut off. I could become angry in an instant because I was so disconnected. I was more aware of my words and my criticism of others. I knew how much I did not like to be criticized. It became evident how much shame and self-hatred I carried.

On the outside I looked beautiful. I dressed nicely, looked attractive and was a kind person for the most part. I loved animals and nature and did my best to help others. My words were sometimes hurtful, even to my children. I often blurted things out without thinking and hurt people I loved. I did the best I could, but I knew I could do much better. I realized that my relationship with Mike was extremely abusive, but at the same time I could not leave him. I would rationalize that he was good to me in so many other ways, taking me out to exquisite places and traveling with me. I let the material things overshadow the emotional imbalance.

Canadian winters are long and cold. My father loved the water and after his retirement looked forward to driving to Florida and spending several months there after Christmas. It helped pass the time and he met many people whom he liked to play pool with. He loved to walk on the beach and even had my aunt, who was a retired doctor and lived in England, go with them one winter. The boys and I spent a few days with them in Panama City one year. We really enjoyed that time.

My parents let me know that they were coming through Atlanta and asked if they could stop and stay with me on their way to Florida. My father had been diagnosed with leukemia and he was not sure if he would be able to make another trip to Florida. He had begun getting blood transfusions and his energy was becoming limited. While they were visiting, Mike met them and took us all out to dinner. Mike was always a smart dresser, much more formally attired than I was, even on weekends. I rarely saw him in denim. He preferred to wear khaki slacks instead. We all got dressed up and enjoyed a fabulous dinner along the Chattahoochee River. Both my parents raved about how wonderful he was, how well he treated me and what a gentleman he seemed to be. I knew what they were thinking. They hoped that we would get married. My father silently felt that I was safer and better off married than single. I kept silent about the negative side of our relationship, as I did not want them worrying. I never told them what he called me when he was drunk in Hawaii and did not win the salesman of the year award. There was no point.

I went to Marietta one Saturday afternoon and met a very spiritual woman that read palms. I heard that she was very good and accurate. I was excited. Nannette was a sweet, soft-spoken woman from Florida. She had studied for a long time and was a spiritual teacher. She did guided meditations for groups. I liked her apartment; it was different. It smelled of burning sage and incense. Her palm reading took my breath away. She told me things about myself that amazed me. She was spot on! Then I asked her about Mike. She looked at my palm and said flatly, "He will never marry you!" I got hot and flushed in the face. I felt panic in my stomach. I was incredulous. "You are wrong!" I said. She told me she most certainly was not. I could not wait to get out of there. It was all I could do to sit through the rest of the reading. I paid her and left in a rush. I was still angry when I drove home. Before I left, Nannette told me that she had something to tell Mike if he cared to hear it.

I told Mike about my reading. He was very curious about what Nannette had to say to him and decided to see her too. She told him that he would remarry his ex-wife and have two children with her. This seemed to really excite him. How could I have been so stupid? He had been waiting all this time for the perfect opportunity and now he had it. We had been fighting more than we were getting along. He always seemed to feel that something was not right between us. I felt it was because of our cultural differences. I also did not drink like he did. When he called my son a little fag because he wore briefs and not boxers, I had it. Around that time Mike made it clear that he did not want any part of another man's children. He told me more than once, "If it weren't for your two boys..." He trailed off. He would never marry me because I had children. All that time I spent helping him pick out materials for his house, paint colors and furniture. I was never going to share this house with him. Breaking up with Mike meant more than him breaking up with me. The boys had a relationship with him also. We spent several nights a week having dinner with him and I thought we were building a family and moving towards marriage. He had been a part of our lives for three years. It was a difficult decision. I really loved him but our very seductive relationship was headed nowhere. It was very hard to let go.

One afternoon sitting on Mike's back porch with a mutual friend it suddenly hit me like a ton of bricks. The fact that he asked me over and over again about getting back with my ex was because he wanted to get back with his ex-wife. Nannette was right; he was never going to marry me. He had been telling me all along, "if it weren't for your two boys." How could I be so blind and stupid at the same time? I felt like I had wasted the last three years of my life.

It took me months to finally end my relationship with Mike. I had to come to terms with all that I would lose. The gifts, trips and dining were wonderful, but paled in comparison to the abuse I received. Both my parents were disappointed that I ended the relationship. They both thought Mike was a really nice guy.

I talked to Barbara at work about my relationship with Mike. It was like a roller coaster with high highs and very low lows. I recognized that he was an alcoholic by now. I kept hoping through some miracle that he would change. Barbara told me several times that the relationship with an alcoholic is very seductive, but it would never change. That saddened me. I really loved Mike. I knew that we would not be together forever like I had originally thought. The idea of being on my own was so foreign to me. I had never been without anyone for any period of time. I was so codependent and knew it. I read the book *Codependent No More*, by Melody Beattie and examined my life. I realized that this relationship with Mike could not continue. I was dependent on him for so much. He fed the kids and me several times a week. He was a good cook and loads of fun. I knew there was so much drama in our lives because of my addiction to the relationship with him and his to alcohol. I felt like I was cutting off one of my legs, but I did it anyway. I told Mike I loved him very much but I could not continue in a relationship with him.

I grieved the loss of the relationship. I missed him in my life. We tried to be friends for a while until he showed up one evening to ask me what I thought about him remarrying his first wife. I could not understand why I felt so crushed at first. I realized that the whole time he was with me he kept wondering about a relationship with her. I never really had him; he was just borrowed.

After we broke up I had a fling with a younger man. It was a temporary fix and did not ease the pain for long. I knew that I wanted more. The spiritual aspect was what was missing. I knew that the next person that came into my life would be interested in spirituality and being connected and balanced emotionally, mentally and physically.

While I was doing all this soul searching it came to me that I needed to open up about the secrets that I had kept all my life. I called each of my family members and talked to them about the abuse that had happened in my life. There had been so much and several of the people involved had died. However, coming out publicly created a huge rift in my life that took years to heal. Family members were angry at one another and avoided contact. My mother told me, "Get over it, Jennifer!" She said that talking about it was like picking at a scab. She said just as the situation would begin to heal I would pick at it and open it again. She was right about one thing. The more I focused on it the bigger it got. I regretted my decision to tell everyone about it. On one level I felt judged by certain family members. One of my sister-in-laws seemed to really dislike me. She took great joy in seeing me in pain and suffering. She even told another family member after I divorced Phil, "My how the mighty have fallen!" She never could understand why I would divorce someone with so much money. She would never have done it no matter how badly she was treated. To her money was everything. She thought it was a source of happiness. If that was true then why was I the loneliest during the years I was married to Phil?

During my time at GTE I made friends with a girl named Barbara at work. We hung out together a little on the weekends and she introduced me to some interesting books and workshops. She helped me to think in a different direction. Barbara met the boys and me at healing night at Inner Quest metaphysical church in Roswell. We each had an opportunity to have a session on a massage table while six people dressed all in white performed Reiki in complete silence. Soft music played in the background. It was an amazing experience. The boys and I saw all kinds of things with our eyes closed. We loved these experiences and looked forward to the once a month occurrence. The boys did a couple of workshops there with other kids from time to time. They learned about spoon bending and kinesiology.

I read anything I could get my hands on that would help me grow. I read about codependency and divorce. I read books about discipline and single parenting. Since we had a house again I read about gardening and healing with herbs. I did self-healing and learned about traditional Chinese medicine. I was doing okay, but I knew underneath it all I was not really happy. I spent more than I made and my credit card bills had begun to pile up. Not having Mike in my life left a huge void for me. Not only did he help me out financially because he took us out to eat and fed us several times a week, he was a support with my sons.

I knew that the boys needed their dad, but he made me so angry every time I spoke with him. I wondered if we would ever get over this. When he needed to make travel arrangements he would give me a thirty-minute window to make a decision about whether a flight time and day would work with my schedule. Each time he pushed for a quick decision there was always a reason to justify it in his mind. Having to make a decision in a hurry served to keep me off balance and I was constantly giving my power away to him. He made me nervous. I knew he was more intelligent than me. I always felt I lost whenever there was any kind of negotiation. I never seemed to think things through carefully before executing.

The boys and I became really good friends with most of our neighbors. There was one woman that lived across our cul-de-sac that the boys did not like. She complained about everything and was very catty. One day at work I got a call from a neighbor letting me know that she had called the police. It seemed that after the boys had gotten home from school they creatively used their tennis rackets to pelt crabapples at her house. I was mortified. Adam thought it was hysterically funny. He managed to get her really worked up about it. I could understand why they would do something like that to her; she was a busybody and was a little more interested in our lives and what we were up to than she needed to be.

One fall day I returned home from work, made myself a hot cup of tea and called my mother in Canada. While we were on the phone I noticed that the pine straw in the backyard was on fire. I quickly excused myself from our conversation and I called the boys inside to see who had started the fire. It had obviously been a team effort. When I sent them outside to put the fire out Adam turned the hose on his brother and got him soaking wet. There was always something going on at home that I had to deal with. Either Adam or Matthew called me about a fight or being locked outside and not able to get back in. If it wasn't crabapples and tennis rackets it was golf balls lobbed at the back of a neighbor's house. Staying focused on work once the boys were home from school was a challenge.

I had money problems. My spending was out of hand. Although I made a decent income it was fixed. The shopping was like therapy to me, but it got me into trouble financially.

I read about feng shui, the Chinese art of placement to enhance areas of our life like prosperity, health, career, children and knowledge. I had several practitioners come to our house and give me suggestions on ways to improve the feng shui. I learned how to do house clearings and expanded my knowledge base reading three or four books a week.

The boys and I had experienced several occurrences of spirits in our home. We were hearing unexplained noises, tapping noises on pictures in our bedrooms and footsteps when we knew no one was walking. We often had light bulbs burn out instantaneously when they were turned on. I learned through research this can be a sign of entities being present. I would frequently see things that were not there moving out of the corner of my eye. It became a daily occurrence. Although it was not an old home there seemed to be a disturbance on the property that was attracting them. I learned how to smudge and clear spirits and negative energies.

I embarked on a more spiritual aspect of my life. I prayed regularly. I was not sure if my prayers were heard, but I continued anyway. It was worth a try.

LESSONS LEARNED

I experienced the deep seduction of an addictive relationship with Mike Crofton. Long after I recognized that my relationship was not going anywhere I continued to put my time and energy into building a life with him. I received guidance within the first few weeks of dating Mike that he was an alcoholic but chose to ignore my guidance. I lived beyond my means because Mike had money. I bought clothes I could not afford for the trips he took me on. I gave up my personal freedom and time at my own home with my children pursing an end that would never materialize.

He was an alcoholic, but I was in deep denial. I ignored the signs and even his words. He told me point blank "if it weren't for your boys..." I put aside my own guidance in the hopes and dreams that were based on a lie. I had all the signs that he would not marry me for a long time, which I ignored. I stayed in this relationship for three years. I had to be ready to let go.

The boys and I had a good time at Mike's house enjoying fine meals and experiencing a sense of expandedness in his home with luxury items like a big screen television and a beautiful home on a golf course. I was living in a fantasy world thinking that his beautiful home was going to become mine when we were married. I was in my thirties at the time and still very attached to the material world. He offered many wonderful material experiences that the boys and I enjoyed. I learned when you have an addiction, even when you know it is not good for you it is difficult to break free. The ending of this relationship allowed something new to come in and for me to move into a more spiritually balanced life.

Vibration: 245 Between Courage and Neutrality

Life Force: 80%

CHAPTER SEVEN

Holy Shit! Where's the Tylenol?

When I was 39 I had an outstanding opportunity to make a lateral move to a larger and different division of the communications company I worked for. I delightfully accepted. I was hired as an executive secretary for a large department with six managers to work for instead of just one. I reported to the new director of data processing who was very well respected. His office was strategically located next to the president of the division, which gave our department great visibility and cohesion with upper management. In this new division I made new friends and developed additional skills. The director and I developed a good rapport. We started working together from the onset. I set up his office and helped him get settled when he first moved to Atlanta. The fact that he was Indian was of great interest to me. I had longed to travel to India since my Air Canada days. I was very interested in Indian culture and eastern philosophy. I was given a wide berth by my managers and supported when I made a request. I was surprised at the amount of clout an executive secretary could be given when well liked and supported by her superiors. This position gave me additional freedom and understanding from management when it came time for me to take time off from work for my children and the death of my father. I really felt positive about my job and the money I was making.

A month after my father's death I felt that I needed a change personally. I still felt empty and sad after breaking up with Mike, even though I knew it was in my best interest. I became aware of a pattern emerging in my life. I realized that with every failed relationship there was one common denominator — me. I blamed myself for being emotionally unbalanced, unstable and needy. I felt like a little broken doll. I really had not completely grieved and recovered from the ending of my relationship with Mike before my father passed away. I felt weighted down with grief.

I had begun meditating with a group in Stone Mountain. I had done some research to locate the woman that I met as a palm reader. She had moved to Stone Mountain where I continued to visit with her on a regular basis. We became friends although I revered her for her knowledge and wisdom and considered her my spiritual teacher. Nannette invited me to attend a varied group of evolved beings that met weekly in her home. There were many interesting attendees, which made the hour drive worth it. Nannette had a soft melodious voice that was interesting and hypnotic. I experienced small snippets of peace and tranquility through meditation. I had never felt this before and I yearned for more. I read several books on the subject and meditated every day. I knew that the spiritual aspect had been missing in my life and made it my focus.

While browsing for a book at a bookstore, my astrologer, Sherry Henderson, suggested I attend their next tarot class. She intimated that it would be good for me to get out and learn something new. "Who knows, it may become your next profession," she quipped. I doubted that would ever happen. In the past, I would turn to shopping to make myself feel better. I decided to take the class and felt it might pick up my spirits. I had always had an interest in psychics and tarot cards. I was not interested in reading for others, but wanted to learn how to read cards for myself. My mother and I used to go to a tealeaf reader once a year. I always enjoyed the readings and found much of it came true. Sometimes, though, I found myself attempting to make things happen earlier than they should. I was very concerned about the past and future and constantly wondered what it held for me. I found myself running off with my thoughts into the distant future. Questioning who was I going to end up with or where I was going to live. I thought if I could learn to read tarot cards it might help me get a better grip on what I could expect for my life and help me worry less.

I knew that John and Sherry would make the class lively and interesting. The past couple of years were difficult for me. A change would be good and I found myself thinking about the class with great anticipation. I drove to the bookstore, parked quickly and made my way into the classroom. I was typically late and this evening was no exception. Most of the participants were already seated. I chose one of two empty chairs across the table from a Don Johnson wanna be. He was attractive in an unusual way, intentionally leaving his beard scruffy with at least two days growth. It seemed like he was trying to appear nonchalant. I thought it was funny that a guy would try so hard to be sexy and laughed at myself for falling for it. We exchanged quick hellos and turned our attention to our teachers.

John and Sherry kept the class upbeat and challenging. Sherry had done many readings for me over the last 10 years or so when I needed advice, usually about relationships and money. This was a natural progression for me. As the class became more proficient we took turns reading for each other. Before I knew it the workshop ended — just before Christmas. At the end of the class, John and Sherry announced that they were throwing a networking party in January. Mitch asked if I would be attending. It was obvious that he was shy, but interested in me. I had been single now for ten years raising my two sons alone. I was definitely interested in a relationship; this guy seemed promising. I told him I probably would be at the party, but I would bring my mother.

My mother flew in from Toronto to spend what would have been her 50th wedding anniversary with me. I did not want her to be alone so soon after my dad's death. I felt there were many similarities between Mitch and my dad. My mother failed to see any resemblance.

I had a feeling of excited anticipation as the evening arrived. The store was crowded with people but Mitch and I managed to find each other. He was smiling when I found him. I introduced my mother to him. I knew it was early in the relationship to meet my mother, but under the circumstances it seemed plausible.

My mother wanted Mitch to do a reading for her. I could tell he was uncomfortable and seemed to shrug it off, suggesting he would read for her another time. I could not put my finger on what it was, there was something compelling about him. I liked the way he spoke, the sound of his voice. We exchanged numbers and began getting to know each other over the phone. We had many long phone conversations about everything. We discussed our beliefs and what we wanted out of life. We talked about our families and backgrounds. Mitch's mother was Northern Italian and his father was Ukrainian.

I told him about my sons and some of my humorous horror stories about firecrackers thrown through the upstairs window, golf balls, crabapples and other joys of being a single mom with two active boys. Mitch had been a middle school teacher and managed to last a whole two years. He said that was enough. He liked children but felt that being a teacher at this time required a certain personality. Now he was building houses. We discussed our fathers. His died at 52, drinking and smoking himself to death.

Over time I heard stories about his father chasing his mother through the house, and how she was afraid of him. She eventually left him but never divorced him. She was a devout Catholic.

I heard about Mitch's two sisters and his brother who was a Marine. He told me he was not close to his family and spoke to them less than once a month. He had broken away from them, which I understood completely. It seemed as though our backgrounds were similar. I felt he reminded me of my father. When I mentioned this to my mother she adamantly replied, "He's nothing like your father." Meaning that Mitch could never compare to my Dad and the man that he was. In the years following my dad's death, we all canonized him. Remembering mostly the good and forgetting the bad is a human trait.

Mitch recounted his most difficult senior year in high school. He played football his entire high school career. He told me his father worked three different jobs to keep the family afloat. They struggled financially as mine did during the early years. Mitch's senior year his father announced to his family that they were moving to a different town. No one wanted to go, least of all Mitch. It was devastating to all of them. I found out years later from Mitch's mother that her husband had an entire second family that he was attempting to keep from family number one. Apparently he was dangerously close to being found out which was why the move occurred. To move in your senior year is extremely disruptive and upsetting. Groups of friends are well established by this time. Teachers and students have built relationships, which strengthen over the high school career.

For Mitch having to go to the bottom of the heap for football made him feel as if his legs had been cut out from underneath him. He had similar insecurities to my own. Although I ran with the popular crowd in high school and had consistency there, we resonated with each other on all levels. We both wanted better, we knew it was within our grasp and we wanted to try with all our might to get it.

It was clear that I did not have the boundaries or the fortitude to be able to discipline my boys. I did not possess the cruelty that my own mother did. I was a very loving mother, but I could not enforce consequences. I would say all the right things up front, but eventually Adam would weaken my resolve and worked on me until I changed my mind about the consequences. I had a very difficult time with tough love. I found it exhausting. Staying on top of discipline did not come naturally to me. My boundaries were just not there. It was not that I did not know right from wrong as much as it was discerning what to do when. I sometimes found I over punished and felt guilty afterward. I might ground the boys for too long a period and then give in after a few days. I knew this undermined my authority and their ability to see me as a guide for their behavior.

Sometimes I did very well and held up my end giving consequences for the boys' actions. Other times I capitulated, not wanting to be unpopular. I was so afraid that they would not love me if I was too tough or strict. Because my parents had been so strict I went the opposite direction and became too lenient. It was difficult for me to find the middle ground. Looking back now I see how the boys needed consistency and follow-through, but I just was not capable of it because of my past and the fear of them not loving me. I was not a confident parent. My mother often criticized me for favoring Adam and not being hard enough on him. She preferred Matthew and made it clear she thought Adam needed a much firmer hand.

I was tired of holding our household together and doing everything all by myself. I commuted two hours roundtrip and worked an eight-hour day at a minimum. When I got home I cooked dinner, helped the boys with their homework and usually did a load or two of laundry. I felt exhausted and emotionally drained. I had a few friends, but did not have the emotional support I needed. The boys arrived home from school three hours before I did which meant that they had too much time on their hands. Even with their homework and chores to do, they got into trouble after school. I was worn down and out.

Mitch took an interest in Adam who was twelve while Matthew was nine. He embraced being a role model and stepfather to the boys. He was dedicated and was not just going through the motions. He gave me suggestions to help me when I asked. I knew that Mitch was far more disciplined than me. He was a fitness buff who ran and worked out consistently.

I enjoyed Mitch's company and felt as if we had some commonality. We had similar desires as far as wanting to balance emotional, spiritual and the physical. He had studied and was interested in growth as I was. He spoke slowly in a soft voice and seemed very laid back.

There was an underlying uneasiness when we first began dating. It was obvious we were both gun shy having been hurt in the past. We had a couple of dates and shortly thereafter, during Superbowl XXVIII, made love for our first time. We got off to a bumpy start. I felt that I overpowered him and he seemed taken aback by my Scorpio energy and sexuality. I know he had never experienced anyone like me before. I found myself having to govern myself and tone it down. We created steam together, however I was not sure about fire.

On Valentine's Day of our first year together Mitch took me out for a really great dinner. It was our second formal date and we were still a little nervous and on our best behavior. I dressed in a striking outfit. I knew I looked great. I felt really good. Towards the end of our evening, Mitch said to me as if in confidence, "I'll never tell you how beautiful you are, I don't want it to go to your head." This statement was odd, but telling. Here was a man that I was dating and trying to please. He was telling me up front, that he would never be pleased with me no matter what. It was my parents' saga all over again. No matter how hard I worked at school, no matter how many teams I played on or how high my marks were in school it was never good enough. Mitch was telling me "You will never measure up." Like an idiot I continued to date this man who disrespected and emotionally abused me. It was what I was used to. It was what was comfortable to me. I was like the lobster in the lobster pot attempting to climb out. Every time I did, I was pulled back into the boiling water to die.

In short order we fell into a serious relationship even though we really did not know each other. Mitch would come over on weekends and spend the night with me. On weekends we stayed in bed until late in the morning. I felt guilty and torn because the boys would get up and ring the doorbell trying to get us to move from the bedroom.

This bothered me and I told Mitch it did. We discussed several times the subject of our personal time being separate and private from my kids. Mitch wanted his time with me and was not concerned that my sons knew what we were doing behind closed doors. I felt very guilty and uneasy. It felt disrespectful to the boys and me. I was twisted up like a pretzel. Even after our discussion there was no change. Putting my foot down was not easy for me; it took me a while to do so because I did not want to upset Mitch. As with my children I was afraid of him not liking me. The situation caused stress between the boys and me. I was really embarrassed by the situation. It did not seem to bother Mitch at all. My boundaries were not discernible and were constantly being overstepped.

I looked independent. I owned my own home, had a great job where I was well respected and paid a good salary. I felt that something was missing and that I needed to have a man to complete me. After all, my father had imprinted me with unconscious programming that I could not make it on my own. I did not know how to be independent. It was foreign to me. I felt I needed someone to lean on, to complete me. I was like a three-legged table. I needed to have the comfort of another in my life to be whole. I had to have a man in my life to feel stable and complete.

Five months after we met, Mitch and I were at his apartment trying to decide where we would put his office equipment when he moved into my house. He had very little to move, but my house was full to the gills. His cell phone rang and he became very quiet while he listened to the voice at the other end of the phone. He asked, "So where is Terry now?" He listened again.

He asked several other questions and sat on the bed and as he hung up the phone he started to cry. Mitch was a tough guy. I had never seen him emotional. I knew this was huge. As tears rolled down his face he told me his brother had an affair with his sister-in-law and she got pregnant. When she was seven months pregnant she went back to her husband. Terry, Mitch's older brother, had driven two and a half hours to get to his brother-in-law's house where he broke in and stabbed him thirty-five times. This was definitely a crime of passion. His brother-in-law's children were in the house at the time of the murder. He killed his own brother-in-law, his wife's brother.

I did not know how to react. I felt bad for Mitch. I had never known anyone that close to a murder. My brothers were cops and my cousin was a cop. I had cops all over the place. However, no one ever murdered anyone in my family. I knew that Mitch's father had been enraged much of his life. Living with anger in a family impacts the other family members. I knew what it was like to walk on eggshells and have to tiptoe around when my father was angry. Tension was a way of life in my household but no one ever killed anyone.

I was as supportive as I could be. He spoke to all his family members and planned a trip to visit his family and his brother. He decided to help pay for his brother's defense. He did not want him to get the death penalty. We made an appointment for one of the best criminal defense attorneys in Atlanta. It took some time before the entire story surfaced. Terry was an exemplary Marine. He had been a dedicated father to his three sons. I could not imagine how his wife and sons were feeling. I felt horrible for the children who experienced their father's tragic death. Two families were destroyed and for what purpose?

I did not tell my mother or anyone in my family about the murder for obvious reasons. She did not have many positive things to say about Mitch as it was.

Mitch moved his computer, printer and his clothes into my house shortly after he found out about his brother. He sold his bed. Other than that he owned nothing. The two partners he built houses for owned the truck he drove. They paid him a small salary for building for them.

Right away Mitch made changes in our household. I felt very strongly about sitting down to eat meals together as a family. Adam sat opposite me at the other end of the table. It did not seem like a big deal to me. Mitch took exception to this and immediately told Adam that was no longer his place and that Mitch was sitting at the head of the table. He was not the least bit concerned about making waves or upsetting our status quo. I knew this affected Adam. He felt his place was being usurped. Mitch most certainly wanted to remove Adam from the lofty perch he thought I had put him on. From the beginning there was tension between the two of them.

Mitch felt I was too close to my children, in an unnatural way. I found this strange, but accepted this as the way his family dynamic was; they were not as close as my family. I spoke to my mother at least once a week, sometimes more. I visited them whenever I could, at least once every year or eighteen months. Mitch had not seen his mother in years and only spoke to her every few months.

We dated for about six months when the company I worked for had an event at the Braves stadium in Atlanta. I had been instrumental in planning the event along with a couple of other people in my department. My presence was needed to set up the coolers and the food. I invited Mitch to join us. All the tickets were paid for and he met the boys and me there. The kids and I were quite excited about a night that was all paid for by my company. We met at the designated parking lot where we had our tailgate party. The boys knew many of the people who were there, and enjoyed the freedom and the food. Mitch found us in the parking lot. He seemed a little shy and possibly threatened by the camaraderie I had with those I worked with. I was well liked and had a good working rapport with the five managers and my director. I introduced Mitch to everyone in my department. At game time we made our way to the stadium. The four of us sat together with Mitch taking the aisle seat. He had arrived later than we did and wanted a beer. He left with the boys to get something for them as well.

When he returned Mitch discovered that a guy that was known by all of us in the office as a real hot head and a jerk was sitting next to me. He had alluded to wanting to go out with me countless times in the presence of my managers. They had remarked to him not to hold his breath. Like that would ever happen. I did not have an inflated opinion of myself, but I was very attractive, shapely and intelligent. I had certain standards and Chuck was definitely not on my radar.

Chuck decided that this was a perfect opportunity to challenge my date to a duel of wits. Mitch did not know who this guy was that was sitting in his seat. He was also not aware that I had told Chuck very strongly that he needed to go back to his seat at least three times. He flatly refused. His sole purpose was to make Mitch think I had invited him to sit next to me. I did not socialize with him in or out of work. Mitch stood in the aisle of the Braves stadium feeling foolish and small when this pinhead of a man continued to refuse to return to his seat. He would not even turn around and look at Mitch, although he was very well aware that he was standing there. Mitch looked at me like I had glued Chuck to his seat and that it was my fault entirely. He glared angrily at me expecting me *to do something*.

I looked Mitch in the eyes and said, "I have asked him to leave and he refuses." He felt that I should have been able to get him to move. I had seen rage in my father. Watching Mitch's face I could see him getting angrier by the second. The next thing I knew his face was filled with blood and he was clearly ready to explode. He felt both Chuck and I were disrespecting him. He was painfully aware that everyone I worked with was sitting in the bleachers all around us. He blamed me entirely for the situation. After recognizing that Chuck was not going to remove himself, Mitch grabbed his jacket and walked up the stairs.

The boys and I sat in the bleachers uncomfortably and looked at each other. I asked the boys if they were ready to leave. We walked quickly out of the stadium. The whole situation was humiliating and embarrassing. The kids and I ran after Mitch. I felt like I had been hit in the chest with a roundhouse karate kick. I was near tears. I had nothing to do with this situation. I never invited the guy. I had asked him to leave immediately and he would not. What was I to do? The boys were upset. We ran through the stadium trying desperately to catch up with Mitch. When we reached him, he yelled at me about disrespecting him. I was flabbergasted. We ended up having a fight in the parking lot. Mitch was beyond reason. He had his own ideas of how the situation had gone down. He felt that I had hung him out to dry. I could have gotten up and changed seats. Frankly, in the heat of the moment, while the game was going on, it did not occur to me. There weren't any seats nearby. Mitch could not wait to get into his truck. His parting words were he would be moving out when he got home. He was through. He slammed his truck door and flew out of the parking lot, tires squealing.

When we got home, he was loading his clothes up in his truck. I could not understand where this was coming from. We got into a huge irrational fight. I felt I had not done anything. Mitch felt I had done plenty. Fifteen years later, I am in a very different place and a different person. Then I felt like I was dying. My lifeline was being pulled away from me. I was gasping for breath.

We had several big fights. They never had any good reason for starting. One night after a horrible argument with Mitch I drove myself over to the local middle school to get my head clear. I sat in the parking lot to think and feel. I did not feel safe being around Mitch when he was angry. It reminded me of the terror I felt when my father chased after me with a belt.

As I sat in the parking lot reliving the argument we just had I cried. The more I thought about our relationship, the more intense my feelings became. As I cried I noticed that all the lights in the parking lot turned off all at once. It startled me. I stopped crying and the lights came back on again. When I cried again a couple of the lights went out at the same time. After this I realized that driving down the road my emotions, joy or anger, could turn off the streetlights. The more intense my emotions were the more lights that went out at the same time. It made me realize that our emotions are energy. "If I could turn off lights with my emotions what were my emotions doing to me when I kept them inside?" I thought.

While Mitch and I were together the boys and I began talking about getting another Weimaraner. We all really liked Beau who had showed up on our doorstep so long ago. Gunner was wonderful, but was beginning to age. We wanted a dog to transition with when Gunner was gone, plus Gunner would have some company. Mitch did not want another animal and told me he thought it was "not a good idea." These were words I heard from him often about many different issues.

After Mitch moved out we got our new puppy. He was soft and sweet and had beautiful blue eyes. We all loved Jake and he became entrenched in our family life quickly. Gunner and he became good friends and got along famously.

We were separated for three months when I received a phone bill for collect calls that had been placed by Mitch's brother from prison. Being the scorekeeper I could not let this go. I decided he needed to pay his part of the phone bill. I called Mitch to tell him about it and collect the money. Before I knew it we were making up and he was moving back in. I never even mentioned the phone bill. We were like magnets for each other. I had issues with guilt, shame, low self-esteem and money. Mitch shared my poverty consciousness with a large dose of rejection issues smothered in rage. We did not stand a chance. We had no tools at our disposal to navigate all the issues that we shared. We had a large stewpot of crap with which to deal. Mitch had never been married. Now he decided to throw in with two boys, a house full of animals and a disempowered, abused woman with no discernible boundaries.

Mitch was surprised that I had decided to get Jake while he was gone. It was one of his first comments, "So you got him anyway." He was obviously disappointed that I chose to disregard what he said about getting the dog.

Adam and Matthew were active boys. They took karate classes and played baseball and basketball every year for four years. Mitch attended all the boys' games offering encouragement and support. The fact that he had been a physical education teacher in a prominent middle school helped to give him the background he needed to guide and coach the boys when they were off the field. One day when Mitch and I were sitting in the bleachers watching Matthew's afternoon game, another parent climbed up into the bleachers to watch his son play. He sat about three feet away from me and at the same level. While we watched the game I made comments to no one in particular about the plays. He talked to me about the kids and the game as it was being played. I did not think anything of it, as I talk to anyone who breathes while in the grocery store or anywhere I go. I am friendly and open.

Mitch flew up into my face when the man left. He told me that I attracted this man and his attention and that I had my sexual antennae out. He was furious with me that another man would sit down in the bleachers and have a conversation with me. Similarly, at the Braves game, Mitch felt that I caused the interaction to occur with Chuck. He said I would have to pull in my horns as he thought I was sending out a sexual vibe to anyone out there. I knew Scorpios tend to be very sexual and sensual people. I was not consciously looking for another partner, nor was I flirting. I did not understand where this was coming from or why he felt compelled to blame me for sitting on the bleachers and minding my own business. Mike Crofton had been jealous but nothing as irrational as Mitch. This was terrifying to me.

The fight that ensued was horrendous. I felt like I was pulled backwards through a ringer washing machine. Nothing I could say would change his mind. I caused it, it was entirely my fault and I needed to change. We went around the same words and issues until I was so exhausted I could barely see.

By four o'clock in the morning we finally had everything settled. Mitch's anger had subsided and I did whatever I had to make things right. Then we made love. Everything was better after that. The pattern of make-up sex was now set in both of our brains and DNA. It would be our pattern for years to come. He would get angry, I would do whatever I could to make things right and then we would make love.

When we had a problem with the boys Mitch would take the time to talk about all areas and try to reach a solution that we both could live with. I often agreed to a new course of action with rules and an action plan. Later I would feel that it was far too strict for me to live with and then back down on our agreement. This indecisiveness became a pattern that I would repeat frequently. It created a sense of betrayal for Mitch.

The underlying feeling I had was that Mitch felt he was more intelligent than me, as well as a much better parent. He felt he could do a better job as a parent than I was doing. He felt that I was inept and inconsistent when it came to parenting. This pervasive feeling that he was better at disciplining the boys was apparent when he decided to change things up and give them each dishwashing duties. He told the boys that from this point onward they would have a schedule with one of them washing and the other drying and putting away after dinner. What bothered the boys was that Mitch did not pitch in to help with the household duties. His European background was consistent with the role models I had. I followed in my mother's footsteps being the housekeeper, cook and housemaid. Mitch came home and sat down at the table ready to eat and left his dishes where they were upon completion of the meal.

My mother taught me to cook at a very early age. My years as a flight attendant and living in England gave me wonderful culinary experiences and varied recipes as well as those I used in my everyday cooking. I was and still am a fabulous cook. Even though I worked a full time job, I cooked a hot meal every night of the week but Friday. I never served my family canned soup or sandwiches for dinner. I cooked healthy meals with at least two or three vegetables as well as a salad. Friday nights I cut up fresh vegetables served with dip, which we munched on while we watched Full House. It was our family tradition.

I am not certain why, but the pattern emerged that after serving wonderful meals each night Mitch found some fault with whatever I served. "This was too salty." "It wasn't hot enough." "This would have been better if you added cheese." He seemed unable to appreciate anything I did, or even me. Perhaps his father never paid his mother a compliment and he was following in his father's footsteps. I am not sure if Mitch did not want me to become full of myself even though I did everything to make things wonderful. I took turns cooking each person's favorite meal. He was never fully pleased or grateful for what I had created. Eventually, Matthew began critiquing my meals and cooking in the same way Mitch had. The boys identified with Mitch as a male role model.

One day when we were shopping at the nearby mall the two of us went one way and the boys went to look at something they were interested in. I received a call on my cell phone. The boys were picked up for shoplifting. We were called into the management office of the department store. We thought we were lucky; they decided not to prosecute. After this incident Mitch suggested that I quit my job, and work for him taking care of all his paperwork so that he could spend more of his time building houses. This meant more supervision for the boys. It seemed a win-win. I was relieved to be able to be home when the boys got home from school. They needed more supervision now as opposed to less. However, living without my income was very challenging.

Mitch was about to travel up north for his brother's court case. I awoke several weeks before he was to leave from a very intense dream. I received a very strong message that I needed to get pregnant and that I would have a daughter. This girl would be a very special gift for me. It was a gift from God. It sounded crazy, but the feeling was so strong and powerful I listened. I was told I needed to fast and do a whole body cleanse before I conceived. I had never done a fast or a cleanse before. The message was profound and compelling. When I had any doubts the same message was given to me again. I got pregnant right before Mitch left for the opening of his brother's trial. I had always wanted a daughter.

Once I knew I was pregnant I began talking to Mitch about marriage. He was reluctant to get married. He was thirty-six and had never been married. His own parents had not been stellar role models for marriage. He also had little faith in my ability to stick it out as I had already been married twice unsuccessfully. He said if he got married it was forever. The day I confirmed my pregnancy I announced it to the family. The light finally went on for him. He realized why I wanted to get married. That seemed to make all the difference to him.

The boys were very excited about our wedding and we made plans for a celebration ceremony. We were married at a beautiful North Georgia resort a year after we met. The boys were included in the ceremony with my friend Nannette officiating. She gave us $1,200 so that I could have a ring. We spent less than $2,000 for our entire wedding, as it was all I could put on my credit card. I looked radiant and barely able to fit into my dress at three months pregnant. I was happy and all three of the boys appeared to be also.

Mitch had agreed to pay for his brother Terry's legal defense. The defense for Terry cost what Mitch made annually. The court case created issues on so many levels. We had a baby on the way and I wondered how on earth we would be able to make it financially.

Around this time Mitch suggested that I use the equity I had in my house to help sustain us. He was not making enough money from the houses he was selling to keep us afloat. He had dissolved the partnership and was building on his own by this time. I had never used my equity and really did not want to. He continued to pressure me to do so until I gave in.

There was a great deal of tension in our household when Mitch returned. His brother was given a life sentence without parole. The events that followed the sentencing were difficult for both the families to endure. One family lost their son senselessly, while the other suffered a similar loss. Terry was no longer going to be around to raise or support his sons. He would not be there for his wife. I could not imagine how I would feel if it was one of my family. I felt compassion for both sides.

We did our best to put the events of the murder and court case behind us. The memories of that day in May when we found out would continue to reverberate throughout our marriage for a long time. Nothing would ever be the way it was. We had to go on, we had our own family and a baby to think of.

I did my best to put aside my own beliefs about how I ran my department in my previous job. I sat down to learn Mitch's system for billing. I knew shortcuts and faster ways to do word processing and data entry. My typing speed had been in the high nineties when I was typing every day. I had skills and knowledge that I brought to the table. Yet Mitch insisted that I do everything his way. I had worked on computers and done data entry for years. I knew what I was doing. He doubted that I did. We fought every time we sat down to work on his accounts. It did not take long before I told him I could not work with him and wrote a letter of resignation. Although I was getting almost $2,000 a month in child support, there was not enough money to pay me for anything I did. Even if there was, he did not value my work or me.

While Mitch and I were having our own challenges and issues, Adam challenged Mitch and his control. He was in trouble at school. With the lack of money and the court case there was a constant undercurrent of tension in our household. Mitch expected things to go his way. When I challenged his ideas or ways of executing a plan he became angry. He felt disrespected and he would not have that. Often his anger would build and he would punch a doorjamb right in front of my face or clench his fist and push it within a centimeter of my nose, like he would just love to plow me in the middle of my face. I never knew when he was going to explode. The threat of violence terrified me. Even though he had not hit me yet, I never knew when he would.

Within this dynamic of anger and blame, we were also building a family. We went camping together and canoeing as a family. We rented a large camper one weekend and drove up to Lake Rabun with our dogs. Mitch felt the boys should help out more and this became a point of contention on our camping excursions.

Adam became more unruly and started to push back in Mitch's direction. He did not like being told what to do by anyone, never mind his stepfather. Mitch felt I was too lenient with Adam and tougher on Matthew. I had to agree that this was frequently the case. I made excuses for Adam and did not for Matthew.

When it came time for the birth of our daughter, Mitch and I had been seeing a chiropractor that had two home births with his wife. He told beautiful, romantic stories about how wonderful it was for him to deliver his own child in the privacy of his own bedroom. Mitch and I longed to do the same. I had grave concerns about my ability to have a natural birth after having so much difficulty with my first two babies. I felt I had died in childbirth in a past life as I had a very deep-seated fear of delivering vaginally. Mitch felt that my fears were just in my head and I needed to release them and I would be able to go through the birth normally.

My gynecologist discussed his concerns with me and would not support me in my decision. So I stopped seeing him as my doctor. A midwife attended us during the last trimester. We had discussed our options and the plan for our birth with her. Mitch decided he did not want her present at our birth. We had no insurance and little money to spend on my care, although this was not the deciding factor.

As I went into labor we sent the boys to friends' houses until I delivered. Matthew came back nervously to the house to check on how things were progressing. It was so sweet to see him so excited yet concerned. After 32 hours, I developed a strange and severe rash along my back and spine that concerned Mitch. By this time I was in discomfort with nothing for pain at all and not capable of making rational decisions. After several discussions with the midwife and my deep concern, we made it to the hospital.

The doctor in the emergency room was not thrilled with the state I was in when I arrived. He checked my abdomen and raised Holy Hell with me. He told me that both my baby and I could have died as a result of my uterus rupturing. Since I had already had two C-sections the incision could have ruptured. He said my uterus was so thin from the hours of intense labor and that was a risk for me. I could bleed to death. I looked dreadful. I was in so much pain and felt so bad I did not care what anyone said to me.

Ana was finally born, perfectly beautiful and healthy. My recovery was slow. I was delighted as were her brothers with this beautiful little girl. I had my little girl! I was ecstatic. I doted on her. I bought matching hats, coats and dresses every chance I could. She was a happy little addition to our family. Matthew bonded with her instantly. He acted as if she were his child. Adam liked her too. Although he seemed to feel as if his position had been reduced in some way. He had always been my first-born, which cannot be taken away. I knew he was troubled by the attention that Ana received.

I took Ana everywhere with the boys. When they had karate I drove while she was in the back seat. The first three months it was apparent that Ana did not like to be away from her mother for more than ten minutes.

Mitch became hyper-vigilant and overprotective. He felt it was too much to drive Ana all over town, grocery shopping and to karate as it interrupted her "schedule." Other families do the same thing when there are older children and a baby. The baby goes where the older children go. Mitch felt Ana should be napping at home in her own bed. That was a problem. When it came time to put Ana to bed, the only way she would go to sleep was if she nursed herself to sleep. At night I would feed her and put her down in her crib. Once lying down away from the warmth of my body she woke up and cried. I told Mitch we should let her cry as she would get in the habit of sleeping on me and never want to stay in her own bed. He could not stand to hear her cry. If I had to go somewhere and left Ana with Mitch she would cry. She only wanted me. After months of struggling with this issue, I decided to just let her sleep with us; at least I could get some sleep.

Breast fed babies bond very quickly with their mothers. The bond is deeper than what occurs between bottle-fed babies and their mothers. A breast-fed baby feels and smells their mother's skin against their cheek. It is a warm, nurturing experience for the mother and child. Ana was a very smart little girl. She wanted to be near her food and soothing source all the time. We bonded deeply.

When Ana was six months old we bought a brand new van and drove to Canada around Christmas. We enjoyed our visit and everyone loved seeing the boys and meeting Ana. We stayed about five days with my mother and another night with my brother. Mitch did not want me to drive and he became very aggressive on the road back home. He attempted to pass a late model Mercedes Benz for about ten miles on a two-lane stretch of road. A slower driver occupied the right lane while the Mercedes driver sat in the passing lane doing about sixty-five miles per hour. Mitch wanted to get by and cruise at around seventy-five or eighty. Mitch kept pulling up close to the guy's bumper, but he would not budge. I was not sure if the Mercedes driver was oblivious to Mitch's attempt to get by, but I doubted it. Mitch kept pulling up closer and almost touched the other car's bumper. We all became very frightened. The boys and I braced our feet and arms in preparation for a direct hit. It was Mitch against the Mercedes and he would not listen to anything I said about pulling into the right lane and just leaving the guy alone. He pushed the gas pedal down one more time and after almost thirty minutes of this cat and mouse game there was an opening for Mitch to pull alongside him. He reached down to the floorboard where the beautiful gold and white cookie tin rested. My mother had filled it with her homemade shortbread and Mexican wedding cakes for me to take home. He pressed the button on the armrest lowering his window and catapulted my mother's cookies at the Mercedes Benz hood. I shrieked, "Mitch you could have killed us or him! You put us all in danger!" The tension in the van was so thick I could taste it. The stress in my body choked me. Matthew almost put his feet through the floorboards as he tensed his body against the impending crash that never came.

When we pulled off to eat at the next Cracker Barrel, Mitch apologized to Matthew. He never said he was sorry to me for putting all of my family in danger. He did not apologize to Adam for endangering his life either, only Matthew. When I thought of my mother's efforts, and her cookies going to waste on the side of the freeway it made me cry. There was no limit to the lengths that his rage would reach. Another piece of me died on Interstate 75 that cold winter day.

On another occasion, while in Adam's room in our finished basement, Ana jumped on the bed. She fell against the wall and as she did a clock fell off the wall and hit her on the top of the head. Mitch became red instantly and punched his hand through the dry wall. I could not understand his angry reaction to this situation. Where my first reaction was compassion his first reaction was rage.

Adam had been tested when he was seven years old for Attention Deficit Disorder. The results were positive for ADD with a high IQ. Once he was in eighth grade he had more issues with school and paying attention in class. Although he did well scholastically, distractions surfaced which created challenges for him. In high school he and a friend entertained themselves and others by getting into trouble together. Food fights in the cafeteria and gags occurred often enough that if anything was broken or damaged the two of them were hauled into the principals' office. On one such occasion his friend was not even in the state when the "said" incident occurred.

Adam was very ingenious with entrepreneurial tendencies. When he was motivated he became amazingly creative. Since we had a Sam's Club card he discovered he could buy a box of chocolate bars and sell them for a profit on the bus. Between working as a bag-boy at Kroger and his candy sales he was able to buy his own car before he turned sixteen. The bus driver did not like him at all. Especially after Adam jumped out the back emergency exit door of the bus one afternoon. Throwing things out the window of the bus was also a favorite pastime of his. The bus driver turned Adam in when he saw him passing something in a paper bag to another student and receiving money. He assumed incorrectly that Adam was selling drugs. Adam's little covert candy operation was permanently closed.

Mitch had relayed the story of his first car to me. He had purchased his own gas-guzzling muscle car when he was sixteen. He spent every penny he had made on that car. It was his pride and joy. Within six months he had burned the engine out due to lack of experience with mechanics and oil. I felt that this experience imprinted a negative connotation in his brain. Every chance he could he took Adam's car away. If Adam did not wash the dishes, he lost the car. If Adam talked back to me, he lost the car. If Adam did not do his homework, he lost the car. The relationship between Mitch and Adam became antagonistic. I felt like I was being drawn and quartered. I would never have been as tough on him as Mitch was. He said I had an unnatural "love" for my son.

Adam became agitated and belligerent. He took exception to Mitch telling him what to do. I don't think Adam was consciously aware, but he seemed to be jealous of his little sister. He seemed to be bothered by the time and attention that was being taken away from him. Our household certainly was different with Ana in it.

One evening after dinner when it was Adam's turn to wash dishes Mitch walked into the kitchen and saw Adam changing the stations on the radio. For whatever reason Mitch was more aggravated than usual. He said to Adam, "If you don't get in here and do these dishes NOW I'll plant you!" Adam challenged, "So plant me!" I was walking quickly down the stairs as I heard the commotion in the back of the house. I leapt over the bottom stairs arriving to witness the worst moment in my lifetime.

Mitch flew across the kitchen so fast his feet barely touched the floor. He reached up to squeeze Adam's neck. His strong hands encircled Adam's throat so tight Adam could not breathe. He wrestled my son to the ground with his grip tightening around Adam's throat. Adam never tried to fight. He just lay on the floor absolutely motionless. I screamed at Mitch to leave him alone. Matthew was so terrified he kept running up and down the stairs shouting, "Call 911! Call 911!" I stood over Mitch screaming at him, "LET GO OF HIM! YOU'RE GOING TO KILL

HIM!" I had to physically grab him and pull his hands off Adam while Adam lay still and lifeless on the kitchen floor. My body was on fire with adrenaline and my face frozen in abject fear.

This event sent ripples throughout our household for years to come. I will never forget that day, as I am sure Adam will not either. He was a skinny teenager weighing in soaking wet at about 118 pounds. He did not stand a chance against a weightlifting full-grown man.

Mitch was determined he would not have a teenager get the best of him. He told me I had three choices, "Send Adam to military school, or to live with his father in Colorado. If you choose neither of these I'm out of here."

Mitch's father felt that when his sons became of age they needed to get out of the house. He felt that males were competing for territory and he had no use for them any longer. When Adam was of driving age it was apparent that Mitch felt the same way about him. It seemed that in his mind I would have more time for him if Adam was not around to divert my attention.

Phil had never been there for the boys except financially. He could manage money, and run a multi-billion dollar business, but he did not know what teenagers needed. I felt that sending Adam to Colorado was a fate worse than death. Phil loved his children, but he had always been an absentee father. He did not have the emotional connection then to raise children. He did not have any spiritual support. Although he was raised Catholic he did not follow their beliefs or attend church. He did not have the benefit of a strong faith back then. He had recently married a woman, who like Mitch, had never been married before and did not have any children. The boys had attended Phil and Kate's wedding over their summer break. It did not feel like a good situation to me.

Looking back at this situation now I would choose differently. I owned the home we lived in. I was getting $1,500 a month in child support and I had a new baby. I could have told Mitch to get out and gone back to work. Mitch had said repeatedly that I needed to be home with Ana. I wanted to stay home to raise her as well. I felt I could not do it without him. It was what I was programmed to do; get married and have babies. I felt I needed a man to help me raise my children. I was being torn apart on the inside.

Adam never cried. Even when I beat him with a wooden spoon and broke it over his backside he never cried. He begged me not to send him. With tears rolling down his sixteen-year-old cheeks he begged me not to make him move to Colorado. At that time I felt I had no other choice.

I felt like another piece of me died that day in the kitchen. I was terrified of Mitch and what he would do. I was really afraid that if I did not send Adam to Colorado that Mitch would kill him. I could not have that. I did not even think about me. My concern was for Adam, Matthew and Ana. I was worried that when Matthew turned fourteen that he would move to Colorado to be with his brother. Mitch assured me that would never happen.

Matthew and Ana were very deeply connected from before the time she was born. Ana adored both her brothers but was much more attached to Matthew. They were both rat children in the Chinese horoscope born exactly twelve years apart. It felt like they had a past life connection and he was her father before.

After the "I'll plant you" incident Matthew became very angry. I could understand why. From his viewpoint we had been one happy family until Mitch moved in with us. Now his brother was moving to Colorado. Phil flew into Atlanta during the early part of the summer break. He and Adam loaded all of his belongings into Adam's old burgundy Honda that he purchased with his own money and drove to Colorado. The $1,000 car barely made it there.

I was devastated and filled with guilt. I felt I had failed my son. I shrunk back from Mitch. The more violent he was the less I wanted to be intimate. Each time he became violent I felt like another part of the love I had for him died. I became less and less interested in being intimate with him. To me our sex life was unfulfilling.

Sending Adam to Colorado empowered Mitch. He suggested I sell my silver to help pay bills. He also wanted me to get rid of my diamond earrings that Phil had given me. I told him I would when he bought me some. I also sold a beautiful breakfront wall unit that Phil and I had bought in England and used the money to buy bedroom furniture.

Matthew flew to Colorado to visit Adam and his father for Christmas. When he returned he had an anger that I had never seen before. Phil had made sure that the Christmas break was the best ever buying Matthew expensive things and taking the boys skiing. Phil could clearly provide more material things for both the boys than we could. When Phil exerted pressure on Matthew to move out to Colorado he jumped at the chance. I wanted to die.

Phil left nothing to chance. Rather than expecting Mitch and me to put our son on an airplane destined for Colorado, Phil flew into Atlanta to fly back to Denver with Matthew. Phil made it seem that there was no time to say good-bye. He told Matthew his flight was three hours earlier than it really was. Matthew called us the day he was to leave to tell us the plans for his departure; we only had ten minutes to say good-bye. When Matthew came back to the house he had to gather the rest of his clothes that were in the dryer, fold them and say good-bye. I felt gypped and rushed. I could not understand why we were given so little time. Ana was upset as we all were. After they left our subdivision Matthew told me later the two of them stopped at the golf club to enjoy a leisurely lunch before heading to the airport.

Phil had been out of work for months. He waited to tell Matthew the news of his new job until the day he left for Colorado. Phil explained he had good news for Matthew. He had a fantastic new job! He would be in California from Monday to Friday every week and home every week-end. Matthew and Adam would be at home with their new stepmother. If Matthew had this information beforehand he might have chosen differently.

I felt for Phil's new wife, Kate. She had no idea what she had signed up for. His father had snowed Matthew. Phil kept this information from Matthew until he got into his rental car. His job in California changed everything. The boys' father was absent Monday through Friday. Kate and Phil had only been married a year. Now she was saddled with two resentful teenage boys.

When I knew that Matthew was leaving too I did not want to live in our house any longer. Mitch had been pressuring me to sell it so he could build "his own" house. I put my house on the market and sold it quickly. After paying the real estate agent and the equity loan off there was a total of $2,500 left. The $54,000 in equity I had built was gone. I was so angry with Mitch I told him I was using the rest of the money to pay my tuition to become a hypnotist.

After Matthew left, Ana became so stressed about the changes in her little world that she twirled her hair. She also stuttered. She missed her brothers and did not understand what had happened to them. I talked to her about them and sent the boys videos of their sister and our animals. Sometimes Ana would become so intense with her hair twirling that her fingers would become entangled. She would have a huge knot of tangled hair sticking out at the back of her head that could not be brushed out and had to be cut out with scissors.

I was angry and grieving the loss of my two sons. I did not want to stay in the area that reminded me of them. I needed to get away from all the memories around their schools and the neighborhood. I found a little furnished cabin to rent on Lake Blue Ridge in North Georgia. In the beginning of July we put our furniture in storage and attempted to begin a new life. The only issue was that the dogs were not allowed upstairs in the house. We had two great months of swimming weather. At least there was a lake to take my mind off of things.

We swam in the lake whenever we could. Both Gunner and Jake would follow us down the pathway with Katman tagging behind. I swore that cat thought he was a dog. He really was an amazing animal. I loved them all and was glad we could all enjoy the water together. Ana and I saw our first Bald Eagle while floating on the lake one afternoon by ourselves. I was so excited as I had never seen one before. He was a magnificent and beautiful bird. I found the sighting absolutely thrilling. My spirits were buoyed for days afterward. I felt it was a positive sign. I was not sure of what.

I enjoyed being on the water and found it peaceful and relaxing. One day while walking back up the path to our cabin I spotted a little black and tan puppy swimming across the lake toward us. She looked like a tiny dot in the water. As she swam closer I saw she was only about ten or twelve weeks old. She crossed the bay to get to me and entangled herself in the ropes hanging around the boat dock. I held her still while she clamored to get out, unwrapping the tangled mess of ropes from her wiggling legs.

Mitch told me immediately to ignore the dog and not to feed her, but she followed our little band of people and animals home. How could I ignore her? She was a sweet little girl in need of love. She was perfect for Ana, as she had just lost her beloved Matthew.

There was nothing better to divert Ana's attention than a little puppy. She was sweet and adorable. The two of them bonded and became joined at the hip. If Ana went somewhere, so did the little puppy. Mitch insisted I find her owners. I posted signs and contacted the local radio station, but no one came forward. The shelter in the area had recently closed due to lack of funds. I believe someone dumped a litter along the side of the road. She made a beeline towards the first loving beings she could find. After about two months of looking, Mitch stopped along the side of the road as we drove our separate vehicles back to the cabin from Alpharetta. He got out of his truck and ripped down my sign. I said to Ana, I guess puppy is staying. We still had not named her thinking we might have to give her up any moment. We tried many names on her for size. Patti, Puppy, and Lucy finally stuck. She was one of those dogs that your heart opens wide for. She was pure love. Gunner was too, but Lucy came along just for Ana, to help her through this very difficult time.

We drove back and forth during the week while we were building the house in Alpharetta. I took Ana to preschool half days. Then I would spend the rest of my day picking out building materials for the house. The dogs rode in the back of Mitch's truck or my Explorer. Once at our property they would run around and swim at the lake behind the new house while we focused on completing the building process.

Mitch was building four houses in a neighboring subdivision. They were built as "spec" houses i.e., speculating that someone would buy them if they saw them.

Meanwhile in the fall the boys began high school. Matthew and Adam ran cross-country and seemed to fit in all right. Adam was in his senior year gearing up for graduation. They complained about Kate not cooking for them during the week and that they were alone much of the time. Left to their own devices their diet consisted of frozen bagel bites and canned pineapple. Kate came home late, spending evenings with friends or at the gym. Both the boys expressed unhappiness about their father being away during the week. They rarely saw him. On weekends he tried to get the boys up early and walk with him and Kate but they would rather sleep in.

The weather was still warm in Georgia when I received a collect call from the boys. They had been put in a juvenile detention center for fighting at school. Three boys who taunted Adam since the beginning of school, called him "tall boy." Every time they saw him they chanted the phrase. One day they grabbed his skinny body and pushed him backwards towards the railing of the second story atrium. Adam could not see where he was and was afraid they were going to throw him over the railing. His adrenaline and tai kwon do kicked in and he became automatic. He hit the closest face with one forceful punch. The force, coupled with the braces in the boy's mouth, tore up his face and mouth. Others quickly swarmed in to pull them apart. As the boys walked away from one another one of the bullies turned back coming up from behind to hit Adam in retaliation. Matthew stepped in to protect his older brother and punched the kid over Adam's shoulder.

Perhaps things might have been different if Phil had answered his phone. Events happen the way they are meant to. It was six hours before he returned the call from the school about the fight.

He had been in meetings all day. The boys sat waiting for their dad to speak to the school principal for three hours. My number was not on any of the data files at the school. When no one called back they were handcuffed and removed from the school property in the middle of lunch. The boys were humiliated by the experience. No one else was arrested. The administration had waited and could not wait any longer. The boys were taken to the county juvenile detention center. They spent the night in the detention center. They were handcuffed and wore orange jumpsuits when they appeared in court the following day. Once Phil returned from California the boys were remanded to him.

Adam was expelled for the remainder of the semester. Matthew and the other boys were given a two-week suspension. Matthew and Adam were the only ones detained in the detention center. I flew to Colorado for the board of education hearing. It did not matter that the other boys started the fight, or that they tried to push Adam over the second floor railing. The focus was on the fact that Adam's karate back fist punch was so powerful it tore up the other boy's mouth. Their parents were at the school immediately.

I flew back to Denver a second time for the boys' court hearing. This time I brought Ana with me. I felt her presence would be good for the boys and for Ana. They needed to see each other no matter what. I sat in the back of the courtroom with Ana on my lap. At the first sound she uttered Phil and Kate shot me evil looks to silence my daughter and I left the courtroom. I had no one to watch her. Phil was angry that I was there. He and Kate did not speak to me, treating me with disgust. I felt like I was being treated like a criminal and being blamed by them.

Phil was angry about the fight. He did not take responsibility for not being there for his sons. He did not hire a tutor for Adam. Instead, he got him a good attorney.

My friend, Janie, gave me two buddy passes for the boys to fly home for Christmas. The passes were on Air Canada, which did not fly directly from Denver to Atlanta. The scheduled flight took them through Canada. When Phil found out about the itinerary he refused to allow the boys to use the tickets. We had just moved into our newly built home. I lay on the mattress, which was lying directly on the floor, shaking involuntarily from head to toe after getting off the phone with the boys. After our initial conversation the boys were confined to their rooms without the use of a phone. Within 24 hours I had pneumonia, 48 hours later so did Ana.

The situation was getting very ugly for them. Phil and Kate had stopped including the boys in anything. They woke up early in the morning and were gone all day. They left very little if anything for the boys to eat for breakfast, lunch or dinner. One day they told me all they could find to eat was one can of pineapple between them. They had no money to buy anything, and no car to get anywhere. Adam's car had been used as a tax right off for Phil. It was not replaced.

Phil and Kate refused to allow them to use their Christmas wrapping paper, saying, "It isn't family paper." When it was apparent how much it meant to me to have the boys home, Mitch agreed to a last-minute purchase of two regular fare tickets. While their parents were out the boys eluded Phil and Kate, escaped from the house and had a friend drive them to the airport.

When Adam returned to school after Christmas he was so far behind in math he could not catch up. It had always been a subject that challenged him. He failed math and was short one credit and did not graduate with his class. With all the money that was spent on their defense, Phil never thought to get educational assistance for Adam to finish out his high school education with ease. This little pebble in the road became a mountain for Adam as time went on. He paid the price for the fight for many years.

The boys attended Chatfield High School, two miles away from where the Columbine shootings occurred. They called me that day from a friend's cell phone to say that they had been shut inside for their own protection. They were aware of the shootings occurring as they happened. They experienced the terror of the situation first hand. Several of their friends were killed in that senseless massacre. Living through this experience impacted their lives. I was relieved and delighted to have them back living with us again when school ended in June.

I hired an attorney and began the legal fight with Phil to regain physical custody of the boys. All my worst fears were realized. I felt he was inept as a father and this proved it to me. The boys were back living with Mitch and me after Adam and Matthew completed their year at school.

We had built a grand home with a fabulous front porch with a metal roof on two acres. The property was beautiful, slopping toward the back and overlooking a large lake. I loved to be around water and this lot was beautiful. The front of the property had four-board fencing and many horses and cows grazed on farms nearby. Across the street from us were two houses that had been there for years and we got to know these new neighbors. I wanted the boys back home. We overbuilt. We designed it together putting everything we both ever wanted into a home. I was very environmentally conscious, so we had a fabulous recycling area in the mud and laundry room. We had a fabulous eat-in kitchen with a fireplace and a Dacor cook top overlooking it. There was a double oven with one being convection. I was able to cook and entertain guests at the same time. I had almost enough furniture to fill it from my old house.

Within months of moving into our beautiful custom-designed home we received an offer to sell. If I had not been so concerned about luring my kids back with the house, we probably would have been much better off if we had accepted the offer. Both of our egos were in the house. We created it together even though Mitch always referred to it as "his" house. We had hardwood floors all over the first floor. I was astounded when Mitch said that the dogs would not be allowed inside. We had Gunner for eight years. I could not think of him having to sleep in the garage now to save the floors.

We put so much time and attention into building our new home. It had a three-car garage with Mitch's workshop and office over top. I faux finished his office and decorated the kitchen. All the while we were focusing on our house the four houses that Mitch had been building remained incomplete and stagnant.

I cleaned one of the finished houses that was completed with a friend of mine. Mitch gave her $100 for helping me. I was not paid for my efforts.

While I was inside scrubbing drywall mud off the white tiled floor and commode, Mitch was supposed to be watching Ana. We had been working hard for about three hours when I stopped to catch my breath and to check on her. She was standing by the curb in the front yard with the front door of my Explorer opened and focused on something. As I approached her and my vehicle I saw with horror that she was decorating the interior of my SUV with lipstick. Dark red-brown lipstick was all over the inside of my passenger side door, the upholstery and the dash for as far as she could reach. I thought to myself, "Where the heck is your father?" I was so upset that Mitch had left her to her own devices. I let Ana know by the tone of my voice I was not happy with her artistic creations. I grabbed one wrist and I smacked her backside five times. When Mitch came up from behind he yelled at me for spanking her. He said to stop beating her. I was not beating I was spanking. I was furious that I should have to deal with supervising our daughter when I was in his house on my hands and knees cleaning crap off the bathroom receptacles. I knew I had one chance to make it clear to Ana that this kind of behavior was not acceptable. This was the one and only time I ever spanked our daughter. I felt it was warranted. She never wrote on another vehicle or wall with lipstick again.

I did whatever I could do to make the houses that were partially built look presentable and more energetically inviting. I cleaned windows and picked up construction debris in the yards. Mitch was depressed and had a hard time doing anything to get the houses to sell. The subdivision was having difficulties and all the builders seemed to be losing their houses back to the bank. We did not want this to happen. I felt like we were on top of a slippery slope.

Matthew graduated from high school while living with us. I was glad we were able to have a party for him to celebrate. His father came in from Denver to attend. We had healed our relationship to the point that we could be with him comfortably. It was better for everyone. We all had matured and gotten over our past fears.

I took a master gardener course with a neighbor. I loved the learning process. The Georgia Master Gardeners were a great group of people and we worked together on several projects as well as a cookbook. The creative process was exciting to me. I really enjoyed the women and the get-togethers as well. We split up and worked in teams to promote the cookbook. One of my assignments was a neighborhood Ace hardware store. Lily and I stopped by together and left a letter with our contact information on it. Two weeks later I received a call out of the blue from the owner of the hardware store. I was offered the lawn and garden department managerial position. I was not even looking for a job and one landed in my lap. I realized that this was a gift from the Universe and I accepted it, after talking with Mitch.

Mitch did not want me to take the job. We knew by this time that we would lose our beautiful house. None of the houses he had built were selling. They were going back to the bank after paying thousands of dollars in interest out of our money for almost two years. He felt it was useless to even get a job. His thought was if he was going down he would go down in flames. Mitch also felt that Ana should not go to a daycare center but he would not watch her while I worked. He was going to do research and not be available. I invited Mitch's mother to come and live with us to take care of Ana. It was the most wonderful time on one hand but a nightmare on the other. I loved living in the house, working and being a master gardener. I loved what was happening in my life. So many good things were falling into my lap.

I wrote articles for the *Oracle 20-20* magazine for Sherry Henderson. I found I loved to write and that I was very good at it. I was jazzed with adrenaline, feeling good, looking good and at the same time it seemed inevitable that we would lose our home. That also meant filing bankruptcy. I never thought that would ever happen to me. I knew if I had not been married to Mitch it would never have happened. I felt I should have kept my house and stayed there.

We did everything we could think of to get the houses to sell and bring in money. We had gone to see a Shaman who helped us with some of our relationship issues and how we related to one another. We had also been going to a healer who was a social worker in the past and did some counseling with us as well. In the ten years we were together we had been to three different counselors. The first one was as afraid of Mitch as I was and terminated our sessions after his behavior became so outrageous and enraged when she pointed out his behavior.

While I was at work at the hardware store I received a call from Mitch one afternoon asking me what I was going to make for dinner. I became very angry to think that he and his mother were home all day together and he called me at work to ask what I was making for dinner that night. I attempted to implement a rotation of the cooking duties so that I was not the only one making dinner. Mitch's mother did not want to step on my toes, she said, by cooking dinner without my assistance. After working all day I would sometimes have to stop at the grocery store to pick up what I needed to cook. I walked in the door and immediately prepared dinner for our family. The fact that two adults were home consistently and did not take it upon themselves to start dinner before I got home really put my anger on a slow boil.

In December we gathered for our annual master gardener Christmas party. Husbands, wives and partners were invited. I made a crab dip and put it in my Evesham bone china baking dish. Mitch really did not want to go, as they were all my friends. It was at the home of Lily and her husband who was formerly a Delta pilot. Their house was the most spectacular private home I had ever been in. It was like a ski resort in the mountains with huge, exposed beams in 20-foot ceilings. Mitch did not feel good about himself and where he was. He pulled his beer out of the fridge and set it on the kitchen counter. I suggested that he put it in a cooler because it was easier to carry.

I don't know what nerve I hit, but he went off the deep end. He became instantly enraged about my evaluating everything he did. Earlier that day I had given Mitch the directive that he should get a job. I did not even think that was the case but I do have a tendency to say some remarks over and over again. "Why did it matter how he carried the beer? Who did I think I was with all my fancy friends and job?" I am not sure what I said that set him off, but he flew after me. He went off like an incendiary bomb. As I was going out the door to my car, he grabbed my wrist that held my crab dip, shaking my arm until all the crab dip was flying all over the ground. He continued shaking to make me let go of the china dish so he could break it. He wanted to hurt me anyway he could. He was yelling foul words at me in a rush. I didn't even know what he was shouting. The next thing I knew his mother was standing outside on the landing screaming at him to stop. He ran after me and tried to stop me from opening my door by barring the way. Mitch claimed that he never hit me. Apparently kicking and grabbing did not count as striking but he bruised my leg and arm despite the definition. I got around him somehow and locked myself in my car. He stood outside screaming at me to get out of the car, something about, "Jennifer if you go…" I refused. I told him to get out of the way. I was crying and hyperventilating all at the same time. My whole body was shaking with fear.

I arrived at the party and composed myself in the driveway. I really did not want to go at this point, my beautiful crab dip destroyed. I had nothing to bring inside. I breathed deeply and after a few minutes went into Lily's home.

I think that Mitch felt like he was losing control of me. My daughter felt that he had an affair at this time. I have no proof, although I knew he did speak excruciatingly sweetly to one of his high-end Buckhead clients. I had never heard him speak to me that way and I told him so. I confronted him and asked if he was sleeping with her, but he denied it. I knew that did not feel right. The tone of his voice and the way he spoke to her belied something much more intimate than a client/builder relationship.

While our marriage and financial world were falling apart I was working. People liked me. Everything was going well for me but our personal life and our home were turning to shit. Mitch suggested that perhaps my aunt in England would lend us some money. I said it was worth a try. I knew if we did not get help for the house and our lives, as we knew them to be, were over. Mitch's sister gave me a free ticket and I flew to England to meet with my aunt. She was a very shrewd woman. She knew it did not make good business sense to invest in a losing proposition. She allowed me to stay at her home but would not give me any money. Her business associate sent me a response after I returned home; it was not even from my aunt. I wrote her back and expressed my dismay at him writing to me instead of her. She sent me my inheritance in advance, which was gone in a month and a half, and we still lost the house.

With Mitch's encouragement I started my own business. At first I had a difficult time deciding what to do. I considered everything I loved to do. I wrote, did faux finishing and was a master gardener. Mitch encouraged me to start a landscaping business. He said that whenever I had a spare moment I was working in our gardens. I loved growing plants and had been reading books about perennials, trees and shrubs. I had just become a master gardener. I decided he was right. Landscaping was the best idea. We brain stormed at our kitchen table one day. I wanted a name that denoted Heaven and Earth in it. I suggested Zen Gardener. Mitch came up with something much better, For Heaven Scapes, Ltd. It was creative and a double entendre. I liked phrases and names that were creative. This one certainly was. I used Mitch's trailer and pulled it behind my Explorer. I could cram an amazing number of shrubs and perennials into that car. My first client was Mitch's client in Buckhead. I did her entire landscaping job for $5,000. I needed to cut my teeth on a new client and she benefited from my knowledge without the cost of a huge landscaping company. It was a win-win for us both. My dental hygienist's mother, also in Buckhead, needed someone to maintain her property. I offered to do it. In July 2001 I quit my job at the Ace hardware store and incorporated my newly formed landscape company.

A neighbor and business owner heard about our financial difficulties when I went by his nursery to buy shrubs for an installation of mine. While I was at the nursery he mentioned that he had several buildings that needed drywall and said he would be pleased to offer the job to Mitch. When I discussed the opportunity with him that night he became upset with me saying that he had not had his "tool belt" on in years and was not about to put it on now. I could not understand why he would not want to do something that would bring in some income to our household. He felt he was a builder and that doing dry wall was beneath him. I suggested that he get a job even at Home Depot or Lowes. He became very angry with me for my suggestion and as time wore on I recommended it more than once.

I enjoyed doing the landscaping work and being outside. It was very beneficial for me. I felt comfortable meeting with clients. Where I had difficulty was with consistency and pricing with my clients. My low self-esteem reflected in my under valuing what I did. Drawing was not my strength. It took some time for me to establish myself as an expert. Once I did, I never looked back. I was in my element. I loved what I did and my creativity flowed. Landscaping gave me a purpose. I felt passionate about my work and threw myself into creating a website and finding new clients.

I began working on my spirituality in earnest. I meditated separately from Mitch and prayed every day. We attended a large Unity church sometime after Ana was born and she loved to go. One particular Sunday Ana did not want to go to church with us. She wanted to stay home with her grandmother. Mitch's mother was not feeling well otherwise she would have gone to her own church. We both felt it would be too much for Ana to stay home with her. I had let the dogs out before we left and they were nowhere to be found. I called and whistled for them and checked the time. I knew if we did not leave now we would be late. Mitch was already in the truck and was impatiently waiting to head down the road. I hesitated and then thought, "Well, they can just stay outside." I thought of going back into the house and asking Mitch's mother to watch out for them and let them in. Even that would take time. She lived in our finished basement. The walk from the door to her room and back would take almost five minutes. Five minutes can change everything. I wish I had taken the time.

While we were at Unity, we received a call from Mitch's mother. He called her back once we were outside. She told her son that a single car traveling down our road at a very high speed hit both Jake and Lucy. Jake was killed instantly. Lucy was still alive but in bad shape. A policeman was there and wanted to shoot her to put her out of her pain. We needed to get home fast. I had so many thoughts rolling through my mind as I prayed for them both. A single car driving fast on our little dirt road hit Jake head on and dragged Lucy underneath its wheels. They were running under our fence chasing a squirrel. Once home we assessed the situation. Jake looked perfect; like he was asleep. There was not a scratch on him.

Lucy, on the other hand, was a mess. I cried over her and talked to her softly while she whimpered to me. She did everything in her power to wait to say good-bye to me. I loved that dog like she was a part of my soul. She had been an earthbound angel sent to protect Ana from anything and everything. They had been inseparable. Lucy went everywhere Ana went, even out into the road one day when Mitch and I were distracted. Had it not been for the dog being with Ana, I am sure that woman would not have seen her in the road. God sent Lucy and I knew it. Now she was gone. Mitch picked her up and placed her on a blanket in the back of my Explorer with the seat down. I held her and talked to her all the way to the emergency vet on the other side of town. I prayed over her and told her how much I loved her, all the while she responded softly talking back to me. Two minutes from the vet's office Lucy stopped breathing and slipped back to where she came. I wept from the depth of my soul for my sweet little angel dog. Only three years earlier she came into our lives and how quickly she was gone.

We lost our house. Two weeks before our move we had an estate sale. Mitch dropped Ana and me at Macy's to price out crystal and furniture for our sale. I had no idea what to charge for anything. I wanted to have the truck and drop Mitch off at Lowes because we had two stops to make. Mitch said, "No. I'll drop you and you can walk to Macy's furniture store." I was totally shocked because the furniture store was not inside the mall but about a half mile away. There were no sidewalks from the mall to the strip plaza where the furniture store was. I found this absolutely unbelievable that he would be so inconsiderate of his wife and daughter.

Ana and I looked at the china and crystal, figured out the pattern and what everything sold for, then walked to the furniture store. The weather was warm and the walk was pleasant. I was angry that Mitch made us walk and took the truck instead. It felt disrespectful to me. It was not that I wasn't capable of walking but the principle of it. As we walked I held Ana's hand only letting go as she tripped over her own feet and lunged forward. I tried to hold her hand but she fell so quickly I could not stop her. She skinned her knees and was bleeding. She cried as children do when they hurt themselves. I got her settled down and we walked the rest of the way. It took us about fifteen minutes to walk. Her knees hurt as she bent them. By the time we looked at couches and prices we were done in another ten minutes.

I asked to use the store phone to call Mitch. When I told him we were at the Macy's furniture store he asked, "How did you get there?" I replied, "We walked just like you told me to do."

His reply shocked me, "I never told you to walk!" I was standing in the store using their phone having an argument about something so inane I was embarrassed. When Mitch picked us up he took one look at Ana's knees and demanded, "What the heck happened to Ana?" I said simply, "She fell." Mitch went from zero to sixty in seconds, "Why weren't you holding her hand? Anyone can see that she fell! The question is where were you and why didn't you protect her? You are her mother and you are supposed to protect her! Why weren't you watching her?" When I was able to get a word in through his tirade I told him what happened and he yelled at me, "I never told you to walk!" I felt like I was in the twilight zone. I was furious. Not only did I have to walk because this stupid man made me walk, now he was yelling at me for doing what he told me to do! I shouted back at him. "You made me walk! I wanted to take the truck but you would not let me!" " I should have driven my own vehicle!" "This is your fault!" he yelled. "This should never have happened!" You didn't protect our daughter! Why didn't you call me?" During this shouting I became aware of Ana sitting in between two angry people yelling over her head and the energy that was bombarded at her. The yelling continued until Ana cried out, "Mommy! Daddy! Stop!" I could not explain the irrationality of the situation. If I had not been there I would not have believed it.

I advertised in the newspaper. We had a great turn out at the estate sale and we made money. I sold everything I loved. Mitch sold nothing. My Oriental carpets, my white couch and chair that Phil and I had recovered in England, my table and chairs, my dining room furniture that I bought in England were all gone. The rational part of me knew we needed the money to live on. The emotional part of me was sad and angry that Mitch did not sell his exercise equipment. He had a treadmill and a corner weight system that we paid several thousand dollars for as well as mats for the floor and free weights. He sold none of it.

I wondered why Mitch was not selling all his fitness equipment. He did not sell his table saw or any of his prized tools. We traded our gorgeous home for a hodgepodge of a rental ranch with a swimming pool. All the furniture I sold paid for our rent for the next several months. Ana was terrified of the place we moved to. I did my best to be happy.

When we moved into the rental our oldest cat became frail and thin. She acted as if she had dementia. We eventually had her put to sleep. She was the third pet in a matter of months to die. Then two more pets died shortly after that. The past was dying. There was death and destruction all around. It was an ending.

In November my friends John and Sherry Henderson asked if I could mow their place in preparation for Thanksgiving. Mitch did not want me to do their yard for some reason. They paid me cash and I got three flat tires. Maybe that was why he did not want me to mow their place. On the way home however, I took a road I was never on before. I drove past several beautiful properties with rolling hills and pastures. I was in awe of the large mature oak trees on the property and then I saw a "For Lease" sign. I said to myself, "No way!" I pulled up the driveway, as there were no vehicles parked in it and walked back to the sign. I called the agent expecting a machine, instead a man's voice answered. He said he could meet me in five minutes. I was excited. This place was so much better than where we were. It had two pastures and a barn where I could store my landscaping equipment and mower, the house was old but really cute. Mr. Baldwin met me in the driveway and said he could let me see the place.

I told him I was most likely getting divorced but would move in with my husband. The rent was slightly higher than the place we were in, but not by much. I told him I would have to talk to my husband but I was fairly certain we would take it. We moved into the old farmhouse on Birmingham Road on December 12. Our rent was $1,500 a month.

We moved all our belongings into the house. We found it cold in the winter. The house was quaint, but my hair blew when I sat in the dining room on a windy day. There were many quirks, like rolling floors and cracked glass. I loved it. The house suited me perfectly. If I liked the property this much in the winter I could not wait to see it with the pond and the oak trees all leafed out in the springtime.

I knew I had had enough of Mitch and our marriage the day I was on our healer's table in Marietta. I thought about the last several years; losing the house, the boys in Colorado, all the things I sold. There was inequality in our relationship. There was the fact that Mitch was not interested in helping me with housework or cooking and about Lucy and Jake. I loved Jake, but the relationship I had with Lucy was different, special. I felt the presence of Lucy, our sweet angel dog. I cried about her and how much I loved her. I knew I loved her more than I loved Mitch now. It was profound. I imagined life without him and felt a relief. There had been a time that I loved him, but not now. Lucy was always sweet, kind and loving. She loved me no matter what I did, said or didn't do. I heard someone say that animals do not have a soul. I knew that was not true. I knew that most dogs were more highly evolved than the people they love and protect.

Three more months went by before I told Mitch it was over. I received a call from a man who was talking to me about seeing my ad in the *Oracle* magazine. I was in a dark place at the time. He said that my phone number came up in meditation. Like a complete fool, I listened to his spiel. He had called me a couple of times to talk and I took his call outside. Mitch took exception to the fact that I drove to the grocery store while on the phone with him and was still on the phone when I came back. This man was extremely intuitive. He told me things about Mitch that were absolutely true. It was uncanny. When I came back into the house Mitch was giving me a really difficult time about my phone call. I told him, "You know, Mitch, you are hanging on too tight. I think it's over. I have had enough."

For me that was it. I was done. At least I thought I was done. He told me he would never give me full custody of Ana. He would never pay me child support. He would not support me. He said many other things. It was Easter weekend. I told him he needed to be out by the end of May.

LESSONS LEARNED

Mitch was a protective father. Since he had not had children before he became hyper vigilant in carefully monitoring his daughter's well-being and diet. Considering he had not experienced fatherhood before Ana's birth, he jumped into family life with my boys becoming very involved in their fitness and extracurricular activities. He spurred them on to become avid runners, and ran the Peachtree with my oldest son for many years.

His discipline and consistency balanced my inconsistency with my children. My boys have fond memories of our family movie nights. Mitch was a movie buff and influenced my sons in many positive ways.

Although the boys were not biologically his, my difficulty post divorce was that I missed our family life. Mitch was the glue that helped hold us together and build closer relationships. Mitch's interest in spirituality and personal growth helped encourage me to get to the bottom of my issues.

Due to Mitch's building profession and entrepreneurial spirit, I benefited by his encouragement and started the first of several businesses when we were married. I opened my landscaping business and he came up with the very creative name for my company while we brainstormed together.

Mitch was one of my most formidable teachers and I honor him for all I learned through the years we were married. I continued to learn about myself and finally surrendered to the process instead of fighting with my ex. Once I surrendered everything fell into place. It was a powerful realization and cathartic experience. I was in tremendous fear of him throughout our marriage and until I stopped fighting him. When you fight with someone, they have to fight you back. It is the law of attraction in action. Fight out, fight back. Love out, love back. I choose love!

Vibration at the End of My Marriage to Rich: 150 Fear

Life Force: 58%

Ana and Isabella

Ana and Gunner

Jennifer with her Dogs, Isabella and Karma

CHAPTER EIGHT

Catalysts and Fairy Tales

Catalysts come in all sorts of shapes and sizes. One thing is for sure, in the presence of a catalyst change will occur.

I spent the nine months following the breakup of my third marriage unwinding. Being married to Mitch had been like walking on eggshells. I was so afraid of him erupting into fits of rage. I never knew when he was going to punch his fist through a wall or a hit a doorframe right in front of my face. The threat of violence was pervasive. Having him out of the house was incredibly freeing.

I spent any time I had alone at home. I reflected on the past nine years. I wondered what got me to this point of feeling thoroughly disgusted with myself. In this space of separation I did not date. I was not interested in having a relationship. I was in a state of healing. I did not feel the need to be divorced. I worked hard in my landscaping business, spent time with my daughter and had time in quiet solitude.

In October of 2003, I drove up to Murphy, North Carolina to visit my longtime friend and spiritual mentor, Nannette Lacey. I had been in awe of Nanette's gifts for many years. Nannette had an interesting but difficult life and was an extremely gifted and intuitive reader. I had a palm reading with her 15 years earlier to get some answers about my life and a man I was dating after my second divorce. I was absolutely positive I was going to marry him. In that reading she told me I would not. I was so angry with her I was almost breathing fire. We both laughed about it years later. But at that time I was so addicted to the relationship I could not imagine life without him. What began as a one-hour appointment with a stranger turned into a relationship of deep friendship and codependency.

Nannette's life as a military wife had taken her all over the world. More recently she had spent time with the Native American people in the pueblos out west. Her favorite part of the United States was Canyon de She. Being somewhat of a nomad, she spoke of being called to go to a certain place. When she had those feelings she would up and move to wherever she was called. She was a woman I aspired to be like. It seemed to me that she came from a place of unconditional love and was always talking about not giving energy to negative issues. She taught me that doing so would just create more of the same. I really needed Nannette in my life as a guide and teacher to help me grow and change my thought patterns. I did not realize how much I leaned on her for guidance, wisdom and knowledge until years later.

Nannette was a kind and loving woman. She seemed independent to me and lived alone in a lovely doublewide trailer in Murphy. She had lived all over the world and had similar relationships with men to me. Her home was very comfortable and serene. It was filled with beautiful sculptures and lovely Native American artwork. I enjoyed spending time with her in her home. I trusted Nannette and her guidance. Over the years we were there for each other during rites of passage. She was there for me during my loneliness and tumultuous marriage with Mitch and finally our separation. It was on this particular visit she handed me a flyer for a buffalo drum-making workshop being held November 1, 2003, in Hiawassee, Georgia. As I took the flyer from Nannette, she said, "I feel there is something for you there and that you really need to do this workshop with Ann and me." I had just purchased a handmade drum at a garage sale. Why on earth would I need another one? I did not even use the one I had.

The flyer was printed on brown parchment and had a small photo of the presenter on it. The photo showed a stocky man standing with his hands stuffed into his pockets. He was wearing a black cowboy hat, denim jeans, and a jacket. He looked rather like the Marlboro man. I read his bio and the course outline. It said, "John Many Voices is a ceremonial leader and pipe carrier." John was a white guy with a Native American feel. I read further and learned he was a Sundancer, Earthdancer and Earthkeeper from Sedona, Arizona. He traveled all over the United States performing medicine wheel ceremonies and teaching Native American ways. The Native American thing was more on Nannette's path than mine. Knowing how accurate Nannette's guidance was, I told her I would check my calendar. If it turned out that Ana was with her Dad the November 1st weekend I would consider attending the workshop with her and her friend.

Friday, October 31, 2003, was a monumental day for me. For years others in my industry had told me that I needed to buy a pickup truck for my landscaping business. I sold my old Ford Explorer for cash and finally made the leap of faith and purchased a used pickup truck. This meant I was committed to staying in the landscaping trade for a while longer. I found a nice-looking, white F 150 crew cab with tan interior, exactly what I wanted. It felt like a woman had previously owned it. After opening the glove box and reading the registration, my confirmation that it was a woman's truck was what I needed. It felt really good. I had been landscaping as a temporary thing out of my Explorer for two years. This was a momentous occasion. It symbolized change for me and called for a road trip. I was excited about my nearly new vehicle and could not wait to take it out on the highway. I called Nannette that night and said I would drive up to Murphy and pick her up at 9:00 a.m. The class began at 10:00 a.m. in Hiawassee.

I woke up at 6:00 a.m., showered and got myself ready. I was getting intuitive guidance to dress very casually. I wore layers and took off my diamond earrings. This was very interesting. I didn't remember getting guidance like this before. I would get intuitive guidance about certain things, like taking a different route to avoid an accident. This was different. I decided to wear a flannel shirt with a turtleneck underneath and rose quartz earrings.

It was a sunny, crisp and frosty morning. I could see my breath as I rushed around to put my cup of hot tea in my clean cup holder. I threw my overnight bag in the front seat of the truck and cranked the engine. I opened the passenger side door of the crew cab and called Gunner, my 14-year-old rescued Golden Retriever, and Karma, a Border collie mixed breed, over to the truck.

I folded down the back seat in an attempt to keep dog hair off the upholstery. Getting Gunner up and onto the back seat was a chore. He was beginning to feel his age, which meant I had to hoist his 80-pound frame so he could climb into the truck. Everyone loved Gunner. He had a special relationship with Nannette and her wolf German Sheppard cross named Pawnee. Gunner groaned as I got him into the truck. He must have pulled his groin as he was obviously in pain. He loved the Explorer, as it was much easier for him to get in and out.

I lifted Gunner out of the truck when we arrived at Nanette's home. We made the drive in less than two hours two hours. I felt pretty good about only being 15 minutes late. However, Nannette was upset with me. We still had to pick up Ann and she did not want to be late for the workshop. It was almost an hour to Hiawassee. On our way down her gravel road we saw six deer grazing on the grass at the edge of the woods. Nannette was of the opinion that animals and nature show us signs about our world and what is going on with us. Deer represent gentleness. One of the does looked up and stood watching us. It was going to be a great day and we both knew it. Ann lived only 15 minutes away in a little cottage. On our way down Ann's drive we spotted a flock of turkeys that was feeding. Nature was giving us all kinds of signs on that day.

Turkeys are thought to be the Give-Away Eagle or South Eagle of many native peoples. Turkey was the medicine of many saints and mystics. The turkey sacrifices his life so that we may live, where all life is sacred. What you do for others you do for yourself. Many of us who have much more than we need would be well served by giving selflessly to those less fortunate than we are. Sometimes a tribal member would give away all he or she owned and do without to help their people. We live in a society of acquisitions, where we need to have the newest phone, car or the most toys. In Native American society he who gives away the most and carries the burdens of the people is the most respected. Turkey medicine occupies the space of enlightenment. When turkey medicine is present, you are being given a gift. I knew seeing turkeys on that morning was a good sign.

Our drive to Hiawassee was filled with conversation and excitement about John. Nannette knew the metaphysical storeowner where the workshop was being held and had been asked a few days earlier if she could help guide John around the area. Nannette spent the whole day on Wednesday with John and really connected with him on a deep level and learned about him. She read his palm for him and remarked she had never seen a hand like his before. She said it was extraordinary. His palm was very wide and square. She remarked that he was extremely intelligent with a photographic memory. He was an extremely gifted, intuitive and special man. She explained how evolved he was. She said that John was a geologist as well as master douser. He manufactured his own dousing rod called the radionic antennae. He taught dousing with empirical feng shui. He was a healer, spiritual counselor and a shaman, although he did not call himself one. Nannette went on to say that he was very humble. She was not often impressed or in awe of anyone. She said John was very, very different.

Besides teaching classes while he was in town, he performed property analyses for clients. The word spread like wildfire that he was in town, and everyone wanted to meet him and learn from him. In the process of analyzing someone's property he taught his clients how to move ley lines to improve their health, wealth and happiness in their homes. He explained to Nannette the different ley lines had special purposes and that if put in the wrong place they could create havoc in your life. He had published a book about working with the earth, ley lines and underwater sources that can affect health and prosperity. Being an Earthkeeper showed his deep reverence and respect for the earth and all peoples. Nannette went on to say that he had been "on the hill" and performed the ritual of a Sundance, hanging for hours by the skin of his punctured chest.

The Sundance is the major communal religious ceremony of the Plains Indians and celebrates renewal, a spiritual rebirth of the participants, their relatives as well as the regeneration of the living earth with all its components. Many contemporary Native Americans practice the ritual, which involves sacrifice and supplication to insure the harmony between all living beings, even today.

John was the revered and honored leader of the Sundance. He ran the entire ceremony and taught others the way of the pipe and red road. According to Nannette he also taught and assisted the others on the building of the tepee and sweat lodge. This was no "ordinary man" she went on. He was very special.

Nannette was beaming and excited as she talked about their day and the fun she and John had together. He apparently was also very witty and an interesting conversationalist. He had really lived life fully. Our drive to Hiawassee was over before we knew it and I made the turn off the highway to find we were one of the first to arrive.

As it turned out there was no need to rush. We walked across the leaf-covered ground and noticed a large, white conversion van parked behind the bookstore. The rear doors were open and a denim-clad man was unloading large plastic totes from the back of it. Nannette said a cheery good morning to John as she crossed the drive towards him. Nannette said quietly to us, "There's John, he must have gotten here late." Oddly, I noticed he was wearing huarache sandals and bare feet on this brisk November morning. As we walked towards him, Ann and Nannette moved into the foreground as I walked behind them. As John lifted his head from his task, smiling an impish grin, he said hello to Nannette and Ann. Then his eyes locked onto mine. I felt as if I had been hit by lightning. This was very strange. He felt so familiar to me although we had never met. We said quick hellos and walked to the store to register. I felt like I was walking in slow motion slightly above the ground.

We went inside the store and paid our tuition and were told our class would be taught in the gazebo. We walked around the store looking at books and candles for a few more minutes before we walked back into the cold. The gazebo was hexagonal with seats all around the interior, large enough to accommodate the four attendees and the drum-making materials. The plastic totes were scattered all around the floor of the gazebo. John came in carrying the last of his totes and beamed his smile in our direction. One more woman arrived even later than we did and interrupted his teaching. John had an impish demeanor. He seemed very humble, unassuming and natural. We were all handed our drum frames and given directions on how to sand the frame to get the wood nice and smooth. During the sanding process, John explained how we would construct the drum out of buffalo hide, which was very sacred. The hide had to be soaked in water at least an hour and then stretched, as it was very tough and hard. We used sinew to attach the hide and pulled it tight on the frame. Once complete our drums were to be awakened through a powerful ceremony.

The process of drum-making was difficult and required a lot of effort. We had all kinds of questions and at some point we all wanted to quit. It was tiresome. After about an hour of this, I am not sure why Nannette stood up suddenly and announced to John, "I have not had my hug from you today!" He laughed and taking his hands out of his jeans pockets gave her a big hug. Gradually everyone stood up to get her hug as well. I stood up slowly from the wooden bench, being the last in line to get my hug, I felt unsure and vaguely uneasy. As we moved tentatively towards each other, our eyes connected. His were such a deep watery blue. I moved towards John slowly and slid my arms around him. He hugged me close to him and we ceased to be aware of our surroundings. I was enveloped in wave after wave of beautiful energy. I felt tremendous love but from where? There was so much that I was feeling; none of which was sexual. Where was this all coming from?

I had never experienced such a deep love for someone I did not know. We stayed in our embrace so long that we became aware of others watching us. Nannette had been standing next to us and had stepped back and away with the strangest look on her face. I could not place her expression. I was trying to steady myself and get my bearings. I felt like the earth beneath my feet was moving and my head was swimming. I was trying to understand what had just occurred. It felt like we went into a time warp and left the others for what seemed like a very long time, but then again no time at all. It was the weirdest feeling I had ever experienced.

It was obvious that John was shaken as well. He had a very difficult time remembering where he was and what he was about to do next. He made light of what had just happened between us. He was very lighthearted. He began asking me all sorts of questions. I noticed his expression changed when I told him I was Canadian. He looked at me and asked in a strange questioning voice, "You're Canadian?" It was as if a light went on in his head. A connection was made. It felt like he had been told something about meeting a Canadian woman. He went on to say, "*and your name is Jennifer?*"

When it came time, John hand-selected a hide for each of us. Nannette was angry with me as she felt John gave me the better hide. In fact, I got one with a huge lump of fat in it, which made the hide look deformed and uneven. I did not know any better, as this was my first and last drum-making class anyway. Stringing the hide onto the frame took some strength. Ann asked John to help her with hers. John sat down next to me to assist Ann. He opened up a dialogue between us while he assisted Ann with her drum. He asked me what I did for a living. I explained I had a landscaping business and used feng shui in my installations all the time. He responded, "You do feng shui too?" "Yes," I replied, "although most of the time my clients are not even aware I am doing it!" I expressed my excitement over my new vehicle and explained that I finally broke down and bought a pickup truck the night before. I made the commitment to be a professional landscaper, complete with pickup truck. We laughed about me feeling that I was not a pickup truck kind of girl.

After the three hours it took to sand, string and tie the sinew, we completed our projects and the awakening ceremony began. We stood in the center of the gazebo holding our drums as John sang. The strength and power of his voice startled me at first. I jumped when he sang. He belted out a Native American song so beautifully it gave me chills and tears started to stream uncontrollably down my face. His voice was so powerful it made me vibrate. I looked across at Nannette and she gave me a look as if to say, "I told you this would be amazing!" She smiled back at me. He moved slowly around the circle, blessing each woman with a drop of rosemary oil on her third eye as he sang. His voice was so powerful. We all knew instinctively how sacred this moment was. I watched John as he blessed Ann, then Nannette, then moving around the circle to me last.

It felt as if everything was happening in slow motion. As he approached me I felt so completely aware and alive. He looked into my eyes unwaveringly and I cried. I closed my eyes as he touched the sweet smelling oil to my skin. I could feel his presence so close to me. There was such a pull between us that felt bigger than the both of us. I knew more than my drum was being awakened as I felt the powerful energy surging between us with my eyes closed. When I opened them he pulled himself away. I stood dazed in the circle for a long while afterward. It was as if I could not move. I felt like I had just received a powerful download of energy from Spirit. I knew I felt different. I hesitated to pack up my things. I did not want to leave this energy. Nannette and I exchanged knowing looks. This was why I was here. It was to meet John, not just to make a drum!

As the workshop ended, each woman thanked John for the wonderful experience and hugged him. We helped him clean up some of the debris and leftover materials. As everyone scattered to gather her belongings I excused myself to use the restroom. When I returned, the gazebo was empty. I wondered briefly if John had left already, but felt his energy was nearby. I walked around the side of the building to say thank you to John. I found him washing out the basin from the buffalo skins. I handed him a business card and suggested that we have lunch when he was in the Atlanta area the following week. He said he would like that and we hugged again briefly and said good-bye.

Once we got into the truck, Nannette exclaimed, "What was that?" I smiled and retorted playfully, "Whatever are you talking about, Nannette?" We both laughed and she told me that the energy from our embrace was so powerful it nearly knocked her over. She did not believe me that it was not in the least bit sexual. As we drove Ann home we talked about the workshop and John all the while.

Once back at Nannette's we let all three dogs out to play for a while. Gunner was very sore and moved very slowly. Nannette suggested that she take me out to dinner in exchange for me driving everyone to Hiawassee. We drove into the little town of Murphy and ate at the local barbeque restaurant. Once we sat down to eat, Nannette asked me about my experience. She was very interested to hear my perspective about our day and my experience with John. The energetic connection between John and me was palpable to everyone in the class. Nannette knew me well enough to be able to see the light in my eyes and read me. She playfully teased me about not wanting to do the class and that she had been right about there was something in it for me.

I kept on marveling at what I experienced. I experienced many different things, but never anything like this. I kept saying, "Holy cow" and smiling to myself. I was definitely lit up. This was definitely going to be interesting.

After dinner, we drove back to Nannette's. We were tired and I got myself ready for bed. The day had been a long one. Gunner stayed under the kitchen table and would not move. It was very unusual for him not to sleep in my room. I had a design to do the next day on my way home for a church, so I needed to get some sleep. I was so keyed up energetically that falling asleep did not come easily. I awoke early from a dream about John. I felt his body spooning with mine. His arms were wrapped around me and his large hands covered my breasts. It was strange, like he had been there with me. I could still feel him there. I could not get back to sleep. I was too excited. I left earlier than I had planned, sadly leaving Gunner with Nannette, and got a start on my day.

At home on Sunday evening, Nannette and I spoke on the phone. I thanked her for dinner and a nice soft bed to sleep in. I told her about my dream. She suggested that I call Diana, the friend that John was staying with as she had heard he might need a place to stay while in Atlanta. I was not divorced, and had no desire to date anyone. Somehow I felt that this meeting was destined. I could not put my finger on it, but there was a feeling of inner knowing. It was something I had to do. I felt uneasy suggesting it, but with encouragement from Nannette I made the phone call. I dialed Diana's number not knowing what to expect. Diana answered the phone and I introduced myself and I asked to speak to John. I sensed Diana's curiosity and unspoken questions in the space between her words. I had no idea what her relationship to John was, which made me feel a little uncomfortable and uneasy. Had I make a faux pas? Were the two of them dating or in a relationship? My inner dialogue stopped as John came to the phone.

John sounded really pleased to hear my voice and remembered me instantly. I asked him if it was all right to call him at Diana's. He laughed and said Diana was very interested in this woman who was calling him. He went on to tell me that he and Diana had a very long and close friendship and he was very glad I had called. My insecure feelings vanished into thin air. We talked a little about his other classes and what he had going on in Atlanta. I asked if he had a place to stay while in town. He said he had an offer but it was not concrete. He sounded interested in this turn of events, so I decided to just throw it out there and ask. John was delighted to be able to see me again and thought it would be a good way to have more time to talk and get to know each other better. We made arrangements for him to stay with me for two nights. I laughed and told him I had a spare bedroom, but there was no door on the room. He laughed, a little uneasily, as to what that meant.

John had been borrowing Diana's van. He would be without a vehicle for the two weeks he was to be in Atlanta. At Nannette's suggestion, she would drive with Gunner and meet Diana in Cleveland, Georgia to get John. Then they would all drive to our designated meeting spot where I would pick up both John and Gunner on the way back to Atlanta. When I arrived at the end of GA 400 just north of Dawsonville, my daughter Ana, aged seven at this time, was in the back seat of the truck watching out of the back window. She watched through the window as Nannette and John got out of her Jeep and said good-bye. Ana commented, "Boy, he looks old." John did look like he had really lived life. The mileage showed on his weatherworn face. We all needed to get back on the road, so we thanked Nannette. John and I picked up Gunner together and loaded him into the back seat of my truck. Nannette hugged John good-bye and I thanked her profusely for all her help and making the long drive in order for everything to work out for us. She had to turn around and drive back to Murphy and did not like driving in the dark. She told me she felt very good about us being together and would do whatever she could to help us. She told me she loved me, smiled and then hugged John good-bye and we drove off. She was very happy to help. What I did not realize at the time was that this was the last time Nannette and John would be together.

As John and I talked in the truck Ana pretended to be asleep in the back seat. John turned around and looked at her with interest. He told me she was playing possum. She was quiet the whole ride home as she listened to our conversation.

Once we arrived at home, it was almost dark and Ana was asleep. John helped me lift Gunner out of the truck and set him on the ground. I carried Ana to the door and opened it. John looked at me and hesitated. I paused on the step holding Ana, waiting for him to speak. He scanned the property slowly stopping to look at the rolling pasture and beautiful trees and then at the house. He glanced from Gunner, Ana and then me and said, "You have a rich life." I had not thought of it that way. I struggled to make ends meet and I worked very hard. I was still fighting with Mitch. This was definitely a new perspective.

I watched as John lugged his huge army-like duffel bag upstairs as I showed him to his room. I pointed out the railing at the top of the stairs without a door and left him there to get settled. I got Ana ready for bed. Ana opened her eyes smiling at me. She told me she liked him. She said he was like an Indian. He did feel Native American, very distinctly earthy. His dirt-stained feet spoke of many miles of barefoot walking. I stayed with Ana until she fell asleep. She had many questions I could not answer.

I gave John a tour of the house and a cup of hot tea. I said I did not have anything stronger. He was fine with that, as he had given up drinking a long time ago. We sat on my comfortable flowered couch and talked until our mouths were dry. Nannette called to tell me she was home safe, and chuckled. "What are you laughing about?" I asked her. She just laughed. Being an intuitive, she always knew something she did not want to say.

Listening to John's stories of how he uncovered the "people's pipe" on a geological dig I found him to be funny, impish and interesting. He kept his cowboy hat on and I wondered if he ever took it off. Beneath his huarache sandals his bare feet were stained with earth. He stayed barefoot all year, he said. He really did not like shoes at all. He had amazingly varied interests and a tremendous wealth of knowledge. He had a great interest in history and geography and had an amazing ability to recall detailed facts, dates and information he had read years ago.

He was different from anyone I had ever met. He was deeply concerned about the earth and what we were doing to her. He talked at great length about the Native American peoples and keeping their traditions alive. He told me stories about doing the Sundance every year and the required piercing he had experienced. He spoke of his meditations in preparation before the dance would begin where he would sit "on the hill" all day in meditation. He would have visions and hear messages for the people of the dance that he would share with them. It felt like I was going back in time.

John was on a Native American elders' council in Ohio and would be traveling there to meet with them in two week's time. They planned the annual Sundance together and John was in charge of it. He spoke of his dear friends, Tammy and Dade and their daughter, Julie, on the council and the work they did together. He said they were the closest things to family for him. They built sweat lodges, did ceremonies and did teachings together. He had passed on his eight years of study with Hollis Little Creek, his teacher, to Tammy and Dade.

He spoke about being guided by Great Spirit, being on a geological dig out west. On this particular project he had unearthed a peace pipe. Knowing that it was of great significance he took it to the elders of a nearby Native American nation. His intention was to gift it to this tribe. The wise elder told John that the pipe was meant for him and that he was to carry this pipe and do ceremony with it. This was his path. It was a great honor to uncover and find a buried pipe. John gave up his home and all his possessions to study the Native American way. For eight years he traveled and lived with Hollis Little Creek, a respected Midewiwin from the Marten Clan of the Anishinabeg nation, who taught John. John apprenticed for years before pouring his first lodge.

The training was extensive and involved teachings passed on from one generation to the next. He learned how to honor and smoke the chanupa, or sacred pipe. He also learned how to use tobacco as an offering whenever something was taken from the Earth. "You always give back, you never just take." He learned how to build a proper sweat lodge and how to perform or "pour" the sweat lodge ceremony, honoring the pipe, the stone people, standing people, Mother Earth and all the people. Pouring lodge involved a very sacred ceremony that would usually start at around 3:00 p.m. with people gathering and talking while the Fire Keeper began the sacred fire. Everything, including the "standing people" or trees, was revered and honored in these ceremonies. The stones were carefully picked and honored as well. They were placed carefully near the bottom of the fire and brought into the lodge one by one by the Fire Keeper. There was never any fee for attending and they were all done in a respectful and safe way.

John told the story of how he always got into "hot water" because he was listening to Mother Earth when he was supposed to be listening to Hollis. When it came time for John to pour his first lodge, he told Hollis, "I cannot pour in your traditional way. I can only pour as Mother Earth guides me." John expected he would not pour lodge. However, Hollis not only had John pour, he honored him by pulling the stones for John. Additionally, he had John awaken Joseph Many Horses' chanupa (pipe) in the lodge. Hollis taught him, "So many make the mistake of listening to Great Spirit without having the foundation and knowing Great Spirit. It has caused many hard lessons on the path. You have the foundation, John, and hear true." John commented, "I don't know why Hollis saw that in me as I caused him such grief with my screwing-up." John laughed about his screw-ups. He was the most humble man I ever met, unassuming and natural.

John talked about being aware and living in the present. He spoke of people's lack of awareness of the present moment, which rob us of our golden opportunities to witness the joy and beauty all around us. He said that the power to change lies in the present. He spoke of Mother Earth with such reverence and love and the uplifting qualities and gifts of nature. John went on to speak of jealousy and other negative qualities many people exhibit that remove our attention from the blessings we receive each moment of every day. He also talked about metaphysical people and how they were the most derisive group of people he knew. He was not awkward about speaking his mind, and he did it often.

We talked for hours about the drumming, singing and dance that John did. He felt it helped to Strip the dark smoke of illusion. His way of speaking, the slow cadence and rhythm sounded like I was listening to a great Indian chief – none of whom I could name in that moment. All of this Native American tradition was very new to me. It was not something that I aspired to. I was reverent toward Mother Earth and nature in my own way. I prayed over plants when I planted them and was always doing the best for Mother Earth in an honoring of my own.

He talked of acceptance of all and especially the past. It releases us from our past. He spoke of having faith and relinquishing total control to free us from the future. He said that living in the present unleashes our energy allowing it to flow into everything we do and everything we experience. He said the authentic, sincere being that is us produces the future one moment at a time and in the present. I listened until I was so tired I could barely keep my eyes open. I did not want to go to bed and leave the present moment. It was so perfect, so magical. I was riveted.

John was extremely intuitive with a strong connection to Spirit. He heard the voice of God clearly. He talked about his guidance and his knowing. He told me that he felt the love of his life was out there in the ethers moving towards him for over ten years. He said he felt her name was Jennifer and that she was Canadian. He talked about also feeling that there was a point in which he felt that she was no longer available, either not on the planet anymore or married. He recalled the instant that he knew something had changed. He was in the Grand Teton national park camping with another woman named Jennifer at the time. At first he thought that she was the one because of her name. Although they had a fleeting relationship he realized she was not. He talked to her about his feelings and about the woman who was to be the love of his life. He looked at me with a certainty that I was indeed "The One." We both traced that time period to find what was going on in my life. I had just gotten pregnant with Ana and was getting married to Mitch. Getting pregnant with Ana was a pivotal point in my life. I had been guided to get pregnant no matter what at the time. Spirit told me that as late in my life as it was, I was being given a gift of a girl child, and the beautiful daughter I always wanted. Even though I had my doubts about Mitch, I was compelled to get pregnant and not focus on anything else.

I was beginning to understand what Nannette was getting at and how she kept urging me forward. There was something very special here, almost magical. I wanted to savor it. Although he was a Leo, he was very different from Mitch. I thought I would never even think about having another relationship with a Leo after Mitch. We had clashed on every possible level. John was deeply spiritual and obviously very evolved. He talked about his connection to Great Spirit. He was very knowledgeable about astrology and asked me what my sign was. We laughed when I told him I was a triple Scorpio. I actually have five planets in Scorpio and most people don't understand the significance. John had a better understanding of astrology than I did. He told me he had been with several Scorpios over the years and every relationship had ended badly. He said that he had a feeling about his own death and that it had to do with a Scorpio woman. I told him I no longer threw things and promised not to hurt him. We both laughed. His birthday was the day after Mitch's and I mentioned my misgivings about Leos. I told John about my marriage and that I was not divorced. I explained the fight we had over Ana and how sensitive she was. We talked about Ana at great length. I explained how important she was to me and how gifted she was.

I talked about Adam and Mathew as well. John talked about his son, Sun, and his daughter, Moon. He explained that at the end of his marriage he and his wife were both sleeping with the same woman, her best friend, and it ended very badly. After the end of their marriage, his children sided with their mother and did not want anything to do with him. It was obvious that it saddened him. He knew he had missed out on so much of their lives. I suggested that he contact them and work on salvaging the rest of their lives together. He was doubtful that could ever happen. We also talked about the meaning of their names and how his relationship was stormy with them.

John was open about his life. He hid nothing. He told me that the reason he had been celibate for the last 18 months was because he had a lot of problems with women, lots of women. He laughed sheepishly about it. He said he was just not good with relationships. He felt women were attracted to him because of who he was. Doing ceremonies all over the United States people witnessed how he connected to Great Spirit, raising their vibration and they all seemed to want some of it. John was not boastful or full of ego. People could see his power and light and were attracted to it. This is very common for great spiritual leaders and people with power. Others are attracted to it. He did not tell me this. It was obvious to me. It was part of why he was in my house at that moment.

I had not been looking for an affair and had not even thought about dating. Had it not been for Nannette's encouragement to attend the workshop I would not be sitting with John right now. I knew that this was something to pay attention to. There was an underlying current of God's hand in this and the power of the Universe. The Divine had orchestrated our meeting. We both knew that this was more than a chance meeting. He said to expect the unexpected. No day was like another and we needed to notice everything as it was happening.

I had been watching John talk animatedly all evening. He seemed tireless. He was incredibly charismatic, funny and cute all at the same time. There was a deep resonance to him. He was very connected to the Earth and to, as he said, Great Spirit and all there is. Eventually, I could not stand it any longer and I felt compelled to kiss him. The thought of sex did not even occur to me. I just wanted to kiss him. I finally got up the courage to strike and leaned over to him and planted a kiss on John's mouth. It was electric. I felt badly that I had made a move on him after he had made it clear that he was celibate. I started to move away and apologized for kissing him and he said "Whoa, where are you going?" As he tried to pull me to him his hat careened off his head. I got the first glimpse of his balding head. So this is why he kept his hat on. We both laughed. He looked sheepish again. We laughed a lot that night. He was so much fun. He had a different way of looking at things that I admired. His love and connection to the earth and all things in nature was something he frequently talked about. He was positive, wise and witty. He was very intelligent without being heady. I really liked him. He was a really amazing man.

The energy between us was so electric. I got up to use the bathroom. When I returned and stepped in between the coffee table and the couch he stood up to meet me and pulled me to him. Our height difference was very slight. As I stood enveloped by him the space between us closed at once and we were entwined and standing together as one, the energy was very intense. The feelings I had inside the gazebo returned. So many lifetimes of us being together were swirling around us. The energy was dizzying. There was so much passion between us just kissing each other. I had never felt such intense feelings with anyone before. He held me so tightly that when he let me go I nearly fell over. I was not sure where this was going. I was afraid, excited and amazed all at the same time. I was getting tired and said I needed to get to bed. I helped John make up the bed upstairs for him to sleep in.

As I started to leave the room, I kissed him goodnight. "Big mistake," I thought. Once we started kissing each other we could not stop. I would never get to sleep now. I pulled off his shirt and threw it on the floor. As he lay back on the pillow, I had a vision of his heart. I had never seen inside anyone's body before. In the middle of all that I was feeling I knew this was significant. What I saw was a very large heart covered inside and out with white. I interpreted it falsely as calcification. I told him of my vision. He took me very seriously and said he had had severe pain in his left arm while in the middle of a drumming ceremony recently. He continued way past what was comfortable and felt what he thought may have been a heart attack. Maybe even two. He said when he was camping alone on Maui the previous Christmas he felt he had had a heart attack. He downplayed it like it was no big deal. He did not go to doctors and would not go now.

John's mother had died recently. She had been hospitalized for a simple procedure and died from complications due to the doctors overmedicating her. After his mother's death John had experienced such anger towards the medical profession for their ineptness and lack of concern that he would not go to a doctor even if he were dying. John told me he and his mother had been very close and her death had been such a shock to John that he shaved his head completely as a show of reverence and grief. He grieved for her for a year, as was the Native American way.

She had been a piano teacher, raising John as a single mother. She struggled to feed her family. This gave John great respect for other single mothers and women in general. She had a profound impact on his life. She had influenced him musically, which led him to studying the cello and voice.

I wanted John to make love to me. The passion that we experienced was rare. Our kisses were so amazing. I felt like we became one being just with our kiss. There was a depth of love that was beyond explanation. Both of us were making decisions on the fly and we were both swimming in the deep end of the pool. John kept his swimming trunks on. His internal strength and conscience were put to the test. He was sure he wanted to wait. Although we did not make love, we both fell asleep. I was awakened by a presence and found Ana in the room. This was bad, really bad. I did not want her to see John and me in bed together and here she was. I did not mean to fall asleep, but it felt so good to be snuggled beside John's body, even with his loud snoring. It just felt like we had to make every second of our time together count. Everything was being sped up. We both sat up and John quickly pulled on his shirt and talked with Ana.

She said she remembered him. That he had been her brother and they were both as she put it — "Indians." Ana described a hut made of sticks covered with animal skins. John said, "What you are describing is a wiki-up." Ana went on to say, "You were my father too." John conversed with Ana about ceremonies and drumming. I left the two of them talking and went downstairs to make breakfast. Before long I heard the sound of a Native American flute that John was playing for Ana. He had taken many lessons from some very learned musicians. It was not surprising that he was so musical. He had spoken lovingly the night before of his cello. When he saw my piano he told me he wanted to give the cello to me. Someone up north had it. He would have to get it when he returned there.

Before long, Ana got her own flute and was playing for John. He sat quietly and listened while she played for him. When I went back upstairs, Ana and John were seated on the floor so deep in conversation they did not even notice me. John showed Ana his buffalo and elk fur. He explained that these were sacred and he carried them everywhere he went. He pulled out his rattle and large buffalo skin drum. It was much larger than the one I made. It was very heavy to hold. I imagined that playing it for any length of time could be very tiring. He also had eagle feathers and many different hawk feathers. He gave Ana a crystal and a blue heron feather. He told her that he worked with the Blue Heron People. He also worked with the four directions and winds. He spoke of tobacco offerings, tobacco ties and making prayer ties for sweat lodges. He talked about how powerful prayer ties were and that you could repair the earth with them.

I had to drag Ana away to get her to school. She did not want to leave. I was amazed at the connection between John and Ana. I had never seen a child connect on such a deep level with a stranger so quickly. But then again, after Ana's crystal clear statements this morning, she already knew John. She remembered him. The depth of this connection and understanding between them was so loving and sweet. It felt so good and so right. They immediately felt a deep love for each other that I had never seen before.

John had appointments that day. I accompanied him on his first one, which was a feng shui consultation. The woman with whom he consulted had her house up for sale and it would not sell. John suggested that we could work on her house together. We were enjoying just being together and neither of us really wanted to go on his appointment. We dallied over our tea and getting ready. We had so much to share with each other. John soon found that I could read his mind. It was as if his mind was my mind. He laughed and asked me to get out of his head. I am intuitive, but this experience was something I had only had once or twice, and not on any consistent basis. We were late leaving my house so we had to stop talking and stalling. It seemed John and I had similar issues. I was always late too.

We arrived at John's client's home. It was obvious she was disappointed that there was an attractive woman with him. It was also obvious that many women were attracted to him and his energy. John introduced me as a friend and said we would be working together to find the issues at her home. John handed me one dousing rod and stuffed an extra radionic antennae in the back pocket of his jeans. It bounced happily up and down from its perch in his pocket as he walked down the middle of the street. He looked so out of place in his cowboy hat and barefooted in his huarache sandals carrying his dousing rod in Marietta in the middle of winter. I felt like everyone in the neighborhood was watching us. John talked about ley lines and prayer to correct broken lines. He spoke about the different types of ley lines, Tiger and Dragon, and what they did as he finished up outside.

We moved inside and walked through the house. I mentioned feeling something in the living room. I picked up on arguments about something where a wall was bare. The client confessed to moving the piano out of the room. She and her husband had argued about whether to sell it or not. After completing the consultation, the client suggested lunch with a girlfriend of hers. I felt uncomfortable. It felt to me that John was used to having women trot after him like little puppy dogs. That was not for me. After driving to the restaurant, I asked if he would mind if I did not join them for lunch. I had some landscaping work to do. I said polite good-byes to John and his client and drove off.

The following day, I had a landscaping project to do. I was not able to be home when Ana got off the school bus. John and Ana watched a movie together. Or rather, Ana watched a movie while John slept. Ana talked John into letting her have some Halloween candy, saying it would be all right with me. It was obvious very quickly that John had a soft spot for Ana and would indulge her every whim. John bought Ana's story hook, line and sinker. Ana happily had John wrapped around her little seven-year-old finger.

When I returned home, John had made Chinese food. They both met me at the door with a single flower in each of their hands. John did as Ana told him. He stood at the door looking goofy and impish and dutifully holding a single flower. It did not seem to matter to him that he looked silly or foolish. He was in the moment and interacting with Ana. He had no qualms about acting like a child or being silly. He was present and loving it. It was obvious he was cherishing this time with Ana. After dinner he looked up at me while I was clearing the dinner table, smiling at Ana he said, "It is no small thing you do." I looked questioningly at him, he said, "You are raising your daughter with such love and connection and teaching her so much. You are giving so much to her and with everyone she comes in contact."

Ana told me that John had played a game on our trampoline that she had invented called "Bird and Dog." Ana was the bird and John played the dog. The dog had to stay in a certain area and only when the bird crossed an imaginary line was the dog able to dart after the bird. Ana clearly had the advantage in this game. They both laughed a lot and had a really good time together. John was playful and boyish, even in his 54-year-old stocky frame. He lived in the moment and enjoyed it.

Dinner was excellent as well as entertaining. Ana decided to spill the beans and tell me John's little secret. While making dinner he left my best pot on the burner to heat up. He was multi-tasking in the kitchen and totally forgot that the burner was on under the empty pot. When he smelled something and lifted the pot off the electric eye, the bottom of the pot fell completely off and crashed to the stove. Ana was delighted to tell me John's embarrassing little secret. John was bashful and sheepish. His demeanor was so endearing I could not help but laugh. Then he turned to Ana and said laughingly, "We had a deal. You promised not to tell." He did not get a chance to tattle on Ana; she could not help herself. "John let me eat all my Halloween candy!" I could see they had a little conspiracy thing going on. He was a friend to Ana. John was clearly wrapped tightly around Ana's little finger. She felt completely free to be a child. It was good to see Ana feeling happy and joyful. The past year for her had been anything but.

We took a day trip to Stone Mountain, as John had never been there. Ana, John and I hiked the mountain, stopping to do a ceremony on some moss growing on a rock and lay down tobacco. John taught that if you ever took anything from nature, you should give an offering. Native American people gave tobacco to Great Spirit. Ana did her own ceremony after watching John. On our way out of the park I experienced a severe whirling of dizzying energy. It was so profound that I had to pull over and let the energy pass before I continued to drive. We sat there for about 15 minutes while I was too dizzy to drive. John offered to drive, and then explained he was not a very good driver. Ana and I both agreed that we should wait until I stopped feeling dizzy.

Sadly our week with Ana had to end. She went to her Dad's the following Monday after school. The day that she left, John cried. I did not understand it at the time. Ana was up at 6:00 a.m. to catch the school bus. I was very surprised to see John up in time to say good-bye to Ana. He loved to sleep late; he was not an early bird. He hugged her tightly and told Ana how much he loved her. He would always be her friend.

While Ana was gone, John and I had time for us. For the first time in my life I found making love to be a spiritual experience. I felt the closest to God as I ever had. John was loving and tender. He tried very hard to be present with me afterward, but physically he just could not. He fell asleep soon afterward and was snoring loudly. His breathing was odd. Like he was huffing and puffing while he slept. I was concerned about his physical body. I knew his kidneys and heart were stressed. I knew he was smoking in ceremony, but I was not aware until later that he smoked other times as well. He slathered mayonnaise and butter on his bread like there was no tomorrow. He loved what he loved and that was it. I encouraged him to take Hawthorne berry and Evening of Primrose oil. He was very concerned about taking any kind of medication, as well-meaning doctors had overmedicated and killed his mother. John was adamant about medication, no matter whether it was an herb or vitamin, only one a day.

Our days were filled with lively conversation. It was definitely not dull. I learned about the earth and myself. I also learned that I had work to do with my ex, Mitch. We did many ceremonies during this time we spent together. We smoked the pipe together in a sacred way. We walked my beloved rental property, around the lake and into the woods. John saw many twisted trees with honeysuckle growing on them. He said they would make amazing walking sticks. He did not miss anything. We saw a Great Blue Heron near the lake on a daily basis. He told me that when we were apart he would send them to me.

Ana was very excited to tell her dad about my new friend. She had no idea what a tornado of energy would be unleashed by the misunderstanding of what had transpired. Mitch called me in a rage. What was the meaning of me having an Indian man sleep at the house with Ana present? I have no idea whether Ana told her father about John being her father in another life, but he certainly felt very threatened by John's presence in our lives and definitely in my house. He made it clear that as long as John remained at my residence that Ana would not be allowed to be present. Now I was beginning to understand why John was so sad when Ana left.

The following Wednesday, I dropped in to see Ana at her dance class after school. John wanted to come in, but I was concerned that Ana might feel uncomfortable about me bringing a man that was not her father into the school. It was too much explaining for a seven year old. I knew John was disappointed, but he did not complain or comment. He sat in the front seat of my truck and dozed. He was very tired.

Mathew and his girlfriend joined us for dinner right before Thanksgiving. Ana was allowed to join us for the day. She helped set the table and played games with John. They spent time on the trampoline. Mathew could see how happy I was. He really enjoyed John. He told them stories while we sat at the table after dinner. Everyone loved him. They were able to see what I saw in him. It was a fun day with lots of laughter. Mathew commented that he had never seen me so happy. He was really pleased for me, as was his girlfriend.

While Ana spent Thanksgiving with her dad, John and I drove to Diana Davis' home in Sautee, Georgia. They had been long time friends. Diana met John out west at a ceremony and continued their friendship even though miles separated them. Diana had helped to promote John, setting up appointments for healings, feng shui, dousing and drum-making workshops while he was in town. Diana had a beautiful home overlooking Mount Yona in north Georgia and a really nice group of friends. I was warmly welcomed. We exchanged phone numbers and promised to get together after John was back in Sedona. Our kids were similar ages and our interests made it seem like a good fit. While we were there Diana laughed at being curious about the strange woman that called John at her house.

Shortly after Thanksgiving, John left for a northern tour. He was scheduled to attend an elders' conference near Chicago. I drove him to the airport. Neither of us wanted to say good-bye. I parked at the curb and he slid over on the seat next to me to say good-bye. A very fierce looking policewoman approached my truck. She shouted sternly, move along. I looked at John and said, "I need to move." He made no move to get out of my truck and said he had to get one more kiss before he got out. He kissed me as the policewoman moved over to my window and rapped on it. He kept kissing me as she wrote the ticket. He got out of the truck and insisted on taking the ticket. He said the $50.00 ticket was worth it. It was the most expensive and memorable kiss he ever had. I waved good-bye as I drove off. Fifteen minutes later as I was getting onto GA 400 northbound, he called to tell me he missed his flight. By the time he asked me to come back to get him I had driven three more exits north.

I stopped at the curb in front of the ticket counter. John smiled that bad boy grin. We had two more hours together. We discovered we both loved Chinese food weeks earlier. The choices around Atlanta Hartsfield airport were limited. We managed to find a restaurant that worked. I made sure I returned John to the airport this time with room to spare. We said our good-byes and I was back to my life as usual.

We talked on the phone while he was gone with one exception. He called to tell me he had been invited to dress a hawk and a Bald Eagle that had been brought into a center where his group got together. Only Native Americans are allowed to have hawk or eagle feathers. He was accepted and included in that group.

There was some missing time in John's schedule. I found that I could read his mind. I could also sense when he was lying. There was one conversation we had that was unsettling to me. I was in the middle of a landscape project in Marietta. He had his friend's borrowed car and said he did not want to keep them up talking to me late at night, so he sat in the car instead. He and I talked into the wee hours of the morning. A policeman approached him and asked for his ID while he was sitting there on the phone with me. Due to the lateness of the hour the policeman asked what he was doing. I excused myself from our telephone conversation so that he could tend to the business at hand. I did not like the feeling I had that night. I could not put my finger on it.

John spent two more weeks with me upon his return. It was wonderful although sad at the same time. Although I felt our time together was very precious and short, I was not able to have Ana during this time. Choosing John over her brought up all kinds of emotions for me. We missed being together every other weekend that she spent with her Dad. Having two whole weeks without seeing my daughter was very difficult. I felt guilty and a sense of disloyalty. Ana was very important to me. She would be with me for many years to come. I did not know about John. I also did not know how my being with John so early in the divorce process would affect the result of my ability to get custody of Ana.

I made plans with Diana and her friends. She invited us to attend a drumming circle that she was having for John in December. About 20 people attended. John led the ceremony. He asked Ana and me to participate. We smudged everyone with sacred sage. Ana and I cleared each person together. The feeling of family and the connectedness of John, Ana and me was felt by everyone who attended. We drummed and sang together, nearly lifting Diana's furniture off the floor with the beat and the energy. Diana sang a solo. I felt in awe of her being able to do this in public. I thought to myself, I don't think I could ever do that. She did a beautiful job singing one of John's own songs, *Beauty All Around*. John taught us other Native American songs. The atmosphere was warm and loving. It was a night to remember. It was as if the room was filled with a golden glow of Spirit and sacredness. Afterward we felt such a deep bond; there was a magical quality to what we had experienced. We all had been raised to a different level and we did not want to be apart.

On another occasion, John taught us about the power of music. A single and attractive woman asked John a question. I sat on the sofa across from where she was and watched as John talked directly to her for over 15 minutes. He was lost in his own world and shutting the rest of us out. I brought this up to him once we were alone. He denied that there was anything there between them. I mentioned if that was so, then he would have repeated the question to all and talked to everyone in the room, not just one person. This event disturbed me and I would not let it go. We talked for over an hour about the subject. John commented at the end that he wanted a partner that would bring up his "shit", as he put it, and not let him get away with anything. He said he clearly found that in me. We did not argue, but I did not let him bullshit his way out of it. I lovingly held his feet to the fire. He had been in denial of his own responsibility for the situation. He said he would work hard not to allow this to occur again.

Soon after our deep and serious discussion, John brought out his sacred pipe. He did ceremony often. He had me sit on the floor of my bedroom with him. As I had done ceremonies with him in the past I knew John was always being in the moment and listened to Spirit for his ceremonies. What he did this night was a marriage ceremony. He linked us together through the pipe in a Native American wedding. Knowing I was not divorced, through the eyes of Spirit he felt it would be honored. It was our intention that mattered. It was done in a good way, not to hurt anyone. Afterward he told me with a smile that he owed me some horses, to complete our ceremony, and what kind would I like? "Appaloosas," I replied. He smiled at me and said; "Only the best for you. I am not surprised at your choice."

While he was visiting us, we watched *It's A Wonderful Life*. I had never seen it. The three of us sat on the couch in the living room together. He asked me if I had seen *Serendipity*, or *Made In Heaven*? I had seen *Serendipity* but not the other. He purchased the movie and had it sent to me from the Internet. Ana, John and I watched it together. It was a sad, poignant movie made in 1989 with Kelly McGillis and Timothy Hutton about two lovers meeting and then being separated by death, then meeting again. He said it was our story.

John eventually had to return to Sedona. He was well known by many people there. His Medicine Wheel ceremonies and sweat lodges had been going on there for 15 years. At one time, he gave jeep tours for tourists to make extra money. It was another way that our paths had crossed. I was in Sedona during this time by myself. I had wanted to do a Jeep tour, but felt it was too much money. I was probably not meant to meet him at that time. We continued our relationship across the phone lines and Internet. We talked about life, work, and Ana. We talked about Mitch and my divorce. He expressed sadness at how long it appeared it would take. He threw himself into creating beautiful websites and doing computer programming for large companies. He was very busy and frequently worked through the night. It was during one of our late night conversations I heard the unmistakable expulsion of air, like that of one smoking a cigarette or pipe. I asked him, "John are you smoking?" He laughed and said he could not get anything by me. "Yes," he was. I was concerned for his heart. I knew that having sex tired him out terribly. It took him days to recover. Smoking was not good for him and it continued to trouble me.

John returned to Sedona the second week of December while Ana was still with her father. The latter part of the same week I got a call from the school clinic. Ana was ill. Could I come and pick her up. I went to the school even though she was with her Dad that week. Something told me I needed to get her quickly. I took one look at her and knew she had pneumonia. We went home and she slept on the couch while I finished an estimate I needed to complete. I tried for over three hours to wake Ana and could not. I knew she was really sick. When I finally got her up, she leaned on the countertop while I put her coat on, "Mommy, I feel like I want to go to heaven", she said. "Oh no, honey, you don't want to go there now." I was very concerned. We drove all the way to Kennesaw where I knew there was a Children's Healthcare Center. I told the receptionist that it was an emergency. There must have been 20 or more kids in that waiting room. We were seen within an hour. After taking Ana's vital signs, they rushed Ana in and did a breathing treatment on her. She was very ill.

Lungs are the place that we hold grief. Ana was only seven and very attached to me. It was natural; I was her mother. She had been away from me for two weeks. I felt that it was too much time for her to be away from me. Was she so sick because she missed me so much? It was definitely too much time for her to be with her dad at this juncture. "Was it worth it?" I had to ask myself. I felt that familiar guilt rushing in. Worry, too, plagued me as I wondered what the impact of my affair with John would have on my custody of Ana. Mitch had expressed deep concern for Ana. He had proven over and over again that he would protect Ana from anything and everything that he felt would have a negative impact on her life or health. At that point in time worry seemed to be my constant companion. How would I pay my bills? Would I have enough money?

I was angry that Mitch had sent Ana to school so ill. He did not know what to do with her when she was sick. I was regularly at his house bringing medication, or remedies for Ana's allergies, as he seemed to be at a loss of what to do, or how to take care of our daughter. I had done all the cooking for our household when we were married as well. Mitch had hated to cook and always refused to do so when I asked him. His method of cooking was ordering pizza. His favorite food, being half Italian, proved to be too much for Ana, as it congested her and caused her to have difficulty with breathing among other things. He had asked me to write down some of my recipes so that he could learn to cook some of the family's favorite foods.

John had offered to meet Mitch to stave off any negativity from his involvement with me. John wanted Mitch to know that in no way was he trying to usurp Mitch's role as Ana's father. John felt his role was that of a friend. Ana made it known that she never wanted Mitch as her father and felt that John was more of a father figure to her than Mitch was. I found this odd for a child of seven. But I remembered when Ana was five years old asking me, "Remember my dad?" I responded, "You mean Mitch?" Ana replied, "No my other dad." She talked of her past lives and her own children. She told me that her own children and she had died in a fire. I knew that she and I had died from deaths together by burning at the stake. It was one of my first past-life memories.

Ana was a gifted child. She was born connected to Spirit. She saw angels in her room as an infant. I witnessed her looking up at the ceiling and smiling and flapping her own arms as if they were wings. She watched something on the ceiling that I could not see with such sheer delight. I knew they were there playing with her. She told us of beings that would come to her at our old house and speak with her. Ana described one such being as wearing a long, red robe and a red hat. She also talked of men in long orange robes. Only she called them dresses. Some of the beings made her afraid, most did not. Mitch and I were both aware of her gifts and how special she was. We were both protective of what she was taught and by whom. She came in spiritual and expressed a desire to attend church at a very young age. She did not learn the way other children did and had difficulty fitting in with her peers. Matthew and Adam were concerned about how we protected her from the world. They felt we had insolated her. This was probably true. One thing was for sure, Mitch would continue to be hyper vigilant and protect Ana from me as well. He did not want Ana to witness her mother going through a slew of men. That was not where I was. John was different and special. I knew I could not stop what was happening with him for anything; it was too important. Decisions have consequences. I would have mine in due course. This was only the beginning.

I felt that Mitch was still in love with me and thought that we would surely reconcile any moment. I had to admit I missed the "family" that we had in the past. Mitch had been very involved with my sons and their lives while we were married and continued to do so, even though we were separated. He still bought them birthday gifts and talked with them on the phone. Mitch was more involved in my sons' lives than their own father was.

Soon after meeting John I filed for an uncontested divorce. Suddenly I had a reason to be divorced. Afterward, I realized that I had done so in error and had to get an attorney because of Ana and custody. I thought it would be over and done with quickly. However, Mitch made it clear that however hard I tried to win full custody of Ana he would fight just as hard to get 50-50 shared custody. I felt he did not want to have to pay me child support. Having shared custody meant that there probably would not be any child support paid to either party. He also did not want me to win. He was a Leo. He felt he was clearly the better parent and had to protect his beloved daughter from me.

John expressed to me more than once that he felt Mitch and I were not done. I felt the idea was preposterous. I was so angry with Mitch, how could we not be done? I had so much to learn about relationships and myself. John listened over the phone as I recounted this conversation or that argument with Mitch. John was patient and understanding. He felt helpless and knew he could do nothing to assist me with my healing and moving forward. He allowed me to be where I was. I was aware that being in a relationship with John had elevated me energetically. He was at a much higher place than I was when we met. Being with him moved me more swiftly through my process of healing and put me in a very different place on my journey.

Ana and I made it through Christmas. John did not believe in Christmas or typical gift giving. He said that it was trite and meaningless. It was man-made holiday that held absolutely no meaning for him whatsoever. Gift giving was a commercial event and he did not buy into that. He was adamantly opposed to commercialism. So much so that he ran for mayor of Sedona to keep commercialism at bay and the natural beauty of the place preserved. He was a man with powerful convictions. His life was in danger during this time. The moneyed powers that be apparently hunted for him to try and get their way. He slept in the woods in hiding for months. It sounded far-fetched then, but now knowing what lengths people will go to for personal gain, I believe it. Diana witnessed that it was true. He had no reason to tell me lies, certainly not about politics. He was able to get legislation passed to keep the hotels, motels and buildings to a minimum and with a height restriction. To this day, Sedona is beautiful and the beauty is preserved.

On several occasions, John called me late at night from high on top of Schnebly Hill, in Sedona. It is a beautiful place, isolated and free from lights and commercialism. John would go up there to meditate and heal the Earth. He would sing to me while he was there, his booming voice bringing me to tears.

One evening we were on the phone together and John said we needed to have a phone date! I wondered what he meant by that. He was creating spontaneity and excitement in our relationship even though he was so far away. We both agreed to see *Cold Mountain* with Nicole Kidman. He told me that it was a story about him and one of his past lives. We talked on the phone on the way to the movie and then he called me afterward and we spoke on the way home.

It was during the movie I had a violent experience of the past life memory. I was John's girlfriend then. Before I knew what the outcome would be my legs shook uncontrollably. I wept before I knew what would happen to him. It was as if I already knew. Of course I did, I had been there. The memory was in my soul. I knew that John and I had many past lives. We did not explore them in conversation, we just knew. It was evident when we first met. Our love was deep and survived through our many lifetimes and incarnations. I had the revelation that love never dies. It cannot. Love is energy not an emotion. I wept and wept. I did not know what I was crying for. I sat alone in the theatre in Alpharetta, having my experience and reliving our past life, weeping uncontrollably.

When John finally reached me he sounded frantic. I was not sure why. It seemed over long that I had left him by phone until he reached me again. We talked while we both drove home from our respective theatres. The dirty bird, though, ended up seeing another movie – something far lighter than the one I watched. "Typical," I thought, "allow the woman to do the grieving for you. Escape the emotion of the moment."

We were both very emotional on the way home. I told him what I felt. There was so much emotion over the cell phones that both of our phones went dead. When we finally reconnected we were both weeping. Our souls were so connected that without the conversation about what I experienced and even with the dropped call, John felt what I was feeling. He saw the images that I saw and was right there with me even though he was over a thousand miles away from me in Sedona. No matter what space and time was between us we would always be connected. This was an amazing revelation. The power of love is amazing.

While John was back in Sedona I began a friendship with his longtime friend Diana. We spent a day together hiking near waterfalls in Helen, Georgia, or took our children out for Mexican food in the Helen area. One afternoon, we visited a friend and neighbor of Diana's. She was a psychic who had recently sold her metaphysical bookstore in the Naples, Florida area and moved north. When she heard about John and me and our "magical relationship" she asked the details of our meeting. That explained why I could read John's mind so clearly. We knew what each other was thinking most of the time, even long distance. She then went on to tell me about her Twin Flame experience. She said they were so connected in a way she never experienced before or since. They were so in love. It was amazing. Then he died. I cried when she told me her story. I told the women in the room that I felt something was going to happen to John. I could not put my finger on it. I felt like we only had a very short time together and that was why everything was sped up for us. Diana said very strongly, "You need to clear that." I did all that I knew to do to release patterns and energy. I felt that whatever it was, it was karmic and there was nothing I could do to change it.

Our relationship was before the days of Facebook or MySpace. We instead used instant messaging. I was unfamiliar with it, but when John sent me the link and suggested it, I grew to like it as it kept John from spending too much on his cell phone and we could still "converse."

John sent Ana and me a package for New Year's. He regretted not being able to be with us over the holidays. My attorney was concerned about how the court and Mitch would feel about our relationship and wanted me to keep everything on the up and up. I was surprised at this being the case; after all we were in the 21st century. Weren't things more progressive than that? Apparently it was not the case in Georgia. We live in the Bible Belt. It is the opposite of progressive.

The small package arrived New Year's Eve. Ana and I excitedly opened it together. John was different; his gifts were no exception. He carefully chose each item from his own belongings. John had chosen a Herkimer diamond in a little crocheted sock for me that he had mined and found himself, a turquoise heart-shaped stone and a blue piece of fabric from his own altar. This was a perfect gift from a romantic geologist and Earth keeper. He carefully chose a little turtle for Ana. Turtle represents Mother Earth. He also gave Ana a flat piece of crystal you could look through and a jade stone he found. On the front of the card was a photo taken of a natural rock formation that formed a cave with light shining through to the bottom of it. The interior walls were filled with color and beauty.

In John's printed scrawl his carefully chosen card read:

Prayers for the New Year: For Jennifer - In the Furry Container

1 For the Protected Heart — that doubt and pain cannot take up residence -
And that the Earth speaks softly to you
2 A diamond mined by my own hands — wrapped in the rainbow of light which I feel each time I think of you — for harvesting the Abundance and Wonder of Life on Earth

The Card —

Texture and Color wrapped around the essential gift we all share — life itself —

A symbol of God's eternal
Presence —

Love You Two John (across the second page before he wrote to Ana)

Prayers For the New Year for Ana —

I for Clarity — to see the world for all its beauty and love

I for Patience
To walk the Earth with patience & strength —
Let nothing get you down
for Adventure — Jade
    the Magic Protector
    will take you places
    that only the heart can
    go — from an Oregon
    Beach — (I found it)

In my conversations with Nannette, she reiterated over and over that John was very special. He was not your typical man. I knew it with my heart and with all my soul. I could not wait to be with him again. John felt the same way. After being away from each other over the holidays, John had a compulsion to be with me — he wanted to see Ana too, but that was not to be because of the situation with her Dad. He said he had decided he was coming for a visit. He made his flight arrangements and arrived at Atlanta Hartsfield the evening of January 20, 2003. I spotted his black cowboy hat before I saw his face. When he found me in the crowd he looked exhausted and gray. He hugged me as soon as he saw me, burying his face against my neck and in my hair. He held me like there was no tomorrow and said he never wanted to be away from me like that again. When we got into my truck, John expressed an urgent need to be with me and make love to me.

We drove home holding hands. While I was driving John reached over and kissed my cheek. We did not make it out of the kitchen before our clothes were off and John got his wish on my Formica kitchen counter. It was incredible to be with him, this man I loved so deeply. I held on to John's round belly and sat on top of him on my bed. I felt the presence of God in the room as we both climaxed together. John snuggled close to me and was breathing heavily within minutes. I lay next to him touching his ample belly, smiling to myself. "Wow!" was all I could think. John had expressed some disturbing feelings to me, which prompted me to light a white candle and keep it lit whenever he slept in my room. I had one burning the whole time he visited me, as I knew he was frequently out of his body traveling at night. I knew that we had experienced each other this way prior to meeting in this lifetime. Our souls had been searching all over for each other for years.

134

John awoke to tell me about his crazy dream. He said that Mother Earth was recruiting him and he was to do advertising and PR for her. It was the wildest thing, he said. He always dreamed in color. There were many more details of this dream that I do not recall at the present. Suffice it to say, it was profound and strange. He was being recruited to do a very special job. He was an Earthkeeper and this did not sound strange to me at all. John had such a love of Mother Earth, being a geologist, and was so spiritually connected to the Divine. It all made perfect sense to me. I just did not know how he was going to do it, or what the job entailed.

John wanted to make love all the time, three times a day — it was if he wanted to make up for lost time. I loved making love to him, so I was equally interested in joining his plan. We made love as soon as his eyes were open; we made love in the afternoon and then took a nap. I would get up and write or take care of my animals, leaving him to sleep and rest. When John was in Atlanta the last time he moved my television into my bedroom. It remained here now and we rented several of John's favorite movies, like *Serendipity, Made in Heaven* and the last movie I rented was his absolute favorite, *Lord of The Rings*.

John called me the love of his life. He had waited for me for a long time. We both had had many lovers. He loved me without reservation. He loved me completely. He loved me in ways I had never been loved before. My animals loved him and he loved my home and property. He dreamed of a time when we could purchase it together and do sweat lodges on the property. I suggested that we go up to Diana's to visit her, and possibly do a sweat lodge with her. I knew she wanted to see him and would be disappointed if she did not. John declined. He just wanted to spend this time alone with me.

I had made plans to see a friend and shaman, Frances Summer. Frances had known of John for several months and actually brought me a frozen bird that she had found on the side of the road. She was sure it was an eagle, but wanted confirmation from John. He was an expert at bird recognition, even better than I was. I was really impressed with his knowledge. He had an amazing knowledge of trees and natural vegetation, being a woodsman and Earth keeper. I should not have been surprised. The so-called eagle that Frances found was actually a turkey vulture and Frances and I argued with him through several e-mails when John was in Sedona. Eventually, John said, "Okay, it is an Egyptian eagle." When I looked it up, I found that in John's inequitable sense of humor that it was actually a turkey vulture. He was just tired of arguing with Frances and me about what he already knew to be the truth.

John was funny about truth. He spoke the truth even when it pissed people off, and he often pissed people off. He would argue with the council about Sundance and Earthdance. When he felt what he suggested was better for the good of all he would not back down. John taught me how to use his radionic antennae to heal. It was profound in its ability to find and clear blocks in people's energy fields. I did work on John to heal his relationship with his ex-wife and his children. He would not be moved. He felt that they would not forgive him so he did not want to try. We spoke about his calling Sun and Moon again in January 2003. Sadly he would not.

On Wednesday, January 22, we woke up, showered together, and then made love. I found it funny that no amount of showering could erase John's dirt-stained feet. Afterward I dragged John over to Frances Summer's for a DNA reconnection session. John was not happy about this. He was clearly tired and wanted to spend his precious time alone with me, not with others. I had wanted Frances to meet John and asked him to do this for me. When Frances began and plunked in a CD she had purchased from another healer, John was livid. He wanted to leave. He did not want to pay $20 for a session that she was conducting through someone else's CD. John whispered to me that he did Medicine Wheel ceremonies for 200 hundred people in Sedona and never charged a dime. He was very angry. He would go through the motions, but he wanted me to know in no uncertain terms he was not happy. I told him we would leave as soon as it was over, no chitchat. I kept my promise.

We left the Dunwoody area and I asked John where to? He said, "Do you have a Chinatown? I want to make you a Chinese dinner tonight." He knew it was my favorite food. I was delighted to show him around the shops in the Chamblee and Buford Highway area. We went from one place to another looking for items to go into our Chinese dish. We had fun showing each other the weird and wonderful condiments and different noodles at the specialty shops. When we arrived home, we made love and took a nap.

When John woke up, I remembered hearing an owl hoot outside our window the night before. John was extremely interested in this and asked me many questions. I had no idea of the significance at the time.

John prepared dinner. He asked me to play the piano, which I had not done for a very long time. I had such negative feelings about playing for people because my mother made me "perform" for her friends. I was not that good and I knew it. I hated to be put on display like that. I felt like a performing monkey. She spent her hard-earned money giving me piano lessons and I should be grateful, as I was told repeatedly. I still have a piano in my home, but rarely if ever play it.

This night, I looked at John's face and said I would. I played better than I played in a long time. I surprised myself. John then played his flute for me. He did so in a strange way, though. He lay down on my green brocade Broyhill couch in the living room. I sat at the dining room table listening to him play. While I sat there my legs shook as they had done while I was watching the movie in the theatre all alone — *Cold Mountain* with Nicole Kidman. I could not get them to stop. It was not due to too much caffeine. It was out of shock that they shook in the movie. Whatever could be going on? I tried to stay focused on John's flute playing. The man could really play.

I showered and changed into a little surprise outfit for our special evening. I came out of the bedroom wearing a gorgeous cream-colored lace bustier. I also found some cream colored stockings with bows at the back. The pairing of these two elements gave me a beautiful, ethereal quality. I added a couple of strands of pearls. I knew John would love it. I picked a white floral Asian silk robe and walked into the living room where John was playing the flute. His eyes lit up and he smiled at me, his eyes crinkling at the corners. He had such character in his face. He told me I was beautiful and that he loved me. I undressed him while he lay on the couch. It was not long before he pulled me up and I sat over him while he looked at me in awe. He was so sweet. I knew he loved me just by the way he looked at me. He had no reservations about showing how much.

As John climaxed he told me he loved me and that he would never leave me. He would be with me always. He sat up and I moved off of him so he could catch his breath. All at once his blue eyes glazed over and they had the shield of death on them. He slid off the couch and urinated. I watched in horror, as he lay there on the floor naked except for his amber necklace he always wore. I screamed at him, "John don't leave me! Please don't leave me! Please don't leave me!" I raced to call Diana Davis. I told her John had just died! She said, "No he hasn't." "Yes, I am sure of it, Diana." I told her how he slid off the couch and urinated on the floor. His eyes had a glaze of gray over his beautiful blues. I knew it with all my heart.

All at once Diana told me that John and Diana had been joking around in the kitchen while he made himself a ham sandwich in early November. He became intense and very serious all of a sudden and told Diana he had been afraid to come to Atlanta. He felt that if he did he was going to die. He thought maybe his plane would crash or something like that, he felt it profoundly. Diana quickly changed the subject and said, "Well you're here now and safe. Let's not talk about that." Oh my God, I felt something was going to happen early on also. I quickly got off the phone and called 911. I told them what had happened.

I performed CPR until they arrived and knew it was no use. He was not coming back. It was meant to be. Within minutes the paramedics, the fire department and police pulled up with their sirens screaming. They broke the silence of our little village. The police and fire station were less than half a mile away from my house. I stood in my living room clad only in a bustier and white stockings with bows on the top when I heard the first step on my front porch, I ran to get my robe on. This was not good. Before I answered the door I removed John's amber necklace, as I felt he wanted me to. I also took his "Dream" ring off his finger. It was a silver ring that a woman had given him from up north. I would soon come to find out that she had thought that she was the love of John's life.

They walked in and looked at John's naked body lying there and then at me. I knew they were all thinking the same thing, "What a way to go, lucky bastard!" I felt like a murderer. I knew I raised him to the highest of heights and he loved being there. This time he just exited his body on his kundalini. It was a perfect death for a spiritual master.

I knew instinctively that the medical profession would find that he had a blockage. I knew he did not die of a heart attack. This event was preordained. He was needed to promote Mother Earth where he could be of the greatest assistance – the other side. Within two days of John's death, Wallace Black Elk and two other Native American elders died as well. I knew this was significant. John was going to do what he was meant to do with his brothers.

The men worked on him asking me questions. By this time they had John trached. I knew he would not like having his body cut up. They asked me exactly what happened. They asked if I was his wife. I explained. They all looked very grave. I stood there dumbfounded, crushed, and broken while the man I loved absolutely lay on the floor lifeless and soulless. I knew he was watching me while I cried, watching me while I paced. I wanted to scream at the top of my lungs, but I held it in.

I told them he would not want an autopsy. The paramedics were sorry but since he died out of state that they would have to. That was the law. They loaded John's lifeless body onto a stretcher and into the ambulance. They took him to North Fulton hospital on Highway 9, in Roswell. I called Mathew and he said he would meet me at the hospital, but his girlfriend would come and get me and drive me to the hospital. He did not want me driving under these conditions. I was grateful for his understanding and quick thinking. His girlfriend lived within five minutes of my house. She would be here fast. I did not want his body alone long.

I called Diana back and told her where they were taking John. She said she would meet me there. As Diana was coming from north Georgia, I knew it would be a while before she would get there. Several others arrived in the waiting room. John was loved and people came to support him and me. Esther and her husband, Joey, came. They stood there uncomfortably. No one wanted to go and see his body, but I did. He was my husband maybe not in this lifetime, but in several others. I had to see him. Mathew, my son was there and then Diana arrived. She flew in the door and blasted me with her words, "I told you to clear those programs around death with John!" I felt as if she was blaming me for his death. I knew John had a special place in Diana's heart. She had known him for ten or was it 15 years and had lots and lots of history with him. She had told me countless stories of women who threw themselves at her charismatic friend. I took her sweet, impish friend away.

I let it go, but my son, who is ever my protector, was absolutely livid. He told me so. I let him know that I understood where she was coming from. Death was like that. Everybody processed it differently. Her first reaction was coming from old pain and she blamed me. It was easier that way.

We sat and talked for a while reminiscing about John's antics and character. I was feel-ing exhausted and Mathew suggested that he take me home. I thanked everyone, including Mathews' girlfriend for bringing me, as Mathew helped me into the car. I felt like every particle in my being ached. I sat in the front seat of Mathew's car. He touched my hand without say-ing anything. What could be said? When Matthew's girlfriend picked me up to take me to the hospital, the night was calm and dark. As Mathew pulled his car into my driveway a huge wind picked up and encircled the house. Mathew looked at me and said knowingly "John is here." I was surprised that he would say that. Of all my children, Mathew seemed to be the biggest nonbeliever in anything that I believed. It was about 3:00 a.m. when we got out of the car. The wind howled and moaned around the house. Mathew helped me out of the car asking if I was all right. I felt stiff and lifeless myself. Mathew told me he would sleep here with me to make sure I was all right. I thanked him. Right now I wanted to talk with John. I went into the living room where John's body had been lying only hours before. I had not been afraid of the dark since I was a child. I sat on the couch in the dark and felt his presence and the softness of his energy. I could see the outline of him like a white cloud. He said he was sorry. He never meant to leave me. He still meant he would be with me forever. I could hear his words in my head. I did not have to speak out loud for him to hear me either. We talked for about 15 minutes. He told me all I had to do was call for him and he would be with me.

Mathew came and got me; he was tired and worried about me. I shuffled numbly into the bathroom to wash my face and brush my teeth. John's black leather toiletry bag was sitting on the bathroom counter. The natural bristle hairbrush I gave him was sitting next to his bag. I could not bring myself to move it. I finished washing and somehow I climbed into bed. Mathew got in next to me. I was really surprised. He had not slept with me since he was five years old. He said he could keep an eye on me and it would give him peace of mind. I think he thought I might hurt myself. The thought never crossed my mind on a conscious level. As I drifted off to sleep I felt my soul lifting out of my body to join him. I wanted to go too. Every time I fell asleep the same thing occurred. My soul was reaching out to him, wanting to be with him. I had never felt like this before. God, I hurt. I hurt so badly. Please, God, take this pain away from me. Please!

The next day people came and supported me. An old friend and acupuncturist made a house call. He stuck needles in my heart chakra because of all the grief I had stuck there. He shoved needles a few other places as well. I really could not care less what he did. He was concerned I would have a heart attack myself. God I hope so I thought! I lay on my bed. I barely moved or ate. I called Mitch and told him. His reply surprised me, he said, "Really?" As in "I did that?" I had felt for some time that he had done some voodoo on John and me. I really felt that he had played a big part in hurrying up John's death so he could get back with me. Or was I going insane? No, I wasn't. I wanted to talk to Ana and tell her. He felt it was not appropriate, as she did not have a relationship with him. "What?" I thought. How typical. A very important man in Ana's life dies and you think she did not have a relationship with him? I hung up the phone. I did not have the strength to fight with him right now. Let him believe he was right. He always was, right?

Mathew stayed with me and went through John's cell phone. He copied every name and phone number from John's phone and compiled a list. I began calling everyone in his phone. I had no idea who most of the people were, but soon I had met many more friends. All the men, especially his dearest friends and elders, said they wanted to meet the woman who sent their brother home with a smile on his face. It made me smile somewhat, at least. I was becoming famous.

I cried on the phone as I made phone calls to the women. I met so many wonderful people who loved John. He knew so many people, and everyone loved him. The people closest to him were Tammy and Dade Yost. When I made the call to them, I found that John had slept with another woman while he was there for the council meeting in November. It seems that John, that little pistol, had fallen off the wagon! That explained the missing time, his sitting out in the car late at night, being stopped by a policeman and the time he could not be reached by phone. I was hurt and upset. But it did not stop the pain of his death. The reality was he loved me. Faithful and perfect he was not. He had to spread that "John love" around. It must have been difficult being so charismatic, having women constantly throw themselves at you even when you say, please no? Diana and I laughed about this later when it did not hurt so much. John was John. We all loved him. We planned a ceremony in north Georgia to honor him.

My menstrual cycles stopped abruptly with the shock of John's death. I heard that this sometimes happened with some women. Strange the ways that death can affect you. I tried to continue to live when I wanted to die.

I am not sure whether Ana felt something and asked questions about me, or if Mitch finally had a pang of conscience. Either way I was grateful that he called and said I could see Ana the third day after John's passing. It was Sunday afternoon. He said I could have Ana for two hours to share the information about John's death — between 5:00 p.m. and 7:00 p.m.

Rather than fight with him, I picked Ana up from her Dad's. I had wanted to drive directly to my house, but Ana said she was hungry. I knew I did not have the energy to cook her anything; I was not eating. I took her to Chili's right around the corner. Once seated in our two-person booth Ana asked me where John was.

Although we were seated in a booth for two, John came in and sat next to Ana. I saw him there just as Ana asked where he was. It is why she asked about him immediately. I tried to wait till we were out of the restaurant. Ana was too sharp to miss a thing. I hesitated. She nearly shouted at me, "Mom! Where is John?" I looked at the small space on the bench next to her and said, "He is right beside you." She turned to look then looked questioningly at me. "What do you mean?"

I haltingly said, "Honey, John died on Thursday night." She started to feel sick to her stomach. "Why didn't you tell me?" she cried. "I tried to. I called but your Dad did not let me speak to you." She wanted to go home right away. We asked for her food to go. When it arrived I put my arm around her and walked her outside.

I could only imagine how she was feeling. The one man she could truly call a friend was gone. She didn't even get a chance to say good-bye. She told me she didn't want to go back to her Dad's. She was angry with her father and sad all at the same time. What conflicting emotions.

When we got home I brought out John's hat, flute and his drum. I let her hold and touch everything. I let her breathe. I answered all of her questions.

Most of all, I told her how John had cried the day she had left to go back to her Dad's. I told her on some level John knew he would never see her again. At this point the dam burst and she really cried. To think she had not been able to see him before he died bothered her. I reminded her that John could be with her any time she wanted him to be.

She slept in my bed that night after we watched *Made in Heaven*. I let her sleep late and did not send her to school on Monday. We watched *Lord of the Rings* and then *Serendipity*, all the movies that he loved. We cried together and we talked about the day he made me dinner and let her eat all her Halloween candy. We laughed at how sheepish he had been when Ana tattled on him about burning my pot. We talked about the magic of his ceremony, the power of his voice and how much he would be missed. He would continue to visit us on the wind, in the rain and he was forever in our hearts.

Diana gathered all her friends together to make prayer ties. Prayer ties are made of black, red and yellow fabric. Diana taught me how to make them using a small square piece of fabric. She told me to hold the fabric in your hand and place a small amount of tobacco into the fabric while you silently said a prayer. The fabric is tied onto a string and either burned or hung in the trees. When the prayer ties hang in the trees everything around them is blessed. When the prayer ties are burned the prayers go up into flames and are carried to Great Spirit. Either way the prayers are answered.

When I spoke to John's children, they wanted all the details, everything that I knew about their Dad. They wished he had called them. They said they would have spoken to him. I told them he felt they would reject him and he did not want that. This was one area that John was not able to complete. Sun talked to me about John's wishes. It was strange that I even knew he wanted to be cremated. John believed, as I did, that burial is a waste. Burial wastes the earth and it wastes precious resources. I told Sun this and he was relieved. Cremation was far cheaper than burial anyway. It took what seemed like an eternity for John's body to be released from the autopsy, over two weeks.

It was a sunny cold day in February when I drove alone to the crematorium. Diana did not want to go. Nor did either of John's children. I brought my drum and rattle and sang and did prayers over John's body alone. I sang the songs that John had taught me and looked at his cut up and blood-splattered chest. "Geeze," I thought, the least they could have done is to clean you up, John! I did everything I knew to do to honor his body. I left tobacco on his chest with my prayers and closed the body bag over his face. I liked him so much better with his soul intact.

I drove home in my truck mulling over the songs and the events of the past two weeks. How my life had changed. I knew this would forever affect me. Ana and I would never forget this man that we both loved for such a short time. As I drove up Hopewell Road, almost home, I felt a spinning. It was dizzying and made it difficult to drive. It was not like the lateral spin of a drunk. It felt as if I was doing forward somersaults in my truck. It made it very difficult to drive. I pulled over to allow the energy to dissipate. I had no idea who was messing with me, but I was definitely being worked on. It is said that the days before someone dies are a very powerful time. The person who is dying passes on wisdom and gifts to the person they are spending time with. I knew that John gave me more than love. What surfaced was a powerful, healing energy within me. I had yet to find out the purpose. When I finally reached my house I had to crawl up the steps into the house. I managed to get myself onto my bed and I fell asleep.

We waited until after John's cremation so that we could spread his ashes at Diana's in ceremony. Someone made beautiful bags to place his ashes in for the ceremony with the colors of the tribes. We all gathered on a sunny Sunday afternoon at Diana's house in the mountains. There were about 30 of us, all honoring and singing John's songs as best we could. Without our leader to guide us, we had to wing it. We placed his drum, rattle and hat on the altar. Diana's son, Forrest, and Ana helped to sage everyone and brought in the food offering for Great Spirit.

I had received guidance from Joseph Many Horses on the smoking of John's sacred pipe. I honored the chanupa and John with the ceremony. I spoke about my experience with John and how short a time we had together, but how powerful it was. I smoked the sacred pipe and passed it. Diana and I gave our kids the choice of smoking the pipe or not. Forrest and Ana did their best since both of them loved John. They wanted to share the pipe as well. They were barely able to inhale before they were coughing and sputtering. Everyone was good-natured about the Attempts. Forrest coughed for days saying he would never smoke again. Ana also said she did not like the taste of the smoke at all!

When it was all over, somewhere around 4:00 in the afternoon, and everyone was feeling good and happy about John, we walked drumming and singing down the road towards Diana's house for refreshments. A big fat possum came trotting towards us and led us down the center of the road as if he was the drum major. We all followed him laughing and singing. He walked right up Diana's driveway and then off into the bushes. We all watched him pass by and into the brush at the side of the road. We all had a big laugh, as we felt this was John in his own good-humored way of saying good-bye to all his beloved friends. This was a particularly odd event as possums are nocturnal. He was not the least afraid of our noise or us.

The gifts of nature surrounded me. While walking outside with my dogs a large male Great Blue Heron flew over Scott's pasture next door and circled around my lake and landed in a tree very high up. I knew this was John saying hello to me. Every day or two a Great Blue Heron would fly by as we were driving to school, or when I walked outside to get the mail. It was comforting to know he was thinking of me and sending me messengers.

Since John had died while he was with me all his sacred objects were in my house. Everyone was calling me asking me what I would do with the items. His large buffalo drum, his turtle rattle, and most of all, his sacred pipe and his hat. I was learning very quickly that women had very few rights to the sacred objects unless they themselves were pipe carriers and traveling the red road. I kept John's hat for Ana. It had a turtle that represented Mother Earth and beads around the brim. She needed to have it, I was sure of that.

As far as the rest of the objects, I spoke at great length to Joseph Many Horses. He was a wise and highly regarded elder. John had spoken very highly of him and I knew he could be trusted to give sage advice. They were not concerned with his CDs, his hat or his clothes. What they were interested in was his drum, rattle, and sacred pipe. They wanted to be sure they went to elders on the council. He gave me several suggestions. I made my decision. I sent his drum and rattle to Tammy and Dade Yost who John thought of as family.

I had several conversations with one of John's friends in Sedona. I liked him. He seemed unconcerned about getting anything for himself. His concern was that the chanupa (pipe) should be honored and buried and that no one should have it. John uncovered it and that is where it needed to return – underground. I carefully wrapped up his precious and beloved carved pipe and sent it to Carlos in Sedona where he would bury it, in a good way. He said it needed to be healed. If it should be found again, then so be it. But no one was to get the pipe now. While Carlos was deciding what to do, he was forced to give a blood offering to Spirit. While working out on his equipment he injured himself on two separate occasions. The pipe was seeking blood. Things were definitely getting interesting.

I smelled John's scent still on his clothes and hugged them to my heart as I folded them and then packaged them lovingly and sent them off to John's son, Sun. He wanted John's CDs. I did not send them. I wanted his music. It was the closest thing to his soul. I would not send everything away. I needed to have something that was John's even if it was only for a little while. Ana and I also kept John's Native American wooden flute and his hippie tarot cards. I knew I had his love always. The things were really unimportant. I would release the rest.

I cut off a lock of my hair and put some things in a piece of fabric and placed it on my altar. A year to the date of John's death, I did a ceremony as I was instructed by Tammy. My grieving was supposed to be over. Why was I was still sad?

It was difficult to return to my landscaping when I felt so disinclined to do so. Six months after John's ceremony in Sedona I moved out of my beloved rental house and property where John had died. It still carried the sadness and grief of John's death. I cried everyday for six months. I could barely function. Had it not been for Ana I would have joined John. It was during this period that John came to me while I was crying and said simply, "Enough." He let me know it was time to move on. He felt grieving was a very low vibration. I could not stay there any longer.

I felt sad about leaving the property but felt that it was best for me to try to get past the memories that were in the house.

LESSONS LEARNED

Although we had a very short time together the impact of the time we did have still resonates in my heart. There was no doubt John was my Twin Flame. I have never felt such an instant knowing and connection with anyone I have met. Hugging him that first time with wave after wave of past life knowing and energy hit us like a Tsunami and affected the other women who witnessed it. Because he spent his last days with me, and had such an impassioned death it left me with an energetic imprint I will never shake. Love never dies. I will have that feeling forever.

Although I know he was not perfect he was nevertheless extraordinary. His presence in my life raised me to a higher vibration just by being with him. The fact that he loved me completely, accepting me exactly as I was, showed me what true love is all about. It is about total acceptance and unconditional love. He knew I was not perfect, but he accepted me warts and all, with all my imperfections. I am truly grateful for this beautiful gift. The fact that he had secrets from me shows he was still human however evolved he was. He always treated me with love and respect. He could not hurt another intentionally.

The time Ana spent with John was very special. She will never forget how he played with her with the eyes and heart of a child. They connected in a very special way that death will never take away.

I recognize the fact that I had this affair with him while my daughter was in my home was the key factor in me not winning full custody of Ana. As hard as this was for Ana she needed this time with John. The result was that she had to endure seven years of back and forth between her father and me. This too was Divine. She needed to have this relationship with her father even though it was not what she wanted.

Vibration before John's death: 550 Love and Joy

Vibration after John's death: 75

Life Force: 40%

CHAPTER NINE

Surrender

Dating several people at once had never been my thing. I was aware I was codependent and this was a behavior I really wanted to change. Bringing awareness to a behavior is the first step of healing and clearing it. Usually after a date or two I would rationalize that I really liked the guy and since I was sending out signals and vibrating that I was codependent a man would show up with similar issues and we would end up in a relationship and that was that. Up until the end of my marriage with Mitch, I was not happy being alone and suffered intense loneliness.

I had heard psychologists say that for every two years of marriage you should have one-year alone post divorce to heal. Using that methodology, it meant I should be single for at least five years in order to heal after my divorce from Mitch. In April 2003, my sister-in-law's brother, Alan, visited for several weeks. He had fortuitously met someone on-line while he was living in England. As odd as it seemed at the time, the woman he met lived in Canton Georgia less than twenty miles from us. He happened to visit Mitch and me just as our marriage was in the throes of dissolution.

It was a difficult period for me, as I was still in tremendous fear of Mitch and his rage. Just the undercurrent of violence was enough to make me feel as if I was walking on eggshells. It was a very familiar feeling for me. Growing up in a household where my father had a violent temper and my mother had erratic and unpredictable emotions, I was constantly trying to please everybody so I would not get beaten. Similarly, while living with Mitch I tried not to rock the boat so I did not anger him. I did not recognize that I had so much internal anger that was still unresolved from the years of abuse in my childhood. Having Alan at the house while Mitch moved out helped to make me feel safe at the time.

During Alan's visit Mitch required Ana to do her homework in the same room where Alan was watching television. Mitch expressed his dismay several times to Ana about paying attention to her homework and told her sharply once or twice to pay attention and stop watching television. Because it was so hypnotic, Ana could not keep her eyes off the program. Mitch came up behind her, grabbed her pony tail, dragged her out of the room and into her bedroom where he screamed at her loud enough for his voice to boom over the closed bedroom door and the blaring television set. Alan was very disturbed by the exchange and Ana's cries in the bedroom. When I got home from work I had an earful from both Ana and Alan.

Mitch had approved Alan's visit with the understanding that he had been a family friend most of my life. Tension was high until Mitch moved out. I knew he did not want a divorce and he was concerned about how much time he would have with his daughter. Alan's presence during Mitch's move kept all of us on our best behavior and prevented any further emotional outbursts from occurring. I was extremely grateful for the synchronicity of his visit. As it turned out his love interest was married. I realized that God and the Universe had orchestrated his visit to see this woman to coincide with the ending of my marriage. After Alan returned to his home in England I began intense healing and nine months of complete solitude, except for my family. I did not want to date and knew it would not be productive for me to do so.

During this time of self-reflection and healing I wrote in my journal on a daily basis. Mitch and I were embroiled in a custody battle, which consumed much of my waking moments and drained my energy. Mitch wanted to have shared custody of our seven-year-old daughter and I wanted to have full custody. Our daughter wanted to live full-time with me. I experienced tremendous anguish over the thought of a seven-year-old having to go back and forth between each of us every other week, especially since she cried every time she had to go to her dad's. Since I had full custody of both my sons, Adam and Matthew, in my previous divorce, I expected the same outcome. I was prepared to do whatever it took to win full custody of Ana and get the child support I felt I deserved. We were both interviewed by a guardian ad litem. She interviewed Ana and me separately at our home at the farm. We had horses at the time, and she did some of the interview outside with Ana.

When it came time for Ana to be interviewed at Mitch's house, the guardian kept interrupting her and putting words in her mouth. Ana became so frustrated and angry that she was feeding back her phrases that she did not say. Each time Ana would speak the guardian interrupted and said, "so what you are saying is...." when Ana was not saying what she repeated at all. She was not able to speak her mind because her father was present. When Mitch was interviewed he made sure that Ana was upstairs and not able to hear their conversation. Ana was certain that her father lied about me to the guardian. Ana was a very intuitive little girl. She could read her father like a book.

Mitch and I had very different ideas of how to raise a child. This had been a huge sticking point in our marriage and was most likely the single biggest issue that had never been resolved, even through counseling. Mitch was very disciplined and believed my lack of consistency with my children and inability to offer consistent consequences for bad behavior made me a poor parent. A healer we had gone to for years also raised the issue of enmeshment as a major issue. She felt I elevated my children to the place of friends and talked to them about adult-type subject matter, which was very inappropriate.

As this was the case with my mother, I could not see what I was doing wrong. I rationalized that I was very close to my children and he was jealous of our relationship. Mitch became hyper vigilant about Ana, protecting her at every turn. He was not going to allow me to get full custody of her. He made it very clear to me he would fight me as long as I resisted. He also indicated that the research he had done about fathers who only had weekend visitation every other week typically would give up and move out of state to begin anew. He would not have that happen. He was committed to his daughter and her well-being.

After Mitch moved out Ana remained living with me for seven months and Mitch paid me child support. Mitch had moved in with his sister and her husband who lived forty-five minutes away. We kept things as they were with Ana leaving every other weekend to be with her father and staying at her aunt's home. Ana was not crazy about leaving me but was happy to spend time at her aunt's house as they had a dog and lived in a large new home. The household was busy with activity including frequent visits with her cousin and grandmother. When Mitch moved he did not take any of our furniture with him. He took only his tools and exercise equipment. He rented a cute ranch near Ana's school and set it up very nicely with some help from his sister. He did everything he could to make Ana's bedroom and bathroom appealing to her with girlie sheets, a cute bathroom and a special phone for her to talk to me.

When it came time for her father to pick her up for her first full week in October, she did not want to go. She ran upstairs to her playroom and locked herself in the room. Mitch tried to be patient but his controlling side overtook him. He demanded that I take matters into my hands and "make" her go. I rationalized that it was not right to force a child if she did not want to. He directed that I had to do it. He was entitled to have her. I cajoled Ana and got her to come down stairs with me. I felt guilty as hell, but picked her up in my arms and forced her into Mitch's truck. Why was I doing this? She kicked, screamed and cried looking out the window at me as they drove away. She did not trust me as I tricked her into getting into her dad's truck. I was in agony. How could I do that to my child? I was in such fear of Mitch; I could not stand up to him. What was worse was that he knew it and took full advantage of it.

Ana begged me not to make her go the next time; I told her she did not have any choice. She had to go with her father. She said she cried at his house and he yelled at her saying, "I don't want to hear your crying!" When Ana begged to speak to me on the phone and Mitch allowed it, she cried over the phone. Mitch became angry and told her she would not be allowed to talk to me on the phone if she was going to cry. Ana was seven and very attached to me. She became depressed because she could not be with me. She was ill almost every week she was at her father's house. I was often there during the week to see her and break up the week for her. I would take vitamin C and different foods to help boost Ana's immune system.

The second week that Ana was to go to her Dad's she railed. She would not go. Mitch finally told me to meet him at Ana's school without her knowledge and again lift her kicking and screaming into his truck. I wept as they drove away with Ana's hand pressed up against the glass screaming, "No, Mommy! No!" I vowed I could not do that again as it felt inhumane for Ana and me. Mitch found a way to work around it. He picked Ana up on Monday afternoon at the after-school program instead.

Every Sunday night Ana would become sad around 4:00 in the afternoon and cry when she went to bed. Every Monday morning for five years she cried. She would throw up because she was so upset about having to go to her father's house at the end of the school day. She said she was lonely there and was often depressed. He spent most of the time in his office while she sat downstairs watching television by herself. It was as if he could not relate to her on her terms. He had no sympathy for her tears and loneliness. She missed our dogs and cats while at her father's house and asked him repeatedly for a pet. He promised he would get one when the time was right. Eventually Ana made friends in her father's subdivision. That helped her feel more comfortable at her father's home.

Ana had many health issues when she was small and they followed her into her youth. The healer we had gone to had made us painfully aware of diet and allergies. Mitch and I had monitored Ana's diet and exposure to different substances very carefully while we were together. However, after our separation it was as though he had a vendetta against anything that might harm his beloved daughter. I had been conscious of these issues while we were married, but felt I was more relaxed about it. The mother of Ana's girlfriend complained about Mitch's over protectiveness. It became so difficult to have Ana at her home for play dates because Mitch maintained her restrictive diet even at friends' houses. Our daughter's dietary restrictions became so overwhelming they finally stopped inviting Ana.

When Ana was at her father's she would return with complaints about her father buying two gallons of ice cream and giving her a small spoonful while sitting in front of her to eat the rest of the carton. She expressed to me that she wanted more and her father would not let her have it. When I mentioned this on several occasions Mitch denied that it happened. There were many occasions where Ana gave me one version and her father another. Ana complained that I believed him when he we lying to me. I knew that Mitch lied. The strange thing was that Ana always knew when he was lying. It was something that she came to accept about him.

Ana's brothers commented to me on separate occasions that we were both overprotective of her and sheltered her from normal life. They were concerned about how she would be able to assimilate with others especially as she got older. I took Ana with me almost everywhere. I involved her in the spiritual activities that I engaged in and she became very comfortable spending time in the presence of adults.

Ana came home crying from a friend's house after an interaction where a group of friends decided to play a game where they left her out. She stayed watching from the sidelines while they had fun ignoring and excluding her from their play. After thirty minutes of feeling uncomfortable being on the outside she finally said she wanted to go home. The kids expressed that she should stay even though they did not want to include her. When Ana told her father about the event he did not side with her, but made excuses for the friends instead. When the friends came by to ask if she was okay, her father told her friends, "Oh Ana is angry at the world!" leaving her feeling embarrassed. He did not take Ana's side in any interaction with friends. It did not matter what happened or what Ana did, he always sided with her friends not her. Ana did not feel her father had her back. Ana was a very sensitive child. She continued to have difficulty with interactions with friends. This highlighted the lack of support her father had for her. Ana had to apologize for events she felt she shouldn't have had to.

Mitch became friends with a divorced woman that lived in their neighborhood who worked during the day. He invited her daughter, Shannon, over to play with Ana. Shannon was a very unhappy child with her own set of issues. Mitch could not see Shannon pinch Ana when they drove in the truck. Ana would complain about what was going on and Shannon would deny it. Even after Ana's complaining it would not stop as Mitch did not do anything. When Ana upset Shannon, Shannon would kick Ana. If Ana kicked Shannon back Shannon kicked Ana ten times harder making her bleed. Mitch had no sympathy for Ana in these going-ons, taking Shannon's side. Ana wondered why he wanted to have shared custody of her because her father was so mean.

It became obvious that Ana was a weapon to use against me. Months after our separation Ana said she was the gun her father used to hurt me with. Mitch acted like Ana's friend to extract information about my love life and what was going on in my household. Then used the information against me. She was the pawn that could easily be manipulated and controlled. He used information and situations with Ana to hurt me. There were times when Ana used information to win the favor of her father also. She became adept at manipulation.

In her twelfth year he would dictate what she should eat. The healer that we had been going to had very strong opinions about food and allergies and continued to be very influential in Mitch's life. On one occasion Ana expressed that she wanted a hamburger in a restaurant. Her father told her she would need to eat coleslaw with the hamburger if she wanted one. She said she was all right with that. As soon as she agreed to the cole slaw he changed the rules. It seemed to Ana he just wanted to make her unhappy. She was told she had to eat chicken and vegetables. When the food arrived the food appeared tasteless and rubbery and Ana could not eat it. She said it felt like it had been microwaved. When she got home she was hungry. Her father erupted in rage about her not eating her food, even though it was not what she wanted to eat.

When Ana was getting ready to graduate from sixth grade she asked her father to buy her a year book. The students in her middle school were splitting up and going to three different schools. She would not be seeing many of them again. He told her he would not be buying one. She had recently hung up on him when she was at our house. She asked him if he was not buying the yearbook because she had not apologized. He responded that it was because of many different reasons. Ana asked, "Can I buy one for myself." He responded that she could. Then he went on to say, "Yes but they are $50.00. You don't have $50.00."

Ana spoke to her brother Matthew about the yearbook issue. She did not ask for a yearbook, but told him she wanted one but did not have $50.00. He said, "Oh you gotta have a yearbook. I'll chip in for your birthday with Mom." The day of Ana's birthday came and Mitch found out that Matthew and I had purchased a yearbook and he was furious. Apparently we were not allowed to buy it either because of what he had told Ana. I did not remember it that way. I remembered hearing it was all right for Ana to purchase one if she came up with the money. The facts were manipulated and I felt confused. Before we all got together at a local Italian restaurant to celebrate he called Matthew and reamed him over the phone. He was so angry that Matthew would undermine his authority and really let Matthew have it. I received a similar phone call. I honestly did not remember agreeing that I would not buy a yearbook because Ana had been disrespectful to her father. It felt like this was an inappropriate way to discipline her since after the school year she could not get one. I remembered hearing that Ana could get it if she had the money.

When we met up at the restaurant Matthew took Ana aside and told her off right before her birthday dinner. He was furious because he felt that Ana had duped him and used him to get a yearbook. He told her he could never trust her ever again because it felt like she had tricked him. Ana was in tears and continued to be upset throughout her special family birthday dinner. I had invited Mitch to join us; this was the last family birthday dinner we invited him to.

Ana continued to hold back tears and I ended yelling at her during the dinner because she was so defensive and upset throughout dinner. I knew she was angry and upset, but I believed her father, because he was an adult. I too felt like I had been manipulated. The master manipulator is one who can cast doubt so that you don't remember the facts clearly. Matthew and I were both angry with the wrong person. To this day Ana has sadness and tears about her twelfth birthday. It was a very painful experience.

Ana's often repeated refrain regarding her father was, "You believed him?" She had told me repeatedly that he lied about the facts and how events really occurred.

I used the time that Ana was with her father to do introspection and meditate. I spent the week quietly reflecting about the past years and writing in my journal. I read self-help books voraciously. The first nine months following our separation I focused on healing and growth. I had taken extensive hypnotherapy training while Mitch and I were still married and became a certified hypnotherapist. I attended workshops to learn other healing methods so that I could work on myself instead of relying on others to heal me.

On November 1, 2003, I attended the drum-making workshop in North Georgia where I met John. Had we been living in another state it might have been different. In Georgia sleeping with another man in the presence of a minor-aged child was a big no-no. Had I been a drug addict or raging alcoholic I might have fared better than I did with this damning evidence. My attorney told me that if I continued to pursue full custody I could lose any custodial rights I might have received. Our first divorce hearing was four days after John's death. I was in no state to fight.

We returned to court the following summer. My attorney had advised me we did not need character witnesses. Alan had volunteered to fly over from England to attend our hearing to speak about the abuse he had witnessed. My attorney said it was not necessary. When we showed up in court I found my ex-sister-in-law, Ana's favorite second grade teacher who had also tutored her in math, as well as the healer Mitch and I had been going to together for the past three years. They were all present to speak on Mitch's behalf and against me. I could understand Mitch's sister, but the other two were really low blows. I had selected our healer. I continued to send her clients on a regular basis and was still a client of hers. Obviously Mitch had something I didn't. I sat alone with my attorney while Mitch and his crew sat together. I was obviously upset by the imbalance and the unpreparedness of my own legal defense. Miss Barton sat in the waiting room for twenty minutes or so and then got up abruptly and walked over to me. She spoke softly so that the others could not hear. "Jennifer, I feel terrible about what they are trying to do to you. I cannot do this, I know how Ana feels about you and that she wants to live with you. I am going home."

Mitch was running his own defense. He had everything carefully planned out. The two attorneys conferred after reading the guardian ad litem report. My attorney recommended shared custody with no child support. I was crushed. How could this be? I was a good and loving mother. My daughter clearly wanted to live with me. I was devastated. My attorney advised if I attempted to pursue full custody with the witnesses Mitch had I could lose what custody I had. He recommended that I not risk it. The guardian ad litem had recommended that if someone should have full custody it should be the father! When Mitch said he did not want to write me a check each month for Ana's after-school care and summer camp, my attorney took me aside and suggested I write the check to Mitch. I could not believe how this was going. So not only did I not receive full custody, I had to pay Mitch child support each month. Mitch got everything he wanted. Ana did not. When Mitch got home he said nothing to Ana about the custody. He waited and let me tell her the following week.

I knew that I needed to have the time I did with John. He had to meet Ana. Ana was completely aware that they had past lives together. She felt a deep connection with him as I had. The relationship with John had a cost. I was rocked to my core that I did not win full custody. Ana was devastated. She could not understand why the court system would work this way and not take a child's wishes into account. She was angry and frustrated and yelled that she needed to talk to the judge. "Why didn't anyone listen to what I said?" Not being heard became a constant theme when Ana was with her father.

Each week we alternated and Ana spent Monday afternoon through the following Monday with one parent and the following week we switched. Ana frequently asked to see me mid week because she missed me. I would drop everything to visit at Mitch's with her for an hour or so and hug her as I left. Ana felt that the years we had the 50/50 custody arrangement were the worst time of her life. She was miserable and Mitch did not seem to care. When she cried because she missed me he lost patience with her and yelled at her for crying. Not being able to cry made her intensely angry. He would send her to her room to settle down.

Sometimes Ana would miss me so much during the week that she would call me when I was dropping my crew off and ask if I could stop by and see her. I would have to ask Mitch first, because if I made any plans without consulting him he would become very angry with me. After making arrangements with Mitch to stop by and see Ana I headed in that direction. Within two minutes of me arriving at his house he called me back and said that he discovered that Ana had lied about doing her homework and she was not allowed to see me. He had not told Ana of this and she overheard our conversation. I could hear her in the background, "No, Dad, no! I need to see Mom!" Then I heard her become hysterical in the background. He quickly excused himself from the phone to tend to Ana. I could not believe he would be so heartless. It seemed as if he wanted to torture her. He would not even let me stop by for a minute.

This dangling carrot theme continued. Every so often Ana would muster the courage to tell her father she missed me, we would set something up and our visit was jerked out from under her for some reason. Ana felt hatred and rage towards her father.

There were many issues about the shared custody that burned me. I had to work with Mitch who I could barely talk to without one or both of us getting thoroughly pissed off. For several years it felt to me that Ana and I would just get into the rhythm of being together and then it was time for Ana to go to her father's. Projects and tests became difficult because the week I did not have Ana with me I was not in the school loop. The following week I would have to play catch up and get up to speed on what I missed. Ana had difficulty in school. Teachers felt that she had attention deficit disorder. I think I would have ADD if I had to pack my stuff up every other week and move to another location every Monday. Sometimes Ana would get to school and realize she had left something at our house. Or I would pick her up on the Monday that was my week and we would have to go back to her father's to get a project or a book she needed for school. The only ones that benefited from the shared custody were the parents. We both had a full week without Ana to do whatever we wished. Ana was the one that suffered the most.

In the seven years following my divorce, I vacillated between dating occasionally to periods of solitude and isolation. Other than work and having my daughter with me every other week I did not get out much. There were long periods when I shut down sexually and did not even dream about sex. I wondered at times if I would ever become sexually active again. I questioned myself constantly while processing my past relationship difficulties on whether I was meant to be in a relationship ever again. During one two-year period I did not date at all. I still carried shame regarding my three divorces and really did not want to have to explain my journey and my past relationship difficulties to anyone on a simple coffee date.

I felt a deep sadness about leaving the Birmingham Road property but rationalized that it was best for me to try to get past the memories that were in the house. We moved to a small rental house on a property less than two miles away that was hidden from the road and surrounded by a thick forest of mature hardwoods. I needed to heal; I wanted to be away from everybody and everything. This property allowed me to do just that. I became reclusive in many ways.

I wrapped my truck with a digitized photograph that I took from a landscaping project I did in Atlanta. The butterflies, daffodils and pansies stood out and were strikingly beautiful. The wrap transformed my truck to a billboard on wheels. People thought I had a slew of trucks as I did so much driving. My phone number and web site were listed on the back and sides. There was no mistaking what industry I was in, and I certainly could not hide. It was the only vehicle I owned and I drove it everywhere. I helped design a new logo with a caterpillar changing into a butterfly. It marked the transformation I knew my soul was going through. The logo represented my life. It was so me. I loved my truck's new look and told my truck that every day. The color and design was stunning. It was one of the first digitized wraps in the area and I was complemented everywhere I went. I even had people want to buy photos of my work for their own vehicles.

Mitch expressed his disdain for my purchase of the truck wrap. It seemed to him that I should be spending that money on our daughter instead of my business. I paid him $142.00 a month for summer camp and the after-school program for Ana. The $142 a month more than covered Ana's camp, after-school program and her back-to-school supplies with a fair amount left over. Each time I went to court for anything with Mitch, I ended up with my face in the dirt. It did not matter what I said or did; I lost. I took him back to court as I had come up with the dollar amount thinking I would be the one that would get it. I padded it to cover a few extras. When I took Mitch back to court to get the amount reduced the mediator had me step outside the room and made a private deal with Mitch in my absence. I felt duped. The amount was increased to $150 a month. Since we had shared custody this money was meant only to cover the weekly after-school program and her YMCA camp in the summer time. I felt defeated and that Mitch had some super power over me. I was in such fear of him and what he could do to me. I lay awake at night worrying. I was late paying Mitch for support and he was not happy.

My work with Pamela, the healer in New Mexico, was deep. She channeled some old-world master that I had never heard of before. It did not matter to me. What did matter was that the information she gave me opened doors to my psyche that I had not looked at previously. She told me that I needed to learn from Mitch. I needed to learn to speak in the moment, and not be in such fear. She also said that I needed to shore up my boundaries and Mitch was the best one to learn to do it with. She went on to say that he and I both spoke "at" Ana and not "to" her. I took the information she gave me to heart. I mentioned what she said to Mitch, but he discounted it because she was not the healer of record with him. He thought his healer walked on water. He constantly quoted verbatim things his healer said to him. When I learned my healer was doing a retreat in India I signed up. I had been dreaming of traveling to India for 30 years. This was my chance to do so safely.

I realized that this longing in my soul for permanence and love was not outside of me, but within me. I made a long awaited trip to India on a retreat. The two weeks I spent there were life altering. I realized while I was there that I wanted to focus on healing and spirituality and do my landscaping as an adjunct.

Mitch did not want me to go to India. He made it clear that there were other and better ways I could be spending my money. On April 15, 2006 I got a ride to the airport. Planet Mercury was in retrograde. Mercury rules travel, communications, computers and agreements. Traveling during a Mercury retrograde can result in missed or cancelled flights and lost luggage.

I happily made my way through security and to the gate destined for Chicago on American Airlines. A group of Americans were meeting at the gate in Chicago to take our flight to Delhi together. The other attendees from Europe and Australia would meet us in India. I had an hour or so to connect or I would miss my flight to India. After sitting at the gate waiting to board for what seemed over long, the ground crew at the gate announced that our flight had been cancelled. I knew if I did not get on another flight immediately I would miss my flight to India. Only because I ran to the ticket counter did I manage to be the last person allowed on the only flight going to Chicago that would make my connection because of a fluke. When I arrived in India with our tour, my checked luggage was missing. I spent the first 5 days there without clothes and only what I carried in my backpack. It was an interesting experience, causing me to realize that our attachment to our "things" is holding us back. Having nothing can be very freeing. It creates a vacuum that Spirit loves to fill. I was waiting to be filled.

I found India to be a place of beauty and wonder. I wondered how so many people could live in such small places. We ate nothing but vegetarian Indian food for two weeks and I was in heaven. The weather was hot and humid. We abided by the native culture and wore modest clothing, our shoulders and upper arms covered. Our travel in the country was tiring and long. The bus rides were exciting dodging Brahman cattle in the road as well as huge potholes and rickshaws. We stayed at five-star resorts wherever possible. The colors and vendors lining the streets and the people we saw were fascinating. I was shocked to see how many people slept in doorways and on the sidewalks at night. Tent cities housed thousands in the city center.

I was very interested to see people sweeping the streets with makeshift brooms. There were beggars. Whenever we disembarked from our bus we were rushed by men, women and children that wanted us to buy their wares. It was difficult to say no. There were so many poor and hungry.

We traveled the northern part of India from Delhi to Varanasi. Rising at 4:00 a.m. we took a rickshaw ride to the holy River Ganges. We had to walk single file through the narrow passages leading to the "ghat" or ceremonial bathing places. After being blessed by a Brahman priest we took a boat ride on the river. Leaving diyas (small candles) on floating leaves to bless all of our ancestors and loved ones that had crossed over. Looking back towards the shore the color and people bathing there was breathtaking to watch. I felt like I had gone back 200 years.

The people of India were incredibly polite and welcoming. I was amazed at how little most people had. They did not have bookshelves and closets filled with choices. They ate little and needed even less. Many people used cow dung instead of a stove to cook their food. They would dry it neatly in stacks that resembled haystacks back home. Once dry it could be burned. Everything was used, nothing wasted. I thought about the way we lived back home and the amount of food most of us living in the United States throw in the trash each day. It is so disgustingly wasteful.

We visited temples in many different places. My favorite was the Hanuman Temple. Bells of all sizes filled this temple. After the ceremony was completed the bell ringing began. Anyone who could reach the brass bells hanging from the ceiling was able to ring them. Each person rang the bell with his or her soul. By the time the twenty minute or so cacophony ended my whole body was vibrating and I knew my energy had been cleared and cleansed. I could not move or walk; I was smiling from ear to ear for the next ten minutes while I continued to be bathed in this amazing energy. Who needs drugs or alcohol when you can feel this way from a bell?

There was very little I did not enjoy about the trip. The twelve of us got along for the most part. I enjoyed meeting other people from around the world who were so much like me in so many ways. We exchanged healing energies with a couple of people who wished to do so. What I was surprised about was the woman who was our tour leader, Pamela. She claimed to be channeling Sanat Kumara. (An advance being, regarded as Lord of Earth and founder of the Great White Brotherhood.) I found it interesting that she commented in a catty way to me that my shoes and lipstick did not match my clothing. I was not sure what she had hoped to illicit from me with these types of judgmental comments. After the trip was over and I wrote my critique of the trip I mentioned that her ego seemed to get in the way. She replied that my neediness was distracting. I wondered why she attempted to needle me. I thought it was very strange, lacking compassion and love. It reminded me of John's very astute musing that metaphysical people can be the most derisive.

I began working on my inner being in earnest after John's death. I knew I had some challenges to work through. Issues kept surfacing with Mitch. I was still fighting with him and trying to get full custody of our daughter. She was so unhappy with the every other week visitation. She cried every Monday morning when she had to go back to his house.

My two-week retreat of idyllic bliss was shattered upon my return from India. The IRS had garnished my bank accounts and I had many business challenges to unwind. The young man I had hired to run the crew had been irregular with his work. I lost five big clients upon my return as well.

As Mitch and I worked together to make the situation work with our daughter we found ourselves at events together at the school. Sometimes we would attend a chorus concert of Ana's and afterward she would ask for all of us to go out for ice cream. We did this for several years. We recognized that we still had feelings for one another and even attempted a reconciliation several times. After seeing each other for a short while I felt that we seemed to be slipping back into old patterns. I made some attempts to work through the issues, but we seemed to end up against a wall. One or both of us felt compromised in some way and things just did not work out. One thing was for sure, we both loved our daughter and we still had feelings for one another. I don't believe you can have a child and spend eleven years with someone and truly hate him when it is over. The anger covers up the love that is underneath.

As we were attempting to get back together, Mitch and I had a strange exchange. He asked that I stop by his house to talk before I picked Ana up from school. I explained to him I needed to go and that I had made arrangements to pick her up early. He asked if I sent Ana to school with a note this morning. I told him I had not. He discounted that it was possible to pick her up early because I always had to have a note. He told me that they would not allow me to pick up a student with just a phone call. He coerced me upstairs and before I knew it he had me upstairs in his bedroom. I really felt anxious about picking up Ana. He assured me that I could not pick her up early without a note. I gave in. I heard my cell phone ringing, he told me to ignore it. When Mitch's phone rang I thought with horror, "It's Ana." Sure enough the school had tried both of our phones. Ana was sitting in the office waiting for me to pick her up. I could not trust him. Ana was not his first priority even though he insisted she was. He came first. I quickly pulled myself together and ran out the door to the school. I would not make the same mistake again. He apologized after he realized that Ana was waiting for me in the office. It was too late. She was sitting there wondering where I was.

I called my previous landlord, Scott Baldwin, about moving back into the farm on Birmingham Road. He said he thought his tenants were moving but was not sure when. He would keep me posted. I signed a contract and was in the bank getting my security deposit for a new rental home when Scott called me and said I could move back in. I laughed at how things happened. I could not back out on the lease I had already signed. I moved again after two years in the small house in the woods, to a subdivision with covenants. Although my daughter loved being in a subdivision, it was not for me. My soul did not thrive there and I was constantly written up for having my landscape trailer parked on the street.

Three years after my initial move from the farm, Scott called me and asked me to return as a tenant. The house had been empty for over a year and it was listed for sale. He made me an offer in exchange for showing the property. He would give me a lump sum should it sell while I was living there. It seemed like a good deal to me. I missed the property, the huge oak and maple trees and the beautiful rolling pasture. I felt so connected to the land and the house, like I was the keeper of the property. I had been regularly mowing the grass for Scott, so it was not much of a stretch for me to move back in. I was excited to be back. Any sadness that was left I now knew how to clear effortlessly. That would not be a problem, I thought.

We made several deals concerning the old house and property before I moved in. In lieu of my last month's rent, Scott wanted me to paint the entire house. He got a good deal because my rent was $1,500 a month. I had to pay my Hispanic workers to assist and Alan flew over to help me out as well as move from one location to the other. Mitch was comfortable having Alan sleep in the house with Ana as he knew that we had a purely platonic relationship. Alan worked like a dog painting the lattice on the porch and making repairs to the woodwork that was rotting. He wanted the house to look good for me. While he was visiting he also put in a stone patio around the back that completed an area that had been an ugly eyesore.

Shortly after Alan returned to England I fought for full custody of Ana. I had never given up the hope that she would have her wish and live with me full time. This time I was prepared. At our first hearing Mitch requested that they investigate me and do a psychological evaluation on my daughter and me. I did my research. I got letters of personal character reference from twenty friends and business associates and put together a book with photographs and a biography of my boys and me for the court appointed psychologist. Ana and I were both interviewed. I was tested, as was Mitch. What was surprising to me was that she used a Rorschach inkblot test. I had done my research and found that many professionals were up in arms about the use of this test for child custody cases because the findings were unreliable. Apparently most reputable psychologists felt that the Rorschach test was dangerously misleading at worst. Those that continued to use this test argued among themselves as to the meaning and even its validity. The fact that this test was being used was mind-boggling to me. If I refused to submit to the test I had no hope of winning full custody.

When I had my first interview I felt judged by the psychologist and found out later that Mitch had managed to get in before I did, even though I called her first. I did not know how he did it. Trying to figure it out was futile. At my second interview when I mentioned something about Mitch's family and his father beating his mother I could tell she did not believe what I was saying. In the final report she cited my family of origin as being the reason I should not be given full custody. What could be worse than a father who drank himself to death, who was a sex addict and beat his wife. Not to mention that his father had a second family in another town and Mitch's brother committed murder?

My attorney told me the result of the psychologist's report. I asked if I could have a copy. She said that they were only for legal counsel. When I heard that Mitch had a copy I was furious. How had he gotten his? Mitch must have lied to have my family of origin sited and not his. I went home and told my daughter I had spent my last money on attorneys. I would no longer fight to get custody of her. If she wanted to take it up with her father she was free to do so, I was surrendering. I was spent literally and figuratively. I had gotten a Target credit card and put my attorney's fee on that. I was spending money I did not have and ending up face down in the dirt every time.

When I told Ana we did not win she was angry. She knew her father had lied. The amazing thing is how others believed him. He sounded so calm and laid back in his interview making me sound like I was not. Being honest is not the way to win in the court system in Georgia.

I told Mitch in an e-mail that I was not going to fight with him any longer. He did not get it. I stopped reacting to the things he said. I let events slide by when I knew he was lying. I stopped standing up for Ana. I let go. I even told God I was done fighting. I had given away my power and my energy. I had other things to focus on. Ana and I made the best of the situation and had fun while we were together. I organized family gatherings taking into account Ana's schedule and making sure she would be able to attend. Although there was a 12-year age difference between her youngest brother, Matthew, and her they remained close. Whenever Adam had a runway show or a benefit we attended together to support her older brother. She was always thrilled when he showed up for her school events leaving her girlfriends squealing with delight. Ana was very proud of both of her brothers and pleased that they supported her as well.

We enjoyed family parties in the pasture having bonfires and wiener roasts in our pasture with the boys and their friends as well. We always took crazy pictures for her albums.

When I called Mitch to tell him that I was getting married to Jessie I could tell he was surprised. I asked if Ana could attend our wedding even though it was during one of his weekends to have her. A month after our wedding Ana was very upset because she and her father had to move out of their rental house which was about ten minutes away. Building had really slowed down and Mitch had not had any projects for some time. He was careful with his money, but it would only go so far. His sister let them both move in with her for six months. I did not complain or give Mitch a hard time about his move. I said nothing when it came time for Ana to go back to school and had to make a forty-five minute drive to and from school from her aunt's house. I knew that Mitch was doing the best he could. I let it go. I knew that the drive was hard on Ana and made her day longer. She mentioned it a couple of times, but really did not complain.

On Monday, January 25, 2010, a day I will never forget as long as I live, I received a call from Mitch after he dropped Ana at school. He asked me if I still wanted to have Ana live with me full time. I said, "I do!" He replied that he figured that was the case. Right before they got to school, Mitch asked his daughter the same question. She said she still wanted to live with me also. He said, "Starting today you can live with your mother full time." He told me that he and his sister had a deal that he could live in her house for six months and no longer. It was right at six months. He said he had to move into a place where he would not be able to have Ana overnight. I did not ask any questions. I just expressed my gratitude. I was absolutely overjoyed. I got off the phone after saying my prayer of thanks and I cried. This had been one hell of a ride. Ana never gave up her dream and seven years later she got her wish.

That afternoon when Ana got home she walked in the door and hugged me. We both held each other and cried. We were both so filled with joy and gratitude that finally after all the anguish and the upset and lugging her stuff back and forth she could be at peace and have one home.

I found it amazing that when I totally surrendered everything fell into place. I had to laugh at myself and all the time, energy and money I spent fighting Mitch. I did not realize that if I fought him he would have to fight back. Once I stopped and gave it all up, everything lined up beautifully.

Since that day I have encouraged Mitch to have time with Ana. I have asked him to stay at our apartment when I have had a conference to attend, or an out of town healing to do. We have come to terms with the fact that we both love our daughter. Mitch loved her enough to fight for her, more than once.

It took almost a year, but Ana finally had the conversation with her father. She told him she forgave him for not giving her what she wanted. She told him she had been angry with him for a long time. She expressed to him that she understood that he loved her and was doing what he felt was best for both of them. This was a very powerful moment for both of them. I applaud her for her grace and maturity at fourteen years old. It is to her credit that she was able to let go of her years of suffering, hurt and anger and had the spiritual maturity to be able to come to this place with her father.

At first Mitch did not make a Herculean effort to see Ana. I think he felt she did not want to see him. After the first two months of sporadic visits I recommended to both of them that they spend more time together and have a special day and plan to do something together each week. I have let go of all my judgment of Mitch. He loves his daughter and wants the best for her. Since I have had two other children I have a tendency to not want to spend time looking up our daughter's test results on line to see how she is doing every week. Mitch is far better at the detail than I am. It is not that I don't care; I would rather Ana tell me how she is doing with school.

We both continue to support Ana together in her schooling and cross-country running. On some occasions we have driven together to her meets. We both know we still love each other and we always will. How can you spend ten years of your life living with someone and have a child together and not love him? We may not always agree but in the end we both want the same thing, for our family to be safe, protected and given the guidance that they need.

LESSONS LEARNED

Adam and Matthew continue to call Mitch from time to time. Mitch gave Matthew and Andrea a wedding gift, although he was not invited to the wedding. For years after our divorce he continued to give the boys birthday cards and Christmas gifts. When you let go of the anger, you are able to feel the foundation of love underneath.

Mitch has been one of my most powerful teachers. For many years after our divorce I was plagued by victim energy. I blamed him for everything. I have learned that by changing our perspective we can look at the same story and see something very different. Mitch has mirrored my pain and suffering back to me. He showed me my lack of respect and low self-esteem. It is impossible to have a successful relationship when you are not happy with yourself. If you cannot be alone and happy with yourself how can you ever be happy with anyone?

When I met Mitch I was empty, expecting someone else to fill me up. I did not feel whole. I felt broken and wanted someone to fix me. I felt that being with a man completed me. I realize now that another can never fill you up. Someone else cannot fix you. There is really nothing wrong with us. It is just our perception coming from the unconscious mind.

There are no mistakes. Marrying Mitch was not one of them. Ana was the gift of our relationship. Had Mitch not come into our lives, Matthew and Adam would not be who they are today. They needed to have the experience they had just as I had to have my experience. They both grew into beautiful, loving, compassionate men. Matthew has become a loving and mature husband. He taught me that without risking it all you could never have true love. "You have to put yourself out there, Mother," he told me. Adam makes friends with everyone he meets and always helps the underdog. I am pleased and grateful that they chose me to be their mother in this lifetime. It has been an amazing honor to be a parent to all three of my beautiful children. I know that Mitch's presence in our lives has also helped to build the character in all of our children.

When Ana and I moved into our little apartment we had just lost everything at the old farmhouse due to mold contamination. Nothing could be moved into our new place without contaminating the apartment. Mitch offered to loan me beds and furniture. We have come a long way from that day in November when we first met. I accepted his offer to use his furniture. My ego is quiet. It no longer runs the show. I follow my guidance in every breath and every step I take. I am grateful for the gifts that Mitch has offered my family and me.

Vibration on January 25, 2010: 700

Life Force on January 25 2010: 100% (Notice how joy effects your life force)

CHAPTER TEN

Make Believe Soul Mates

I received the sign that I was ready to date in December 2008. It was an internal feeling of completeness as well as the small, still voice inside saying, "It is time." Nothing was broken or missing in me. The emptiness and loneliness that always plagued me, even while in a relationship, was gone. I knew that as long as I had a physical body I would be working on myself and there would always be issues. The bottom line was I was really happy with me. I was comfortable and happy being alone. I did not need to have a man in my life. If I had to be alone the rest of my life, I was okay with that. I was happy either way.

The friends and family who loved and supported me without negativity and judgment were still in my life. The ones who did not fell away naturally. Some of the changes were very painful. My deep connection with Spirit had gotten me to this place. I never felt completely alone. The end result was I was loved and supported just the way I was.

I revised my list of characteristics I wanted in my partner several times over the past seven years. On a sunny fall afternoon while getting my hair highlighted, I waited for my hairdresser and picked up a magazine that caught my eye. The cover had a headline about writing a list of 100 attributes that you wanted in a man. Apparently the author was very successful with this exercise. She wrote, if you really wanted to attract the partner of your dreams you needed to write a list of 100 items that you wanted in him. It needed to be very detailed, down to the minutest of things. Once complete the instructions were to file it away and not refer to it constantly. I had done something similar and revised my own list at least three times as I evolved. My final list contained 100 very detailed descriptors describing everything from must have a deep love for his children to height, weight, eye color, good singing voice and must be spiritual.

I love my children very deeply and wanted someone who understood how I felt and did not feel threatened by my relationships. I like to travel and read so I wanted someone who would enjoy doing those things with me. I am very young for my age and I wanted someone who was active like me, and would rather be outdoors participating in activities than sitting inside watching sports. It was also important to me that I would be free to go on spiritual retreats and spend time with my friends — both male and female.

I am a Scorpio. We Scorpios have quite a reputation for being the most sexual sign of the Zodiac. My love life up to this point had been disappointing and unfulfilling. I wanted to have a man who loved sex, for sure, but was a kind, considerate and caring lover. He needed to be someone who did not put his needs or desires first all the time. Being in my mid fifties myself, I wanted someone who would want to make love to me, naturally, without the need for Viagra or other stimulants.

I am in the landscaping trade because of my love of nature. I feel strongly connected to the earth, plants and trees. I desired someone who shared my passion for nature and the earth. I have heard horror stories about women who attracted men and had to buy vehicles for their men. I definitely knew I did not want that, so I included in my list that my partner would have several vehicles. I listed three.

I wanted someone who was talented and handy with tools, as my Dad was a very good carpenter himself. He built his own home and changed his own brakes and oil. I saw how wonderful it was that he could fix anything without having to call a service person. Not only does it save money, but also putting your own energy into a home or vehicle made a huge difference in how the home and vehicle feels. The house I lived in was beautiful, quirky and very old. It needed constant repairs and maintenance. Having a man who was handy would be a very good thing.

Speaking of tools, being a landscaper means I have loads of power equipment. I always wished that I could learn how to service my own equipment instead of having to pay someone to do it for me. This was another area where I really needed to have a man that was good with tools.

I wanted someone who would be a good role model for my kids. I wanted a man of integrity, who could commit, and wanted a monogamous relationship as I did. I wanted a relationship with a man who I could become completely vulnerable with and grow more in love with every day. I wanted a man who was deeply spiritual and accepting of me as I am with all my foibles and flaws. I wanted a man of strong character who was comfortable in his own skin. I wanted a man who knew who he was and loved himself.

I also wrote a detailed account of what I desired in a relationship in my journal. I wanted a relationship that would enable me to grow. I knew in my heart that I wanted to have a true partner; someone to walk beside me who would enhance my life in every way.

On January 2, 2009, my daughter and I created vision boards together. I purchased a couple of bride and fashion magazines as well as some poster board in bright orange. Three weeks earlier my friend, Pam Leinmiller, invited me to a Christmas networking party where Charlene Hicks, a well-known medium and trained psychic, was speaking. Pam knew of my metaphysical interests and had a strong intuitive feeling that I was meant to attend for some reason. Pam has a strong faith and hears the voice of God. She acted on her intuition and I listened.

Charlene spoke at great length of her years of study and that she was one of the few psychics in Atlanta to have taken the formal psychic boards on being a medium. That was something I never knew existed. She also spoke about the power of doing a vision board and then putting it out to the Universe in order to manifest what you wanted. I had done one once before, but her way of doing the vision board was slightly different. She told us if we followed her directions it would be very powerful. She gave us all orange-colored handouts. I was sure to take mine home with me. I knew this was something I needed to do and I put mine in my purse.

Charlene told us to draw a large X on the whole page dividing your poster board into four quadrants. The top quadrant is the relationship portion. The right side represents rest, relaxation, health and fitness. The bottom portion represents money and work. The final quadrant represents home and family life.

In the middle of the poster board I pasted a photo of a big fluffy white cloud that symbolized God to me. Just in case God and the Universe didn't understand my depiction, I wrote "God" in magic marker underneath the picture. That way there was no doubt. God is the center of my world and the One that will bring my man into being.

Next, above my cloud, I placed a recent photo of myself. I picked one my son Matthew had taken of me looking really hot at a cancer benefit called Fashionata in Atlanta. The memory of that night always brings a smile to my face, as all my children were there. Adam was modeling, Matthew, Ana, and I were there to see Adam in the show. We were all dressed up and had a really fun time. I was wearing a slinky, sexy dress and smiling. I wanted a picture of me feeling good. The one I picked was perfect for what I wanted to put out to the Universe.

Around the photo of me, in the relationship section, I cut out some words that were meaningful to me and pasted them here and there. I used positive phrases like "Fabulous at any age," and "The new me." I had done years of work on myself and I was different. In the top right hand corner I pasted a picture of a bride and groom embracing one another, outdoors with a beautiful sunset behind them. To the left of me I pasted a photo of Viggo Mortensen, Whom I adored in the movie "Hidalgo." He was handsome to me in a rugged sort of way and definitely the outdoorsy type. I wanted someone who depicted what I wanted in a man. He was vitally healthy, handsome and unshaven in his picture. I thought it was a really sexy picture.

On the right side representing rest, relaxation and fitness, I used some healthy-looking people doing yoga. I added some encouraging words and a photo of a favorite place, the Taj Mahal, because I would like to travel there again.

The rest of the poster board was not as important as the relationship portion, but I went through the motions as directed by Charlene Hicks. The bottom of the poster board was you in the world and money. I used gold bullion here. Until now I had struggled financially and wanted to do better in this area. I also cut out some words, pasting encouragement for me, "You can do it!" On the left side I pasted a horse and a house, which represented the farm I was renting. I had always dreamed of buying it, even though it seemed out of reach.

I said a fervent prayer, "Creator, I am ready for my Divine Partner. I am open and ready to receive. Send him to me now." I said, "Thank you, God." Giving thanks affirmed that it is done. After my prayer, I visualized what my life would be like with my beloved. I envisioned us together, deeply committed to one another, with unconditional love. I saw us being whole and separate individuals walking side by side, totally accepting of each other as we were. I felt the joy and happiness that my daughter and I would have. I saw her and me, feeling safe and secure. I envisioned family gatherings with all our children present, filled with joy, laughter and love. I saw my older children really enjoying this man, wanting to spend time with us and knowing that he and I were really in love and happy. I saw Ana and this handsome man having fun together, teasing each other, and being playful. I saw my daughter supported and loved by both of us. I also felt the joy of her successes in school and in her life. I saw her living with us full time. I saw us purchasing the home and property I was renting and my neighbor and landlord really connecting with and liking my partner.

I felt the joy and the love deeply in this vision without any doubts, without any buts.

When you pray fervently (or with emotion), you are sending out your desires to the Universe with power. The emotion gives your prayer wings. You let the prayer go and wait. I no longer did the push-pull thing with God, that I had done previously where I said out of fear, "I want a partner, no I don't, I want a partner, I want a partner, no I don't" almost in the same sentence. I was not in fear anymore.

Your prayers are always answered, just not in our time frame. I had no expectation as to how long it would take. I really did not give it much thought. Once I released my prayer and vision I let it go.

I did not go back and revise, or say, "and one more thing…." I moved onto the next issue at hand. On the physical plane it was time to work on my home.

My bedroom closet is very small. My house was built over 80 years ago and people did not have the wardrobes that most of us do now. I read an article in a magazine once that if you wanted to have a partner in your life you needed to make room for them as if they were already there. I began making room for my partner in my life. I cleaned out my closet and made enough room for a couple of pairs of pants and maybe a shirt or two to hang alongside my own. I sorted through my clothes and made a pile to donate to Goodwill. I went through my dressers and eliminated clothes that I rarely wore. I also removed all the extra pillows from my bed leaving only the ones that we would sleep on.

I studied feng shui for 15 years and used it every day in my landscaping business. Like anything else, what you do every day for your customers you rarely do for yourself. I had not really looked at the way I lived in my own residence. I knew that we all had patterns in our homes. I wondered what these patterns said about me. I began really looking at my furniture and pictures on the walls. Did I have pictures with one flower, or one tree that was a reflection of my life? If I wanted to have a partner, I must change some things in my home.

The first thing I did was to start on the outside. I purchased a pair of ceramic chickens at Home Depot. They were different colors so that they looked enough like one could be a rooster (in my mind anyway). I made sure that they sat side by side, touching each other in my flowerbed near my front porch.

Next, I looked at the configuration of furniture on my front porch. I had a pair of white rocking chairs as well as a few white wicker chairs. Looking at the chairs on my front porch, I analyzed. Did it look inviting? Did it look like there was a happy couple living here? What I determined was that there was too much space between the chairs to symbolize an intimate couple sitting in them. Without purchasing anything new, I moved the chairs around so that the two rocking chairs were in close proximity to one another, as if an intimate couple was sitting in them. The other chairs I arranged to sit opposite each other for conversation with another couple. The adage "as without, so within" came to mind. The outside had to reflect what I wanted inside.

I knew from past experience, that I could only make one big feng shui change every two weeks. This is very important to note. A pillow can be moved or a picture, but major furniture changes need to be done with time in between. Just because you can't see anything happening doesn't mean nothing is going on. Energy needs time to settle.

In December I found a feng shui article on the Internet. This article stated if you were a single woman and wanted to have a man in your life, you needed to have two night tables in your bedroom. The tables did not need to match. The goal is one on either side of the bed. This was an eye opener for me. I walked from room to room looking for any physical signs that reflected my inner life. What I found was very revealing.

In every room of my house I had only one end table. Starting in my living room and walking through each room to my family room, my bedroom, and even my daughter's room there was only one end table in every room. My bedroom was small, yet it contained a California king-size bed. The bed nearly filled the room. When I moved into my house, I realized that only one end table would fit comfortably in my room or the bedroom door would scrape the night table on the other side of the bed. This is not good feng shui. I felt at the time it was better to use the table somewhere else then leave it where there was friction, as it can create conflict within the household. So I shelved the idea of having two night tables and moved the second one out to the family room. I never thought consciously that the end tables were a reflection of my wanting to be alone. This observation was cathartic in itself.

The simple furniture inventory brought me to the realization that I thought I had wanted someone in my life all these years, yet the outer reflection of me (all my furniture) told the truth. I really didn't. I had so much fear of recreating another bad relationship that I was reeling against one with all my might. The outer (furniture) told the truth which I previously had been in denial about. My commitment to myself was to have integrity in all my relationships including my relationship with me. If I can't tell myself the truth, how can I expect a partner to tell me the truth?

This was huge for me. I had to really look at all areas of my life where I was still lying to myself. This was definitely what so many people call an "aha moment." I did not like this. It meant more inner work to do. I was not afraid of doing the work. Having uncovered such a big piece of the puzzle was both exciting and disheartening all at the same time. It meant I was getting that much closer to who I really was and what my unconscious mind was thinking. I had to be much more diligent. Being in denial was not good. I had to look at all areas of my life where I was in denial. This took time and effort. I wrote in my journal, analyzed, and really held my feet to the fire on this one.

When we are in denial and dating someone, we ignore red flags that protect us. We may see a sign that the other person gives us of whom he is and ignore it. That is what I did all my life. I saw a bunch of red flags and thought it must be a parade. These can't really be red flags! Ignoring signs that we get about other people is not healthy. Thinking that an issue that crops up is a one-time thing, or that the person will change is dangerous. A dear friend of mine has repeated this quote to me numerous times, "If someone shows you who they are, trust that." In other words, you have witnessed a behavior that you do not like. They are not going to change. You are not imagining the issue.

I recognized that my boundaries were not healthy because of my childhood. I have to be very diligent and aware when someone is crossing my boundaries as I have a history of not noticing. As soon as I notice someone has stepped across a boundary, I have to make the correction instantly and stop it from happening again. Awareness is the first step in making a change. Not doing anything to stop your boundary from being crossed is unhealthy. It creates more codependency and the enabling piece of a relationship. This was something I could not ignore.

I looked at my relationships with my children, especially with my oldest son, Adam. I continued to rescue him, loan him money and ignore his issues. I enabled him to continue in his own self-destructive behavior, playing my part to help keep him there. There were others. I am close with all of my children. Close is good, but codependent is not. I called them too much. I had not released them from the apron strings. I was too tied to them. I had to let go. I had to set them free. I also became aware of how I was still too tied to my own mother at 54 years of age. Patterns were emerging that showed me that my mother was too tied to her own children. Since her mother and father were both dead by the time she was five, it was no surprise that she would want to create what she wished she had in her own childhood.

I made a conscious effort to let go of my older children energetically. I stopped calling quite so often and let them call me instead. Sometimes I fell back into my old patterns and had to remind myself it is better for everyone if I empower them and myself.

Changing patterns of behavior takes time and diligence. We created these patterns over our lifetime. To expect that we can change by doing things differently a couple of times is unrealistic. I continue to watch myself and monitor my own behavior with my children to allow them to live their own lives. I provide support and counsel or whatever they need when they ask for it without having to constantly check in with them to feel secure or needed.

On January 5, 2009, after looking at this information from many different angles I moved the end table I had placed in my family room into my bedroom. I turned the end table 45 degrees on my side of the bed to be able to accommodate the second end table near the door for my new partner. I could not get to the drawers on my side of the bed, but I made it fit. I could feel the gears locking into place. This was a monumental shift for me. I was consciously inviting a man to share my life.

Within a week of moving the end table into my room, I was given the guidance to sign up for on-line dating. I had been on several different dating sites intermittently over the past two years. PlentyOfFish, e-Harmony and Millionairematch. I did not have luck with any of them. Chemistry.com moves you along faster than e-Harmony. I found the process on e-Harmony was very laborious and slow. You could spend several months writing messages back and forth and never meet anyone in person.

I knew that I was in a very different place now, so I wanted to try something different. I wanted someone that I had chemistry with. I saw an ad for Chemistry.com and knew it was the one. I trusted my inner guidance on this. My friend, Diana, cautioned me to wait three more weeks before joining, as Mercury was in retrograde. We both had heard that relationships that began during a Mercury retrograde would end quickly. I was sure this was not a factor for me so I paid my $29.00 for one month and I was off to the races. My goal was to be on the site for three weeks and cancel my membership before it renewed automatically.

Within two days of signing up I had five different matches. Of the five, two sounded very promising and one man who was local was a good match for me as far as his interests. However, there was a vague, creepy feeling about him that would not go away. In another day there were three more matches for me to choose from. One was extremely good looking and never responded to my e-mail. I discounted this one as he was probably using his cousin's photo anyway.

Even though I was not interested in all of the matches, I e-mailed all of them. My feeling was that in order to weed out I needed more information. I had an instant gut feeling about one of the matches and watched as that feeling deepened with each interaction on line. When he started talking about his kundalini snaking up his spine and the feelings that he felt, my stomach turned. It felt yucky. A sick feeling in my stomach felt like I did when I was a child and my neighbor was luring me into his house. I paid attention to the way I felt and wrote him a note stating that I did not feel comfortable with what he was talking about and next thing I knew he had closed the match. I felt relieved.

I corresponded with three or four different men and ended up having telephone conversations with two of them. As soon as I heard complaining about an ex-wife, I excused myself politely from the conversation. They were nixed also.

In the past I made rules of engagement for dating. Most of my rules were based on my past experience. It is funny how we come up with a rule or bias for our life based on something that may have been a one-time occurrence. For example, I found that most Baptists did not understand me because I talked to my angels. I listen to my inner guidance. I used to get psychic readings and astrology readings. Most Baptists just do not like these things. I assumed that a Baptist man was not good for me; that we would just not get along. So my on-line selection rules were: No Baptists, no motorcycles, no men with young children, and since I had a daughter in school, they must live locally (at least live in Georgia).

They must love children, animals, be open to different belief systems or believe what I believe. I also tried to stay away from Southerners. I felt that since my relationship with one man I dated for three years was such a disaster and he was Southern, and me being Canadian, we just did not understand each other. I preferred men with hair on their heads and not their backs, and it had to be blonde or brunette. I also wanted someone 6-foot tall and physically fit. Since I am short I wanted someone that could at least be useful in the kitchen and be able to reach the cabinets that I could not.

As dumb as these rules sound, we all have them. Although I had these silly rules, I have also learned that The Divine does not give you what you ask for. The Divine gives you what you need. So God's will becomes my will. As well as I knew myself I really did not know what was in my best interest. The Divine is never wrong and will always give you what is best for you in the end. So believing that, my guidance was to be open and to trust.

Of the three men I narrowed it down to, one man lit up for me. When I say this, it means that when we are meant to take note of something of great importance, things will be given a slight glow. It is not very obvious, but subtle. When you are paying attention you will notice it. Even walking through the grocery store certain foods will be highlighted for me and be emphasized better for me than others. It used to happen to me when I was in my barn getting my tools for my most recent landscaping project. In the process of loading up my truck and trailer I would walk into the barn and say, I need three shovels, three rakes, a tarp, and so on. One or two tools would have a slight glow around them. Being the stubborn person that I am, I would not only question, but also argue with my guidance. I am laying sod today, now why would I need to bring a leaf rake? What I learned over time was that the one tool that was lit up was the tool I never expected to need. If I did not heed the advice given by this glow I would inevitably regret it. The tool that was highlighted was always the one thing I would need to complete the project. I am a slow learner. It took me at least 15 occasions for me to experience this halo around one or two tools in my workshop. If I argued and left the tool at my shop I would inevitably have to either make the trek back to my home to get the tool, or worse yet, purchase another one at the local hardware store. So the Universe had trained me well. I knew that when something was lit up I needed to take note and act, or I would really miss out.

Jesse's photo was not great. I really could not see his face clearly. In each of the photos it looked as if he was hiding, or did not want to be seen. It was very subtle but there. He was seated on a motorcycle. Another big boy with a toy, I thought. Why is it that men in their 50s all have motorcycles? I don't get it. It was a really nice photo of his bike. It was as if he did not want anyone to focus on how he looked. The photo looked as if it had been taken from 30-feet away, which is supposed to be a no-no in on-line dating etiquette. The redeeming factor was that he had a photo of his dog with him and the dog was really handsome. Since my experience had been in the past that you could never trust that the photo was even of the person you were going to meet, or even taken in the most recent decade, what did the photo mean anyway?

Though I had very strong signs that I should pursue this match, I had my doubts. He lived in North Carolina, and I lived in Georgia. He grew up in Tennessee, which made him a Southerner. On top of the fact that he had a motorcycle he also had red hair and freckles. The only guy I ever dated with red hair was James Sayer when I was 14 in junior high school. We went steady for a couple of months in Ontario. I really did not find men with red hair all that attractive. I was coming up with all kinds of excuses not to be interested in this man. So many of my rules of engagement were being challenged and broken with this man.

At this point in my evolution I was communicating regularly with my angels and guides. Mostly they would communicate with me and I would argue. They laughed at my expense regularly. Sometimes I would have visions of them falling down in peals of raucous laughter. Angels, can't live with them, can't live without them. I looked at his photo again and asked, "Really? This guy? Are you sure?" I got the same answer but more vehemently this time. It was as if someone was pointing to Jesse's photo and shouting at me, "Over here! This is the one!"

Honestly, if I had been choosing for myself, and let me assure you I was not, he did not look like anyone I had ever been attracted to. DING DING DING DING! We have a winner here folks! Everyone I had ever been attracted to was wrong for me! Why would I want to be with someone that was wrong for me again? I had asked, and God and The Universe had responded. Jesse Bonham was chosen for me. All I needed to do was accept.

Our e-mail encounter was short. By the second or third e-mail I had re-named him, "Man-of-few-words" and myself, "Jennifer-who-speaks-too-much."

I write e-mails as if I am talking. So did Jesse. His were short and cryptic. In the past I had gotten to know someone fairly well on-line before agreeing to meet for a coffee date. Sometimes I would cautiously e-mail for a month or two, or even three before even considering a date. I am sure that many very nice men weeded me out as too cautious and fearful. I found out before we met that Jesse had lived in Panama City after graduating with a degree in theology and had his own landscaping business there for ten years. Things were starting to fall into place. I could feel he was similar to me.

I was used to being almost passive in my dating style. I would initiate contact and then leave the ball in the man's court. In this instance I got the distinct impression I needed to be proactive with this man or he would be gone. So I trusted my intuition and became the huntress. I was forthright and upfront. After three e-mail messages, I suggested a meeting. Jesse was more cautious and asked that we have a conversation first. He expressed that he was not much of a typist and preferred to talk on the phone; he was done with the Internet stage.

Remembering our first conversation, I was amazed that the first thing Jesse wanted to know was how I felt about him being close with his children. I replied, "I would not have it any other way." I had the same issue. I expressed concern about his three-hour commute from Kings Mountain, North Carolina. He told me it was not a problem as he was often in Alpharetta area to cycle with his friends. I was skeptical but kept everything he said in the back of my mind to reflect on how things panned out.

I had taken a part time job after the holidays at Soma, a high-end lingerie shop, across from North Point mall. The strange thing was that Jesse frequently cycled along the greenway located right behind the plaza where I now worked. I suggested we meet for breakfast before I had to be at work at 10:00 a.m. I gave Jesse the option of choosing the spot for our first meeting. It was not surprising that this man from Tennessee chose Cracker Barrel. My daughter thought it was absolutely hilarious that we should meet in a "country breakfast" place. She commented that it was not very romantic. She and I laughed so hard we were almost in tears.

I was very excited in spite of myself and found myself thinking it did not matter what I wore for this meeting. I picked a black and white outfit I had purchased on sale at Chico's. Thank God for Chico's. I looked smart, but not too dressy, as I assumed correctly that Jesse was a pretty casual guy. The restaurant was not too far from my home, and I found myself buoyed by the idea of meeting the man the Universe had chosen for me. I went with an open mind and thought to myself I had better not eat as I usually do, I might scare him off. I have a very healthy appetite and usually eat more than most men.

I arrived at the restaurant on time and parked my truck. I scanned the parking lot looking for the vehicle that might be his. Would I be able to pick it out in this sea of vehicles? Would it tell me anything about this man? A quick assessment of the lot and I picked out a dark blue Ford F 250 truck with a high-end bike rack. It had to be his. It was the only vehicle with a bike rack in the whole parking lot. I doubted very much if anyone above the age of ten in the whole restaurant even owned a bicycle.

I walked across the parking lot, looking towards the row of rocking chairs in front of the building. I was able to see a man's outstretched boot-clad feet. I knew they belonged to Jesse before I could catch the first glimpse of his face. They were nice, clean, expensive-looking black lace-up boots. He stood up before I got to the porch, and walked over to meet me. It was a very good sign. This man was well bred, a gentleman. Holy cow! By the time my hand met his in handshake, my face was beaming ear to ear. I could not contain my excitement.

I was very pleasantly surprised in so many ways. He was very handsome and pleasant. I felt instantly at ease, but still very excited. Jesse was soft-spoken and quiet. He listened intently, smiling at me as I babbled on endlessly. I could not believe how much I was talking. It was as if someone injected high-octane fuel into my veins. When Jesse was able to get a word in edgewise

170

he talked about his children, Stephen and Melissa, and how close he was to them. He also talked about his 11-month-old grandson and how much he loved him. His grandson was born with a slight challenge. The skin of his middle and index fingers had grown together in utero and he was scheduled for surgery right before his first birthday. My mind was going a mile a minute. I hoped I would remember at least a small part of what he said.

In the middle of my rapid-fire monologue, I received a phone call from work. Apparently I had written down my schedule incorrectly and I was late for work. I felt like Cinderella rushing off to my truck. I quickly met Jesse's dog, Ozzie, before I left. I told Jesse I really enjoyed meeting him and was grateful to him for making the long drive to meet me. I hoped that we could do this again sometime soon. We set up a tentative date for the following weekend, depending on my work schedule. I hugged him good-bye.

There are no mistakes. Everything is in Divine order. With that being said, in retrospect, the fact that I had to rush off after 45 minutes, instead of lingering too long helped to continue the excitement and willingness to have another date. How often do we spend too much time with someone we have just met and ruin our good chances for love by not saying good-bye soon enough? Our insecurities keep us hanging on way too long, afraid to say good-bye. I have to say thank you to my scheduling angels for helping to create things the way they did. I surely could not have orchestrated a more perfect situation. We could not linger over coffee for hours and perhaps ruin everything with a first meeting that ran on too long. Many dating sites suggest that the first date should run no more than one hour and should probably not include food.

We had one more breakfast date the following weekend before I invited Jesse to my house. Our second date, this time at The Original Pancake House, was pleasant and comfortable. When I mentioned an electrical breaker that kept tripping at my house, Jesse offered to replace it. I was a little hesitant to have him come to my house for a variety of reasons. One, my daughter would be home. Two, my house was a mess. Three, it felt like it was too soon. The fact that Jesse lived so far away changed the landscape of our dating. As far as the house was concerned, I figured if he were going to truly accept me as I am, I would not be anything other than me. Regarding my daughter, I tried really hard not to involve her in my dating situations until I was sure it would be something of a serious nature. I had made that mistake in the past and was not about to repeat it.

Jesse came by just before dark, dressed in a black snug fitting t-shirt and a nice pair of jeans. My daughter and I could not help but notice how fit he was. I figured he had about 1% body fat. I thought to myself, I could squish him if I sat on him! Ana sat in the living room staring at the blank television screen quietly waiting to watch a movie with me, while Jesse fixed the breaker. He cautioned me that the wiring really should be replaced and that I should let my landlord know.

I offered Jesse a glass of water, as it was all that I had. I also asked him what I owed him for his time. He was happy for me to pay him for the part, which I did. I was very appreciative of his help. I introduced him to my dogs and he met Ana very briefly. We stood in the kitchen and talked for almost two hours before he said he had to go as he was spending the night with his friends in Alpharetta. He really did have friends locally. I was relieved to hear he was telling the truth. I was so used to being lied to by men, that I figured it must be a guy thing. This was so refreshing.

In the process of getting to know Jesse I found out that he had been married for 23 years to the same woman. Had things not worked out as they did, he would still be married to her. He had a very difficult time transitioning into single life afterward. This was an indication of a man who could be faithful and committed. I watched and looked intently for red flags but I did not notice any waving. My daughter said he looked like Frankenstein. I interpreted her depiction of Jesse was due to the way the shadows fell on his face. Ana expressed an instant dislike of him. I put aside what she was thinking. Maybe she wanted me all to herself. I was so excited about a new relationship. I would come to recognize this later as denial. My daughter had a gift of seeing through a façade to the truth immediately. I did also, I just ignored it.

During our conversations I was able to see motion pictures or visions (in my mind) of how Jesse was with his wife in their relationship. I knew things had fallen apart partially because when he became upset he had the ability to be withholding. I knew also that this was a protective mechanism. If this was the worst of him, I felt I could deal with it. I could be withholding of my love, affection and even communication. It was in my blood, my parents taught me well.

While we were in the early days of our dating process I did not introduce Jesse to any of my friends. I kept our relationship quiet. I let things unfold and nurtured what we had like a small seedling, keeping us protected. A friend had given me the book, *If The Buddha Dated*, by Charlotte Kasl. I had read the book from beginning to end at least three times. One of the author's suggestions was to stay chaste as long as possible at the beginning of a relationship. Not having sex allows each of you to view your relationship with both feet firmly planted on the ground, no pun intended. Without the lust factor, you look at the other person from a grounded point of view, realistically.

Jesse and I dated over a month before we got close to making out. It was not that we were not attracted to one another, we clearly were. When the issue came up after four dates, I told Jesse that I was using Tony DiNozzo's motto from *NCIS*, "If you keep doing what you have always done, you will get what you have always gotten." I wanted our relationship to be different. I wanted to give "us" all the advantages we could have for success. This way we could get to know each other without the focus of the physical relationship.

Waiting to become intimate was a huge factor in creating a very different relationship for us. In past relationships I have become intimate early on in the relationship. I feel that seemingly small thing created an underlying current of disrespect especially with men who were already insecure. The thought is, if she will go to bed easily with me, she will be easy with other men. It is my belief and that of others that waiting to be intimate until you have gotten to know each other well creates a deeper level of trust and mutual respect. You get to know one another as people and friends first before becoming lovers. It made a huge difference in the foundation of our relationship. So while you are getting to know each other during this time, you are holding each other in high regard. The desire to see each other is based on enjoying each other's company and not making love. Once you step into the bedroom there is no turning back the hands of time. The single act of lovemaking puts you in a very different arena. It changes the landscape of the relationship in which women become more needy and codependant wondering why he doesn't call.

Before we were intimate we were connecting heart to heart. Jesse surprised both of us one evening when he started to talk about his feelings for me. He said it seemed strange for him to be feeling what he was feeling for me so soon. He said it was a peaceful, easy feeling. It was heartfelt and it did not seem the least bit corny at the time. We both had a familiar feeling being together. It felt like coming home.

Jesse was up at 6:00 a.m. every morning in North Carolina working Monday through Friday during the week. Some weeks he would take Friday off and drive down to Alpharetta to visit with me in between my hours at my part-time job at the lingerie store. During these visits he would stay with his friends in Alpharetta.

On one particular weekend, I worked until 10:00 p.m. on Friday night and was scheduled to work Saturday night to close as well. I suggested to Jesse that we skip this weekend because of my schedule. The only time I had available to see him I had committed to attend a Nikken wellness function with several of my girlfriends across town. With Jesse coming into town, I really wanted to cancel, but women have a tendency to cancel plans when something better comes along. I did not want to do this to my friends. So I kept my commitment with them.

On Saturday we had two hours together at this Nikken sales demonstration before I had to drop Ana off at home with her brother who was to baby-sit. Jesse drove three hours each way for a total of six hours to see me in a group setting before we had to go our separate ways. I felt bad that we had such a limited amount of time together and none of it was private time.

What this day told me was that Jesse valued me as a person and cared enough about me to spend his time and energy to see me even if he had to sit through a presentation to do it. It wasn't about sex or what he would get out of it. He proved he would sacrifice for me and give me his time and attention. This was something I had done for others but had not found a man who would do the same for me. It seemed that Jesse was different. He showed himself to be attentive, caring and nurturing. His focus was on me, not on himself.

During this time of getting to know one another, Jesse had to endure a great deal. I had a house full of animals, a landscaping business, as well as a part-time job and shared custody of my 13-year-old daughter. My two older sons lived away from home, but were actively involved in our family and visited often.

Jesse could not spend the night at my house when my daughter was present, nor did he try to. Not only did he show respect for me, but he had a high regard for my children and respected them as well.

It was during this period of getting to know one another that I asked the looming question regarding the church that his ordination was in. He told me it was Baptist. "Oh my God," I thought. If I had really held firmly to my silly rules about whom I could or could not date, I might have given Jesse the fly by. Baptists typically did not understand me. I talked to my angels and to God directly. I did healings and blessings on all my landscape installations. My beliefs and those of most Baptists usually created friction. I was open about my healing practice with Jesse and asked if he had any issue with it. He quelled my concerns by saying that he did not need to have the same beliefs as I did. He said he was fine with it.

Jesse had attended other churches, but his formative years were tied to the Baptist church. Fortunately for me, Jesse was secure enough in who he was to be able to allow me to believe what I believed. The lesson for me was huge. If a person is evolved enough it does not matter who believes what. Judge ye not, lest ye be judged.

He brought flowers when he came to see me. I love flowers, but never told him, how did he know? On the weekend he drove from North Carolina just for the day, he brought a lovely Asian teapot and tea from Teavana. He knew I drank tea. It was a lovely gift, something that really took some thought and consideration for who I was and what I liked. It was given without manipulation or hopes of getting me into bed. Giving without expecting anything in return is the true meaning of giving. These are things that registered strongly for me. I recognized this man was different.

I was definitely "in like" with Jesse. I recognized that Jesse was having deeper feelings and moving in the direction of love faster than I was. I was feeling some resistance and I found the fear of not being able to trust myself surfacing. I had been fooled before. I had trusted my intuition and feelings when I met my last husband. He acted laid back and calm when we were dating. After we were married things really changed. He was controlling, manipulative and unappreciative. Anything but laid back. There was an undercurrent and threat of physical abuse and constant fear. I did not want to miss any subtle signs and lie to myself. I did not want to end up with a repeat of my previous relationship.

I have to mention that Jesse loved extreme sports and being on the edge. He enjoyed extreme mountain biking, snowboarding and other extreme sports. He was not the least bit fearful. He was an avid snowboarder, motorcyclist, had done lots of white water kayaking and rode like a maniac when mountain biking. He was definitely not a wimp. He was a man's man, strong and fearless.

Jesse's friends were calling him at my house, trying to get him to ride with them. He spent as much of every weekend with me as he could. From the end of the conversation I could hear, it was sweet that Jesse felt like he really wanted to be with me. I made it clear that I wanted him to have his relationships with his own friends and be free to cycle with them whenever he wanted to. I found it refreshing that he had longtime friends. Having friends is a sign of stability and loyalty. It is also evidence that a person can probably get along with others. Dating a person with no friends can reveal a great deal about that person's personality and issues. I found it to be very reassuring about who Jesse really was.

By April, just three months into our relationship, Jesse asked me if I would like for us to spend more time together. He had been driving back and forth every weekend, staying at friends. Things were going really well, and the drive was taking its toll on him. My response was, "Of course, I would love that." Then he mentioned he had been offered a job in Roswell and planned to move to within 20 miles of my house, to Cumming or Woodstock, Georgia. When I got off the phone, all kinds of issues surfaced for me. "Oh my God, Oh my God, Oh my God!" I thought, "This is moving way too fast." I am slow to process information. After the phone call from Jesse I had time to think and really felt afraid of this recent development. My concern was that Jesse wanted to settle in to a relationship that I was not yet ready for. Yes things were going well but I needed more time to be sure this was what I wanted.

I called Jesse two days later while he was at work. After exchanging our usual greetings, I hit Jesse between the eyes. In a very firm tone I asked him, "I hope that you aren't moving here just to be with me. What happens if things don't work out?" I wanted to make sure he would not resent or blame me for being in the Atlanta area further from his son and his grandchildren. Jesse was very sure of where things were going. My fears were bubbling up fast. I could feel the current carrying me away. I had a history of attracting men who were not good partners. I was not positive. My self-doubts about my ability to recognize a good partner for myself were surfacing.

Jesse reassured me that he had lived in the area before. He loved the mountain biking trails and had several friends close by as well. There was more in the Cumming and Alpharetta area than just me. He felt the move would be good for him.

The move for Jesse was relatively easy. He pulled up stakes and drove lock, stock and barrel with his home on wheels. After his divorce he really wanted to get away from it all. So he bought an RV and a big truck to tow it and drove out to Wyoming. He loved the outdoors and that part of the country. He also lived in Utah near Green River for several years. The RV was very nicely appointed and furnished.

He had the best of everything in it; complete with a big flat screen television and a leather recliner. Everything was high end. The back of the RV was filled with all his sports equipment including a white water kayak, three snow boards, two mountain bikes, one road bike and his Very hot R6 motorcycle. He had everything he wanted and could move easily in a day. Jesse moved to an RV park in Cumming Georgia, less than 10 miles from me.

The RV thing bothered me. Maybe because it reminded me of John who lived in Sedona, Arizona. He had lived in an RV there. The memory of his sudden death and loss still pained me. My friend, Diana Davis, laughingly asked me, "What's with you and guys with RVs?" I honestly didn't know. But loving the outdoors as I do, everything I learned about Jesse made me like him more. I still had not discovered a thing that really bothered me.

On a warm sunny Friday afternoon in April, only three months from the date we first met, he stood waiting for me at my green-rusted back pasture gate. As I drove up the drive and parked my truck in the shade, I saw him standing there playing with the three dogs. I was awash with emotion. I felt a deep sense that he had my back and I would never have to worry about anything ever again. I wept from the bottom of my soul. As much as I had resisted and fought, he loved me deeply. I knew it with such certainty I cried tears of joy.

For the most part, those three months were peaceful and calm. We talked about our day and enjoyed each other's company. Jesse came over regularly and brought his dog with him. Often one or more of my cats were outside. Jesse had said he would not hurt the cats, but liked to chase them.

One particular day, Jesse let Ozzie out of his truck in the driveway. Toby, a gray long-haired social cat, was under our magnolia tree in the front yard. Ozzie made a mad dash for Toby. I watched in horror as Ozzie ran Toby down without listening to Jesse's commands to come. Toby managed to have the presence of mind to hastily climb the closest tree to get out of harm's way. I could tell by the way that Ozzie ran after sweet Toby that this was a hunt and he would kill if he could. Jesse had to climb the tree to get Toby down. He was so distraught he did not want to get back down. Toby climbed into Jesse's arms and purred.

I expressed my concern about Ozzie to Jesse. Jesse said it was no big deal. He had chased cats before and never hurt one. He said that Ozzie would not know what to do with a cat if he caught one. Our relationship was fairly new and I did not want to rock the boat. The jury was out on this one. I would have to wait and see.

In May, my landlord listed my home and property with another real estate agent. The For Sale sign had a photo of my rented home on it and spoke of a quick sale to me. Although the house I was renting had been up for sale for two years, I became uneasy about it. After living in the home for my second tour of duty, my gut was telling me that it was going to sell quickly. I questioned one of the agents that showed the property about how motivated Mr. Baldwin was and he assured me he was motivated.

That was it. I knew Jesse and I had to buy it. When I asked Jesse if he loved the property as much as I did he replied affirmatively. I told him that the house was going to sell soon, and asked if he was interested in buying it with me. It was a long shot. I really did not expect him to say yes. When he did, I knew his commitment to me was more than on the purchase of the land that I loved. It meant a future together. He was committing his life to me.

On our way home from signing the purchase contract on our property with my next door neighbor, Scott Baldwin, Jesse asked me how I envisioned myself getting married. I was rather surprised that a guy would bring up the subject of marriage. Usually that subject was one that women broached and then men hightailed it out of there. I told him that I would like to get married on the beach with flowers in my hair in a casual ceremony. Not the conversation I had expected, but given the financial commitment we had just entered into and the man that Jesse was, I should not have been surprised. I had to get over my fears and just do it.

This relationship was nothing like any I had ever experienced. It became increasingly difficult for us to say goodnight and not be together. It was not that we could not function apart; we were both independent people. Jesse had been single for 10 years. He had openly discussed his past relationships and the reasons for their not working out. We had both discussed our recent marriages and relationships with others. The concern he had in his most recent relationship that ended was because she was jealous of Jesse's children. This was not the case with me, as I had equally close relationships with all of my children.

We really enjoyed each other's company and by this time were intimate. We had our private time together every other week that Ana was with her Dad. We were very attracted to one another and enjoyed lovemaking and connecting intimately. It was another thing that blew me away. I have to say that when God makes a plan it is amazing. When he reached for me and pulled me to him, I could feel how deeply he cared. I felt he could express himself well even without words.

The last weekend in May after a visit with Jesse's oldest daughter, Melissa, I finally felt ready to take the next step. There was no doubt that this match was made in heaven, created by God. I felt that Jesse was definitely "The One." On one of the first days in June, Scott Baldwin asked us when we were getting married. After all, we were under contract as purchasers of his property next door. Jesse replied, "When Jennifer says so." On our walk through the pasture between our respective farms, I said to Jesse, "I am ready to be married to you."

Whenever Jesse was in town, he attended church with my daughter and me. He also attended the Tuesday evening prayer circles and healing services with us. He was familiar with our church and some of the congregation. The next day I called our minister to ask when she would be available to marry us. The whirlwind began. She told me she would have to run our astrological charts and get back to us the following day. She asked when we wanted to get married. I suggested anytime between July and October.

When we spoke again she gave us three options. The first date offered was June 28th under the influence of Cancer, but was only three weeks away. She gave us two other dates under the influence of Leo and then remarked that the first date, June 28th, would bring us bountiful blessings and would support both Jesse and me in our marriage. She even told us what time would be the best, the most auspicious on that day.

I was reeling at the prospect of everything we would have to do in such a short amount of time. I had been listening to my Divine guidance through this whole process. How could we turn down bountiful blessings and having us both supported in our marriage? I felt we needed all the blessings possible to help us in our new life together. I told her I would call her to confirm the next day. She was excited for us and her parting comment was that we would probably change the date, most people did. It all sounded so bizarre and impossible. One thing was for sure, we did not have a wedding in our budget.

Jesse and I worked like dogs preparing Our home and back yard for our beach themed wedding. Jesse was already worn out from all the work done around our seven acres to prepare for his daughter, Melissa's, visit. I noticed during this time that Jesse had begun to drink on a daily basis. He had always had an occasional beer after he moved to Georgia. I rarely drank, so the increase in Jesse's consumption concerned me and I mentioned it in a gentle and loving way. "Jesse, I am concerned about you drinking beer everyday. It is hot and you work outside. Beer dehydrates you." His response was to snap at me, "What do you think? That I'm a drunk!" His response and his anger surprised me. I had not seen him snap like this before. I pushed it aside and just made a mental note of what was unfolding.

We planned a casual beach-themed wedding and asked our guests to wear aloha shirts and beach attire. After working tirelessly on our property, our yard was beautiful; complete with sand and palm trees and we were exhausted. Jesse and his best man, Joe, took the wheels off my landscape trailer and created a really great and innovative stage for our musical duo. The barn was cleaned out for our bar. Jesse, being the MacGyver that he is, put up an exhaust fan in the barn to move cool air through it. Joe, his best man, had cut himself on the fan when it teetered off of a stepladder, attempting to catch it as it fell. He had to be taken to the hospital the day before our wedding for stitches. It cast a pall over our joy-filled preparations. We borrowed tables from everyone we could think of and all our guests brought food. This was the way that our ancestors used to get married. It was a village event.

Ana painted a scene on the outside wall of our barn for the wedding. She created a sign on the barn as well that said, "Jesse and Jennifer a match made in heaven." Her work was lovely and heartfelt. What troubled me was that she painted two martini glasses as well, complete with olives and swizzle sticks. Since I rarely had anything to drink, I knew that it was what she had witnessed Jesse doing. When Jesse saw the glasses he said he did not like what it portrayed and asked her to paint over them.

Ana mentioned to me three weeks before our wedding when we began talking about my mother coming that she would be upset with how much that Jesse drank. I agreed that Mom would probably not be very pleased. Ana then added, "Well you know mom, you have this pattern of attracting alcoholics." Ana is a wise young woman. She is also very intuitive. I felt she knew more than she was saying, but like I have done everything else in my life, I let it slide.

On the afternoon of our wedding, I found myself hyperventilating moments before I stepped out the door to meet my sons, Adam and Matthew. They both looked at me and smiled.

Matthew said I looked like a princess. Ana was my maid of honor. She was never in a bridal party before. She was thrilled and emotional. She had panicked moments before when she could not find me. Having checked in each of the rooms where she felt I would be, she became tearful as she went from person to person and room to room asking them, "Have you seen my mom?"

I was hidden in her bedroom away from the crowd. I was working to compose myself before the ceremony. I had become afraid and emotional. Due to the heat, most of our guests were inside wanting to be cool. It was noisy and chaotic and I needed peace and space to be alone. I found myself in a state of panic I could not shake. Our minister, Cindy Fuller, found me and sat me down on Ana's bed. She held my hands and helped me to ground myself and breathe.

Within a few minutes, I pulled myself together and breathed deeply. I was able to control the tears as I walked down the aisle, enough to be able to smile at my friends and family. Just as I was nearing the alter, the processional music, *Jesus, Joy of Man's Desiring*, ended, leaving me walking in silence until one of Jesse's friends restarted the recording. The joys of putting on your own wedding! I halted slightly and then continued toward our minister and Jesse after a moment's hesitation. I reached up to hug Matthew first, on my right, and then Adam. It was very sweet to have them on each arm. I took one more step toward Jesse and he grasped my hand tightly. We thought we were both ready. I anxiously put Jesse's ring on the wrong hand.

Our wedding was beautiful and very spiritual. I had known our minister for over 15 years. She spoke about the two of us being born a day apart in different parts of North America. It was one of the things that I liked about Jesse; our astrological charts were so very similar. According to our charts we were very much alike.

Just as we were being pronounced man and wife a wind came from out of nowhere on this still, hot Georgia day causing the wind chine to ring all by itself at the perfectly proclaimed time. I could feel the air filled with angels. I looked radiant and beautiful. I was so happy.

My mother, who had never accepted any of the men I had brought home as mates, was moved to tears and expressed that she had never seen two people so well-matched and in love. She was so happy for me. Our marriage touched a place in her that had long been dormant. She expressed raw, unadulterated love and joy. It moved me to the point of tears.

I felt at peace and joyful. Our day was lovely, even though it was very hot and humid. My mother worked tirelessly in the kitchen washing dishes and cleaning up, as did many of my friends.

In an attempt to keep our three dogs quiet we had taken them to our neighbor's home and put them in a dog pen there. At the time, I saw that the pen was covered with poison ivy. I was highly allergic to it. When it came time to get the dogs, I realized we needed to give them all baths so I would not end up covered in an itchy rash. After everything we had done in preparation, there was more work for us. There we were on our wedding day bathing the three dogs. I would not recognize the symbolism of this until much later.

Jesse and I went to bed that night exhausted and did not make love. I wanted to but Jesse was too tired from working so hard cleaning the barn and setting up the stage. The bedrooms in our quaint old home were very close together. The walls between the rooms were not insulated and the bedroom doors had large spaces under them. We were not comfortable with Ana and my mother in the house. It was not until the next night that my mother suggested that we go out into Jesse's RV to have some privacy so we were able to make love. Jesse was gentle and sweet. He was a considerate lover. I was very attracted to him. I thought I had died and gone to heaven.

After our wedding weekend it was back to work for Jesse and me. We could not afford a honeymoon, and did not even go away for a weekend. We had maxed out our credit cards paying for the wedding items, musical duo and rings. We talked about going to Ireland later in the year to spend some time alone. It would have to wait until we had the money to do so.

My mother commented to me toward the end of her visit that I was calling Jesse, "my husband." She observed that I had never done that in any of my other marriages. It was true. I had never felt so fully vested in a relationship. I was truly committed and happy. Sadly, Mom had to return to Toronto. I had really enjoyed having her with us. She had been a tremendous help. Our relationship had been healed over the years due to my inner work. I had put so much behind me. It felt so good to be at peace with my mother and myself as well.

I threw myself into being the best wife I could be. I prepared dinner every night for my family. I kept up with Jesse's and my laundry, even folding and putting his clothes away each week. Jesse's routine was to be up at 5:45 a.m. and out of the house within 20 minutes. He had to drive across town through traffic to be at work on time. I soon found it easier to set up the coffee pot on a timer at night. This way when Jesse got up his coffee was already brewed. I even heated his coffee cup so that it would stay hot for him on the road. I got out of bed when he did and made his lunch daily and sent Jesse off to work with a kiss.

While Ana was at her dad's, I asked Jesse if he would like to take a shower with me. We did not shower or use the bathroom together as many couples do, as Jesse seemed to like his bathroom time as private time. I respected his unspoken wishes. He joined me in the shower. After we shared the water and the soap, I could feel that nothing of a romantic nature was going to occur. I turned my back to him and shaved my legs. I could feel Jesse cringe behind me. I was shocked that this bothered him. He never said anything about it to me, but we also never showered together again. I found this to be odd, but I swept it under the carpet. It seemed the safest thing to do at the time.

The week following our wedding I was back doing landscaping maintenance for my regular clients. When I went into the barn to find materials for a job, I discovered that Jesse had put most of my equipment and supplies on the far left side of the barn in a dark shutoff space. As there was no light in this part of the barn, it was extremely difficult for me to find things and due to Jesse's equipment stacked in front of my spreaders and push mowers; it was almost impossible for me to get to my equipment.

From a feng shui perspective, putting my equipment in the dark was not a good thing. It put my business into suspension or to sleep. What was obvious to me from this action was that Jesse did not like me doing landscaping and his sports equipment, motorcycle and bicycles were placed in prominent positions in the barn, making what he did for recreation much more important than what I did for work. It was almost three months after our wedding before I had the opportunity for a new project. I had to move my equipment into the daylight.

When I brought the fact that my equipment was in the dark to Jesse's attention, I did so with humor. "Hey Jesse, are you wanting me give up landscaping as my profession?" He had no idea what I was talking about. I asked him if he had an unconscious feeling that he did not like me doing landscaping for my work and did he realize that putting all my stuff in the dark back corner of the barn expressed a feeling that it was not important? He denied that he did it on purpose, or even subconsciously. He said he and Joe had just moved things out of the way for the wedding and that was that. When I needed my seed spreaders in the fall, my equipment was still in the back behind all of his plastic totes full of unused air conditioning parts. I had to ask for him to help me get to my equipment.

Jesse's beautiful sports bike, a Yamaha R6, was situated diagonally in a prominent corner of our old, run-down barn in front of all my tools. It was a beautiful silver-grey bike in pristine condition. Jesse had placed rubber mats neatly on the floor and parked the bike so that the tires did not touch the concrete beneath it. He had expressed to me that his bike was very expensive and implied that I needed to be careful getting my tools out and not to bump the bike while doing so.

To the left side of the bike all my shovels and plastic leaf rakes hung on hooks. Behind his bike was a row of small and large red plastic gas cans as well as a two-cycle mix for my blowers, weed eaters and edgers. Behind the row of gas cans was an open shelf filled with two-cycle engine oil, heavy-duty string for my weed-eater, marking paint, liquid chemicals and other tools. To the right were all my picks and rakes, as well as Stihl blowers. My equipment was fairly organized but not exactly pristine. I usually unloaded my truck and trailer alone. My shovels and picks were usually put away in haste after long hard days and usually had remnants of the day's dirt on them.

Every time I had to load up my truck and trailer for work I had to maneuver around Jesse's sports equipment. He regularly left his expensive mountain bike on a rack two or three feet in front of his motorbike, which made it impossible for me to move my mower without either moving his bike and rack physically or hitting it with my mower.

After several months of trying to be the perfect wife and tirelessly cooking, cleaning, and making lunches, I realized that what I was doing was not being appreciated. I found myself becoming angry. Jesse had yet to thank me for dinner, his coffee or even his lunch. When I mentioned this to him, he snapped at me, "I never asked you to do it!" All I wanted was to be appreciated. I appreciated Jesse for all that he did to clean up the pond and any equipment he fixed for me.

I expected him to do the same. Jesse was not able to express appreciation for the simple daily things I did for him.

I continued to run the house, cooking nightly, doing our laundry, as well as working on my landscaping and healing business, writing my book and taking care of Ana. I felt unappreciated. It seemed to run in cycles. I could give and give for a while, then found myself feeling resentful or angry for being unappreciated. Each time the cycle of feeling resentful would present itself in my body, I would feel it, respect it and say something to Jesse.

Each time I brought up an issue, Jesse rebuffed my effort to discuss it with the excuse that he was tired, or he had just gotten home from work. He clearly did not like to discuss issues. This shocked me. Before we got married I told Jesse that working on myself and our issues was a priority for me. I asked him if he would commit to healing and evolving with me. He said he would. What I came to realize was that Jesse had an issue with conflict. He was unable to discuss any issue of consequence when there were emotional charges. He felt extremely uncomfortable doing so. If I attempted to talk with him when he had just gotten home from work, he would snap at me, saying, "I don't want to talk about this now, I just got home from work." If I waited until later, he would tell me he was tired.

I recalled several times that Jesse became angry with his closest male friend for not respecting his wishes before we were married. He had wanted to see me after he went mountain biking with his friend, Kurt. Kurt was a dentist and used to operating on his own schedule. He had a wife and kids and other commitments. Jesse had been free as a bird for ten years. He had difficulty talking about issues as they came up. He would keep them stuffed until he could not hold them in any longer and then blow up. On this particular occasion, Jesse had wanted to ride early in the day and then visit with me, as he had to drive back to North Carolina later in the day. Kurt put the ride off due to family events and Jesse blew up at him.

I had been this way for years. Being a Scorpio also, I was well aware of the anger that boiled below the surface when issues were shelved and deferred until later. They never go away, as they need to be addressed so that the emotional charges can be released and healed. Constant suppressing of issues creates a steady boil slightly beneath the surface. It is not evident at first blush, but with careful and watchful observation it allows insight into the emotional body.

Jesse's father had been an alcoholic. He was harsh and unfair to Jesse. Being the most sensitive of three brothers and three sisters he frequently found himself beaten by his father for his emotionality. His mother felt very tender-hearted toward this sensitive boy, which created jealousy and rage in Jesse's father. He did not hold back, beating Jesse just because. When Jesse became emotional, he was beaten. It was not long before he shut down his emotions totally to protect himself. He told me stories of his childhood when he would wake up at 5:00 in the morning leaving the house on his retired circus pony, before his father would wake, just to be free of him. If he were at home when his father woke up, he would spend the day toiling on the farm, under his father's steady watch. He was punished for things his brothers had done and he did everything he could to get away. He would rather spend his day in the woods riding alone.

Our generation had strict parenting. I had worked hard myself to overcome issues associated with controlling and overbearing parents. This revelation did not occur to me as being problematic. I felt similarly about my own father when I was a child. In my own family, all of us kids had chores assigned: from cleaning the basement and our rooms from top to bottom to weeding in our backyard garden. Every Saturday was a workday. No one escaped from work at our house even if we wanted to. We did not have much freedom either.

I had become much more heart-centered over the past seven years. I was positive and for the most part in a loving space. I kept myself grounded and in the moment. Rather than being afraid to talk about issues and challenges as I had in the past, I faced our problems head on and discussed them with Jesse. I had become conscious of my words, actions and those of others. Each time I would present an issue to Jesse, I spoke in a calm, loving voice keeping eye contact with Jesse and touching my hand gently to the middle of his chest or heart chakra while I spoke to him.

During the preparations for Jesse's daughter's visit and our wedding, I noticed that Jesse drank more regularly. Since I rarely drank, I did not have beer or wine in my house. If Jesse would like something to drink, he would have to bring it. Most often we did not drink anything when he would visit. On one or two occasions, he brought over a bottle of wine that we consumed together. I did not see anything alarming in his behavior. He went from the occasional beer early in our dating cycle to drinking at least two a night. As my family had some issues with drinking, I was sensitive to the increase in his consumption of alcohol. I mentioned that he was drinking quite a bit. Jesse snapped at me, "So you are saying that you think I am a drunk?" Since he only drank two or three beers at a time, I had never seen him actually drunk. I could not say he was a drunk. It was just a concern. I brushed my concern aside and decided it was his way of dealing with a stressful situation.

We both had a lot on our plate. A new home with a huge mortgage to pay each month, increased responsibilities, three dogs, four cats and many repairs to make on our old home and property. There always seemed to be something that needed work. I was running two businesses; there was the responsibility of my daughter and the issues with an ex-husband. Blending families and animals create opportunities for issues to arise and arise they did.

Our first major issue was about Jesse's Australian Sheppard, Ozzie. Ozzie was a very smart, high-energy alpha dog. He had emotional issues from a time when Jesse decided to move to Utah. He had Ozzie for about a year and felt he could not take him when he moved. Jesse's son and daughter-in-law adopted him while he was away. Ozzie was a very active and aggressive dog. Australian Sheppards are bred as working dogs. Being one of the most intelligent of breeds, they really need a job to do and lots and lots of exercise. Without either of these they can become anxious and aggressive.

Jesse's son, Stephen and daughter-in-law, Kathy, lived in an apartment and both worked while Ozzie spent all day crated in the apartment. He was teased by many of the apartment tenants that were not used to dogs while he was sitting in their vehicle. This repeated teasing and crating created tension for Ozzie that needed to be released. He bit several people and made Kathy afraid. As time went on, she felt more afraid of Ozzie and therefore, he spent more time in the crate. The cycle created a very aggressive dog.

A couple of Jesse's friends came by one evening in the early summer with their 9-year-old son. He played Frisbee with Ozzie under our watchful eyes. While we stood talking, their little boy, Andrew, followed Ozzie to the side of the house where we could not see. The next thing we knew we heard snarling, the unmistakable snap of teeth, and then a scream. Andrew was in tears and said that Ozzie had bitten him in the leg. His father brushed off the incident, knowing how sensitive Jesse was to criticism of his dog, and told him he was fine. Although the child was clearly shaken up, his father also went on to say to Jesse that something similar had happened with someone else's dog and that he would be fine, not to worry. Their little boy was very upset and continued to cry. I felt very badly about the incident and talked to Jesse about it later. His take was that the boy had cornered Ozzie and that it was the kid's fault. He should have known better than to try and take his Frisbee away from him. I found out quickly that Jesse did not see clearly when it came to his dog. He would not hear my concerns and clammed up, refusing to talk any further about it.

While preparing for our wedding, Ozzie jumped almost five feet off the ground and made contact with Jesse's best man's nose. It looked as though he was trying to bite him. When I approached Jesse about Ozzie he got angry instantly. He was in deep denial about Ozzie's issues. He felt that there was nothing wrong with him. Ozzie was very food aggressive and had attacked my Weimaraner, Isabella. Being a hound, Isabella liked her food and anyone else's that was not being eaten. Ozzie did not eat much and often left his bowl half-eaten and pushed it with his nose repeatedly into the corner. Isabella had gone towards the bowl and ended up with deep bite wounds on her rear flanks and neck.

When I spoke to Jesse about Ozzie, I kept my voice quiet and even and made sure I made eye contact with him. Jesse's first response to any issue was to roll his eyes and say in an exasperated way, "Honey!" Which meant he did not want to talk about it. Although Jesse did not want to discuss the dog, I pressed on, as I knew this was a huge issue for us and would not go away if we ignored it.

We talked about Ozzie for almost an hour. I did not seem to make any headway at all. My dogs were problems also, he felt. I expressed to him I would never ask him to get rid of his dog. I felt that we needed to get some help for the dog, an animal behaviorist, or some kind of professional help. Doing nothing was never a good idea. This became Jesse's modus operandi. Deny that there is a problem, do nothing, don't talk about it and maybe it will go away.

Over the next ten months, there were cycles. As long as I did not bring up any issues, things went along fairly smoothly. I cooked, cleaned and worked. Jesse and I cut wood, he worked on my landscaping equipment and cleaned up the area surrounding our lake alone. He cut down trees that were overhanging the pond and dug out behind the damn so that the water level increased by almost four feet. This made a huge difference to the look of the lake. He was frequently off alone by the lake for long periods.

Whenever I asked for help in the kitchen though, or with any household chores, I was told that he worked every day and I didn't. When I got busier with my landscaping business he would pitch in. He also mentioned that my daughter should help more and that when she did more he would also. Although my business picked up in the fall and the following spring, and Ana assisted more, the help never came. Jesse had slipped into being his father, and wanted me to be his mother. He drank at least two bottles of beer every night.

After about two months of being married Jesse announced he did not like eating at the dining room table and that he wanted to eat in the living room in front of the television. When I would mention that drinking water instead of beer would be a healthier alternative, he would snap at me and say, he liked his beer and he was not going to quit drinking it. He also told me shortly after we were married that he did not want to continue going to church with my daughter and me. Sitting in front of the television during dinner, there was no prayer and very little conversation. Jesse became very disconnected from himself and me.

He complained about the mortgage payment and wondered how we were going to come up with the money every month. Somehow we did. We were on time each month for a whole year. I could sense that Jesse was becoming disenchanted with what he felt were his responsibilities of married life with me.

In November, Jesse's youngest brother made a rare phone call to Jesse late one Sunday afternoon. He told Jesse how much he envied his life. He expressed that he had it made. Two days later he was found dead. Jesse did not share with me that Daniel died. I had to pry it out of him. He expressed grief that first night and then never spoke about it again. Jesse felt guilty about not doing more for Daniel. Daniel had a hard life. An alcoholic like his dad, he had three DUIs and consequently had trouble keeping jobs as well as other difficulties. Before Jesse met me, Daniel had been living with his mother and Jesse felt he was taking advantage of her. He drank and got quite ugly when he was drunk. He was abusive to Jesse and their mother. Jesse made Daniel move out and felt bad about it afterward. After Daniel's death Jesse became very depressed.

By November, about five months into our marriage, sex became less and less frequent. I was very attracted to Jesse and loved him. I wanted to be intimate more frequently. I knew that if we were he would open up emotionally. When I asked Jesse about it, I was rebuffed. He told me that me pushing it would just make it worse. He was not interested in making love on a regular basis.

In February, Jesse flew to Utah to go snowboarding. He did not want to make love to me the night before he left. When he came home he was even more distant than he had been before. When I tried to snuggle with him and get friendly he put his arm around me like he was in a coma. He did not hold me or hug me in bed. When I moved closer he snapped that he was tired.

I was shocked that weeks had gone by, without us making love. The fact that he was even less interested in making love after his trip made me question what was going on. I got up and wrote for several hours. At the end of that time I woke Jesse up, I knew what had happend. "Jesse have you had an affair?" He angrily responded from his sleepy state, "What? I'm tired!" I knew in my heart he had been with someone else while he was out of town. Most men would make love to their wife either before a trip or upon returning. Jackie wanted neither.

By the end of January, my daughter moved in with us full time. Up until then, Ana was with us every other week. I knew that Jesse liked our time alone. We tended to reconnect during those weeks. Jesse had expressed earlier that he wanted Ana to live with us, so I assumed that he spoke the truth. Once Ana was with us full time our sex life became almost nonexistent; about once in four to six weeks. I asked if Jesse should see a doctor and get a checkup. He smirked, letting me know there was nothing wrong with him. He just was not interested in me. I thought I was too fat, or not attractive enough. I searched for reasons that he would not want to make love to me.

I knew that this was faulty thinking. This was Jesse's issue, not mine. Between the drinking every night and his depression, Jesse became increasingly distant and disconnected. It was like living with a roommate. I felt like an indentured servant. I took care of all Jesse's needs and he took care of none of mine.

How could I have attracted another addictive personality as my partner? I could not believe this. I tried to get Jesse to go to counseling with me. He was not interested in the least. He felt he did not have a problem. Denial is the first sign of addiction.

Jesse would leave the house at around 6:00 a.m. Before we were married he would call me during his workday. After our wedding he stopped calling me. If I called him and left a message he would not call me back. I tried leaving him text messages. He would not return my texts either.

When the weather was good, as soon as Jesse arrived home, he would play with the dogs for a little and then load up his expensive mountain bike on his truck rack and go riding on the trails off Sixes Road in Woodstock. He came home about two hours or so later, popped open a beer and sat down and watched television. He would get a beer out of the refrigerator in his RV so I would not know and drink it while he cleaned his bike behind the barn. The empty bottle was left out in the barn in the recycle bin. By 8:30 p.m. or even earlier he was heading to bed. The next day was a repeat of the day before. If I wanted to make love, and my teenage daughter was present, it was impossible to be discreet. Jesse knew I could not follow him into the bedroom at that early hour.

I continued to do the laundry, cook the meals, and Ana and I would clean up after dinner. There was no "us." We did nothing together. When I suggested a night out in April, when Ana was staying at a girlfriend's overnight, I suggested several romantic restaurants. Jesse wanted to go to the little village of Crabapple to a pub. I expressed that I did not want to eat at the pub; I had wanted romance and intimacy. Instead we ended up at Chili's. There is nothing wrong with

Chili's. It is a fine family restaurant. It is one of the restaurants that my daughter and her father eat at frequently. What I wanted was a place with quiet ambiance, where we could spark some romance. It became clear to me as I sat in the booth with children screaming behind me that he just did not want to connect with me in any way. This was classic avoidance. I was surprised to feel anger surfacing. I cried, out of anger, out of sadness. I went into the bathroom to compose myself. When I came back to the table Jesse was halfway through his first beer. I wanted to leave. He looked at his beer and me and said we could go if I wanted to. He was exasperated with me. He could not understand what was wrong with Chili's. I ended up telling the waiter we would order. He had come over to our table a couple of times and was a little uncomfortable with the tension and conversation at our table. I felt bad for him. He was an innocent bystander. We got through our dinner, and I managed to discuss what I was feeling. We left the restaurant without any resolution and did not make love while we had the house to ourselves. Reality was beginning to set in. Jesse was in a dark place, where he could not be reached. I was not the cause. He did not want help and it was clear he did not want me. I did not know what else I could do.

It had been over six months since we had what I would call a normal sex life. Jesse went to bed early to avoid it. He had begun wearing boxers to bed every night. The signs are so subtle you have to really be aware to see them. He smirked when I suggested he see a doctor. Jesse's equipment was working just fine, his smirk told me. He was taking care of his needs himself when I was not around. I felt like I had been slapped. My face got hot and I felt a pang of fear in my stomach. This was not a good sign. Ana asked me several times if Jesse was gay. At first I thought, no way, he is always doing extreme sports, with guys. No! He couldn't be?!

I spoke to my closest friends and spiritual mentors about what was going on. I asked for advice and counsel. I did everything I knew to do. The bottom line was, I could not repair our relationship on my own. Jesse had to want to.

In April, we planned to get away to a friend's beautiful rental house in the mountains of Sautee, Georgia. As the weekend approached, I had a sense that Jesse did not want to go. I was not one to sweep issues under the carpet. I faced them head on. One afternoon after Jesse got home from work, I brought up our trip and asked if Jesse could take Friday off, to extend our weekend. He said he could not; he already had work scheduled for that day. I asked if he really wanted to go away with me, that I had a sense that he did not want to. He responded "Silly girl!" Of course he wanted to. On Thursday evening, the day before we were to leave for our weekend get-away, Jesse came home from work with his hair buzzed off. He was doing his best to make himself unattractive. Cutting his hair off the day before our "belated honeymoon weekend" was like a slap in the face for me. He knew I liked his hair long. I had expressed this to him more times that I could mention. Cutting his hair right before his trip spoke volumes. This was passive aggressive behavior.

We had a very relaxing day and a half. We drove up to Diana's on Friday after work, stopping at a Japanese steak house on the way. On Saturday morning we went to Helen, Georgia for breakfast at the famous Hoffers bakery. It was my favorite place to have breakfast. When Jesse suggested it, I offered that we eat at a different restaurant, as it was not a favorite place for him. Our breakfast was delicious and our conversation was enjoyable. I made a delicious dinner on Saturday night, which we enjoyed on the intimate balcony off the dining room, overlooking the mountains. Afterward we actually made love for the first time in over a month. I gave myself to Jesse in his favorite way. When he asked me not to stop and it was obvious that was all he wanted, I made the conscious decision I would be left out. I stopped and changed positions. The fact that he would choose to have only his needs met and did not want to give to me, hurt me. I tried to think only of the beautiful act of connecting through our union. It was beautiful. We snuggled and slept close together afterward. The next morning, after breakfast, Jesse wanted to leave. We had the whole day ahead of us, alone to hike or sit in the hot tub. I was very sad and disappointed. Jesse wanted to be home early to play with Ozzie and go riding.

Our weekend away was the last time that we made love. This was such a disappointment for me as we were so attracted to each other. I really thought Jesse was the one for me. But my needs were not being met. Jesse was systematically shutting me out of his life. We were not marriage partners; we were little more than roommates without fringe benefits.

We had not even been married a year and I knew it was over. Jesse was not capable of giving me anything. He could not connect with me on an emotional or physical level. His religious beliefs had finally surfaced without the mask of subterfuge. Before we were married I discussed my beliefs and the healing work I did openly with him. He was quite effusive when he said he did not have to believe what I believed. I was entitled to my own beliefs and he was fine with that. More recently however, he had told me he did not believe that I healed anyone. Although he said in the next breath that people obviously felt that they were helped as they kept coming to me.

I wondered why he even married me, as he did not like what I did for a living, did not agree with my beliefs and did not want to make love to me.

He was not a generous person, and that stinginess translated to him being withholding of his love. I did not know how I was going to pay the mortgage by myself, but I knew I could not continue to live in a marriage that was loveless. Yes, he felt love for me, but he was dishonest. He lied to me about who he was and the fact that he was an alcoholic. As you do one thing is how you do everything. Jesse was not honest with himself. How could I expect him to be honest with me? Jesse could not give to me what he was incapable of giving to himself.

In retrospect, we got married quickly, which was not my intention. I listened to our minister who said that June 28th was the most auspicious day for us to marry. I wanted to wait until later in the year, closer to the fall. When I consulted with my astrologer after the fact, I was told that a marriage on the day and time we wed would bring drugs and alcohol into my home. I found it interesting that our minister did not mention this aspect.

There are no accidents. It was no accident that I married Jesse. As a result of our marriage I got full custody of my daughter Ana. I felt certain that being in what seemed like a stable environment opened me up to the possibility of having Ana get her wish. She had wanted to live with me since my divorce seven years before.

I found the silver lining. I also recognized that even though I had done years and years of healing work on myself, I still had more to do. I had to release the emotions associated with my past. I had cleared the pattern, but I had not totally released all the emotion. I also had to heal my relationship with my dad. It was obvious although no one in the family would admit that he had been an alcoholic and an addict. He smoked like a chimney for 17 years. Then quit cold turkey. He made his own beer and wine, allowing himself time alone in the basement. No one ever knew how much he consumed down there alone. He came upstairs ruddy-faced and flushed.

My dad was a man's man, like Jesse. He was talented in many areas. He had lots of tools and though he was self-taught, he managed to build two houses and a cottage for our family. He was very disconnected and not available for me emotionally. He also drank until his gout became so bad he had to give it up, probably in his fifties. He used to escape from my mother, by going into our basement to make wine. He would stay downstairs for hours, skimming, filtering and bottling. It was a fine art and he loved it. Wine making became his love. He became very good at it. My mother lost him for years.

Sadly the week after our last discussion I awoke at 3:00 a.m. for the third morning in a row. I lay awake listening to Jesse's breathing and feeling his body next to mine. I could not bear to sleep beside this man that I loved, knowing I could not have him and that he did not want me. He had shown through his actions that he did not want to be with me. I was so sad and angry all at the same time. The feelings of complete and total rejection and emotional abandonment were so overwhelming. I prayed and asked for guidance. After hours of lying awake listening to my guidance, I realized that I was being a victim. That did it! I did not want to be a victim in my own marriage. I knew that I had to make a decision for myself. We were both unhappy. Jesse was depressed and unhappy and my needs were certainly not being met in any way. What was I teaching my daughter by staying with this unavailable man? I got up and went into the kitchen flipped on the light switch to find that it was 6:10 a.m. Jesse's new iPhone alarm did not go off, I chuckled to myself. I walked back into the bedroom and woke Jesse. I told him his alarm did not go off and that I needed to talk with him. I knew he did not like these conversations, so hitting him early in the morning was even worse. I made it short.

I told Jesse that this was the last night he was going to sleep in my bed. He had not been a husband to me in many months, so he needed to sleep somewhere else, either the couch, upstairs, or in his RV. I also said that it was unlikely that we could do an uncontested divorce due to our house contract and purchase. He asked me, "So you are saying that I am stuck?" I said, "Well you signed on the dotted line, Jesse." He said angrily, "We'll see about that!" I also said that I had loved him and been loyal, committed and honest throughout our relationship, which was more than I could say about him. I added that he needed to move out before his motorcycle trip and if he wanted to leave Ozzie here with me, I would charge him $35.00 a day. I also asked him to pay his expenses and the mortgage before he left to go on his trip. Jesse left without his coffee. I knew he was angry and very hurt.

I knew that the first year of marriage should be the best. After the first year, things will either go downhill or stay the same. I could not sleep night after night next to a man who I am attracted to but who does not want to make love to me. What I recognized finally is that withholding love and sex is a form of abuse. This was the only type I had not experienced. Now my repertoire was complete. I understood why I had so much trouble writing my book. Jesse was not the love of my life I thought he was. He was another lesson. He did his job. He was a player in the play of life. I was not going to make Jesse my project and try to rescue or fix him.

In the week following our return from our weekend away, I realized that there was nothing more I could do. I told Jesse that we did not have a marriage, that we were little more than roommates. I needed more. I gave him several different options for therapy. I suggested that he go to Adult Children of Alcoholics, or Alcoholics Anonymous. That made him angry. He could not admit he had an issue with alcohol. I asked him again if he would go to counseling with me. Jesse replied he would think about it. That was not enough for me. I had to give him some sort of a deadline. I told him he had 30 days to decide if he was in or out of our marriage. I really felt that he loved me enough to want to work through our issues.

A week before the 30 days were up, Jesse and I were standing in the barn together and I asked him if he would go to counseling with me. He said that if he thought it would help, he would go but he did not feel it would help. The bottom line was, he told me, he was not going to change, and he was 55 years old. I made sure he knew that I loved him. He said he wished that love was enough, but he just didn't care enough. He would not quit drinking and he would not change.

On Saturday, I called Jesse's cell phone on my way home from visiting a client. His message did not play. Instead I heard that his voice mail had not been set up. Acting on my gut feeling, I called my cell phone provider and found that Jesse and taken his phone off my family plan and had separated his account from mine. When I got home I asked when he was planning on telling me that he had taken his cell phone off the family plan. He said he was going to tell me. He was in the middle of reading an instruction manual and I found that he had purchased an iPhone as well as a new section for a second bike on his high-end bike rack. He did all this without consulting me. The week before he had purchased new clip-on pedals for his bike shoes as well as an expensive two-wheel bike for his grandson. He also went to visit his kids and made it very clear my daughter and I were not invited. Jesse was acting like a single guy. It felt to me like he had already made his decision. He was already gone. Since Jesse did not share his thoughts and feelings with me, I could only assume he was not going to tell me. This was typical behavior for him. He was unable to discuss anything of emotional consequence with anyone. He just was not going to.

In retrospect, I have come to realize that at the end of my marriage to Jesse I reacted as the wounded child. My feeling was that Jesse did not want me. He rejected me and that really hurt me deeply. It brought me back to my childhood when my Dad treated me differently because I was a girl. He was cold and distant. He felt females were inferior. This had a strong impact on my self-esteem. I felt unwanted, unequal and unaccepted. I was relegated to the tasks of a female, doing the cooking, cleaning and family ironing. None of my brothers cooked or ironed. I was programmed at a very early age that females did women's work and men did men's work. We were the "weaker," less intelligent sex.

It could be argued that if I had enough drive, I could have achieved much without my father's support. However, when you are programmed to have low self-esteem you grow up believing that what you are told by your parents is true and that is what you begin to accept as fact.

I felt rejected, so I in turn rejected him by asking him to leave. I wanted to be loved, yet Jesse was hurting so much inside he could not give me what I wanted and needed. What I did not realize was that my pushing Jesse to heal, get counseling and do something only pushed him to shut down even more. It was another cycle. By asking Jesse to move out, the space was created for me to see and accept my part in our relationship. I was equally responsible for where we were. I was wounded too. I was hurting also.

In the weeks following Jesse's departure I became so despondent I could barely move or function. I had a teenage daughter to take care of, a house to keep up with, a business to run, and animals to care for.

I was angry at first, and then I felt a deep sadness. I had spent many days crying on my mower and processing the pain of our ending marriage. I continued to do my clients' landscaping maintenance as if in a trance. I had done this job for ten years now and I could do it with my eyes shut.

Having my own business had many benefits. I could work alone or hire people to assist me. I enjoyed working alone, as I could do the lawn maintenance without interference or interruption. One of my long-term clients lived out of the country in Switzerland and had a large estate within six miles of my home. There were over two acres of grass to mow and many large islands filled with shrubs to prune and weed. Although the work was physical and tiring, I enjoyed it and used the time to commune with God in complete privacy while I worked.

My entire time sitting on my large zero-radius mower was spent in a type of meditation called Ascension. Ascension is a succession of mantras (or prayers) recited silently, while connected to your heart. I had been using Ascension for four years by this time and had become adept at Ascending with my eyes open during my landscaping work. The mantras bring you to a place of deep inner peace and connectedness with God. All fear and worries fall away and only love remains.

Three weeks after Jesse moved out, on a very hot day in May, I spent the whole day sitting in the hot sun mowing my client's grass on my big Ferris mower, thinking about Jesse and our marriage and what was really true about our relationship. I allowed myself to feel the pain fully instead of trying to push it down or mask it. There was no one around to hear or see me. I asked for God's help in allowing me to really feel all my feelings. As I did this I felt very angry about the loss of our relationship and of our dreams.

I felt angry about how Jesse had misrepresented himself before we were married. The person he was when we were dating was not who he became after our marriage. I felt as if I had been duped. He was no longer the open warm, affectionate man who loved to make love to me and wanted to be with me. As I let the thoughts and words fly on the mower, I "talked" to Jesse in my mind saying the things I did not say to him in person. At times I even yelled out loud "I loved you! I really let you in! I was fully vested in our relationship! You really hurt me! You rejected me! I was loyal and honest and you betrayed me! You lied to me!" The anger really started to surface about the loss of my dreams and what I thought we had. As I returned home I unloaded my blower and weed eater, having to maneuver around Jesse's motorcycle, sports equipment, and tools strewn all over the barn. After dodging all Jesse's stuff lying in the barn for over a year and walking back and forth around his expensive motorcycle, I realized that he had had more up, close, and personal time with his bike than he had with me over the last year. I could feel the anger rising and building within me. Allowing myself to feel my feelings fully instead of stuffing them like a "good girl," I realized the rage I had about our sham of a marriage. I was angry that Jesse did not even want to try to mend our relationship. I was angry that he did not want to go to counseling or even talk about our issues with me. I was angry that he did not want to make love to me. I was angry that he would rather ride his bicycle and drink beer than spend quality time with me.

Jesse had changed out the clutch on his truck and left the old truck parts all over the floor of the barn. He had also collected cast-off tools, workout benches, and other junk from friends and had dumped it in the barn. When he removed an air conditioner from a friend's place, rather than take it to the dump he brought it home and dumped it outside the barn. He had also brought home six large plastic water barrels thinking that he would make them into rain barrels and sell them to make extra money. In this mix was also an unwanted ladder rack for a truck that he promised to sell for extra cash, which was lying forgotten in our front yard.

I looked at Jesse's Yamaha R6 sports bike sitting out in the barn. I knew how much he loved that bike. I began pounding his motorcycle. It was not like me to want to destroy someone else's property. I wished for a nearby cliff so that I could push the fucking bike right off of it. I screamed out loud, "I am so angry that you could not give me what I needed! I am pissed off that you don't want to pay the mortgage!" Then I screamed at the top of my lungs, "I am angry you don't want to be with me!"

He had moved all my landscaping equipment into the dark recesses of the barn when we got married. The fact that his motorcycle and his bicycles got more up, close, and personal action with Jesse than I did infuriated and pained me beyond belief. As I let go of all the anger I vented with my voice and my actions as the pain came up. I screamed until I could not scream anymore and then I wept. My sobs and wailing could be heard from the next-door Publix supermarket, but I did not care. I had to get this pain out. I knew that holding it in did not cut it anymore.

I cried for our lost relationship. I cried for my daughter who at the age of 14 was going through a second divorce. I cried at the loss of the man I loved and thought I would grow old with. I cried that Jesse would rather have a beer than me. I cried until the tears would not fall any more.

Some days I got up and felt terrific, free, and fearless. Other days, especially after Jesse had been by the house, I would sink into a dark place where I could barely think straight. My memory on those days was poor and I had difficulty getting my daughter to do anything. I lacked the emotional strength to pursue anything.

The next two weeks were difficult and painful. I felt like I was walking through thick, wet mud. I could barely function. I was in the depth of depression and did not even recognize it. I had to get estimates done because I had to pay the mortgage. I had to eat and feed my daughter. Without any estimates I would not make any money. I had nothing on the table that was going to bring in any money at the moment.

It was uncanny how my oldest son Adam always knew when I had gotten into a downward spiral and could not get out. He drove up from Atlanta to talk with me with his live-in girlfriend because he could feel the emotional space I was occupying.

His Girlfriend, Clara, explained to me that we shared a vibrational bubble and when I was depressed and despondent my energy affected the two of them and what they were creating because of our connection. Conversely we would buoy each other up and raise each other's vibration when we were feeling joy-filled. Right now and for the past two weeks they could feel where I was and their momentum had stopped as well. They had been having difficulty manifesting television and modeling jobs during this time.

I knew this to be true, but being reminded of it helped me. I was surprised that they noticed. Adam had come a really long way in a short time. Only a year ago he was deeply depressed and immobilized himself. He had done 26 consecutive weeks of counseling and it had really done wonders for him. It was group counseling, which frequently brings up more for each of us because we see things in others and then connect the dots for ourselves.

I heard what they said to me and mentioned that I had not even bothered to clear myself in weeks, as I was so deeply depressed. I could not even see that I needed it. Normally when I feel attachments or dark energy I recognize it within a day or two. Letting go of Jesse and our relationship was far more profound a release than I had experienced in a very long time. My sense was that I was clearing something far deeper than just our marriage in this lifetime. I was clearing all the lifetimes that Jesse and I had been together and never been able to make it work. I was also releasing other issues from the past as the sadness came up.

That is the hardest part about depression. When we are in it we can't reach up and ask for help. We are so far down we don't even see that we are depressed and that our energy has been affected. No wonder people commit suicide; they have no idea that they need help. Loved ones need to recognize it and assist in a loving and compassionate way, like my son, Adam, and his girlfriend, Clara, did. They were kind, loving, and concerned. They did not harp or judge. They just brought the issue into my awareness. Awareness is the first step towards healing. I knew that I needed to move the muck and mire I was stuck in. I went inside the house and cleared myself.

A former client turned friend in Florida spoke to me about a fellow healer in Miami that did Akashic record readings. Janice had spoken very highly of Ernesto Ortiz. He was a shaman, healer, and teacher. He was very well thought of not only in Miami but also around the globe. He traveled extensively, teaching in places like Peru, Guatemala and Egypt. Apparently he had done some very deep clearing work on himself and discovered after clearing himself for years that old patterns still remained. He discovered through working on himself that something called "Imaginal cells" located in each person's DNA was what needed to be cleared. This fit in perfectly with my belief that all our patterns are held in our DNA. Clearing the Imaginal cells is like using a microfiber cloth to wash your car instead of a hard brush. All the remnants of blocks and any residual energy is cleared. Janice told me he was teaching a class on how to read the Akashic records and do Imaginal cell work in Bali, Indonesia. I knew immediately I had to go. I had always been intrigued about the Akashic records. The Akashic files contain everything that has ever happened in any incarnation for each person. They are the record books of God. I was ecstatic. A new fork in the road was being presented! Jesse was gone, a vacuum was created, and my new world was appearing before me. I had dreamed of visiting Bali for over 30 years. My dream was becoming a reality.

I contacted Ernesto and made an appointment for an Akashic reading, just to test the waters and make sure for myself he was authentic and accurate. An Akashic reading is different from a psychic reading in that you ask questions you would like to have the answers to. It is absolute and accurate. He told me that Jesse and I had had seven lifetimes together in total. Each time we were unable to complete our relationship – and each ended badly.

We both fulfilled our contract to each other. Ours was a karmic relationship and we had cleared our karma with one another completely. He added that the healing and Oneness Blessings that I had given to Jesse while he was sleeping were planted seeds that would help him eventually heal, but it would be a long time off. Ernesto added as long as I did not create any additional drama in the divorce all would be well. I also asked if I would go to Bali. He answered that I would. My concern was that Matthew and Andrea's wedding was right smack in the middle of the course. Could it be that they were not supposed to be married? Ernesto told me I had to talk to Matthew about his upcoming wedding to Andrea.

My conversation with Matthew would be enough to move the energy. It had already begun to move as we spoke about their wedding date. I was very upset that I needed to question Matthew about his relationship and whether he was sure that Andrea was the right one for him. Matthew had broken up with Andrea after they spent a year living together. I knew that my questioning him would not go over very well.

I had my chance to talk to Matthew shortly after my clearing with Ernesto. As I had expected, Matthew became very angry about my doubts. He said he was in a very good place and he was sure. I reminded him that just a year ago, right before my wedding, I was sure about Jesse also. "Look at us now," I said. Matthew said that was not the case with him. So I dropped the subject. Adam overheard my conversation and was extremely concerned about the damage I may have done and went over that night to repair it.

I wondered about Ernesto's advice when I received a phone call from Matthew less than two weeks after our conversation. As I answered the phone, Matthew said without hesitation, "We cancelled the wedding!" I could not help but gasp. Matthew went on to explain that Andrea's grandmother had taken over the planning and details of the wedding to the point that it no longer was "their wedding." Andrea told her grandmother she would not have their wedding in her grandmother's garden after all. At this point the date was up in the air and they were looking for a new venue. I sighed relief and asked Matthew to please take the dates of my course into consideration and I would greatly appreciate it if they would have the wedding either before September 14th or after September 30th if at all possible. Matthew told me he would see what he could do. I am not sure if he remembered, but the date Was changed to October 2nd on Tybee Island. I knew this all happened so that I could do both, attend Matthew's wedding and go to Bali.

I sat outside under the shade of a large maple tree and allowed myself to really feel what I was feeling. I feel more deeply connected to God and myself when outside in nature. I quickly entered a state of deep connection to my high self. I asked for God's assistance in feeling my feelings that I had about divorce and our marriage being truly over. I was surprised that I cried. I allowed myself to feel the feelings without the story of what happened. I tapped into the sadness, the loss and the fact that Jesse would never share my bed again. We would never travel to Ireland as we had planned and I would never go skiing with him in Utah. Jesse, Ana and I would not be a family. I felt it all. I cried without shame and without judgment. I allowed myself to grieve fully. When I felt totally complete, I got on my Ferris mower and mowed the pasture well after it was too dark to see. The fireflies accompanied me as I mowed. I knew I was safe, protected and going to be fine.

I did not want to date, although the listing real estate agent for our home asked me out several times. I was not interested in dating at all. I was still grieving. I wanted to give myself enough time to process and heal before I moved forward. I told him I was not divorced and would not date until I was. Within a week he called back and asked me over to his house for dinner. My boundaries were clearly being tested. I replied again, I was not divorced and would not date until I was. Did he think having dinner at his house was not a real date?

I had a phone message from this same man regarding showing our rental house while we were visiting family in July for a wedding. After answering his questions regarding the air condition-ing, he asked me again if I was divorced yet? He said he was lonely. I was repelled by his neediness. I was not lonely. I might feel sad from time to time, but lonely I was not. I enjoyed my time alone. This was progress for me. In the past I could be coerced into doing something I did not want to do, because of my weak boundaries from my childhood. I was on my way to healing. I had more good days than bad and I felt good. I also felt strong. I would never date a man who did not listen to me. What part of "no" did he not understand?

I knew that Jesse could not get to the place that I was. Not only did he not know how, he did not want to. He was hopelessly disconnected and in denial of his pain. His bike riding and beer drinking continued to keep him shut off from his deep feelings. He was beyond comfortably numb. Without any hope of reconciliation I knew we would be divorced before long. I would not sit in limbo waiting for Jesse.

I made preparations towards a divorce, changing my name etc. I printed the paperwork off from the Internet and set it aside. Although I felt that Jesse was not able to change, I was not sure this was the right time to file for divorce. I wanted the pain to stop, but I needed to breathe first.

I cleared myself as I would a client. I cleared myself daily or when I felt a dip in my energy. I realized that every time Jesse came to the house there was a ripple effect. I was connecting to his energy and his depression. I was impacted by his sad feelings and where he was emotionally. I could feel that he was lost, but he was unaware of what to do. I knew that my meddling or trying to assist him in anyway would be spurned. He did not want my help. He did not want counseling. He had made that very clear. I had offered to go and he had refused, more than once. He was a grown man.

Every time I thought about going back with Jesse or having him move back into the house, I felt like my body was denser. I felt bad. I knew that as much as I had wanted our marriage to work, it was not in my best interest. The man I married was not who he portrayed himself to be.

I asked myself about signs. Did I ignore them? I did ignore the drinking, although I asked several people for some guidance, because he was only drinking two beers each night, which did not constitute alcoholism. It was more of a self-medication. Jesse was feeling emotions and feelings he did not want to get into and acknowledge, so he rode his bike like a demon and drank to dull the pain. Instead of making the pain go away, it pushed it down and numbed himself temporarily. He was angry from something that happened long before I came into the picture. Unexpressed anger is what depression is. Whoa! I realized after some guidance from Gomati, a dear friend, I needed to express my anger to get through this depression. Jesse and I were mirroring each other.

I found myself alone quite a bit after that guidance and I managed to scream my head off several times in the privacy of my truck. A couple of times I drove with the windows open and screamed at the top of my lungs. It was cathartic. I felt a tremendous release and much better after several blood curdling screams. I lost my voice, but the depression was definitely easing.

I was awarded a couple of small landscaping jobs, which took the pressure off to make money. I loved the work and always enjoyed doing landscaping and being outdoors. After the third week passed and I did better, Jesse came back to the house both on Saturday and Sunday to retrieve some of his belongings. By Sunday afternoon, unbeknownst to me, I was in a deep state of depression again.

It was obvious to me now, every time Jesse came to the house I would get depressed. I needed to make sure that I was not at home the next time he had to pick up more of his stuff. I also had to clear the house, as it was thick with sticky and low depressing energy. I realized I needed to be more proactive and immediately clear the house and myself whenever Jesse came by.

I was beginning to stand in my power with my customers. I was discounting my work less. I had built a good reputation over the past ten years and I was beginning to reap what I had sowed. I was much more confident of my value and myself. I gave great service, was dependable, on time, and did quality landscaping work. The issue was balancing. I could spend all my time working and have no time at all for relaxation or with my daughter. Trying to find time to write was also important and becoming a challenge.

My insight was becoming very strong and accurate. I took a course from Gomati and Vasistha Ishaya to become a Oneness Blessing Giver in March of 2009. In addition to the training to give Oneness Blessings, I did the 64 Deeksha process after becoming a Oneness Blessing Giver. These two events opened me up and made me a better channel. I streamed information from the cosmos. Conversations would come to me that others would have. My guidance was very accurate and I was listening. My visions were also accurate.

I continued daily to process the sadness and disappointment of the loss of my marriage with Jesse. Whenever I had a moment alone I would allow myself to feel my sadness instead of pushing it away. I really tapped into what was bubbling up emotionally for me. Sometimes it was anger, but mostly after the day in the barn when I wanted to push Jesse's bike over a cliff it was intense sadness.

I spoke with Gomati and Vasistha, my Ascension teachers. They were wonderful support people for me. They loved me unconditionally and supported me without judgment. In one conversation with Vasistha he told me that witholding of love, affection, attention and lovemaking is abuse. Oh my God! This was a revelation to me. With all the ways that I had been abused over my lifetime, this was one that I had yet to experience.

I realized that however painful this was for me, Jesse was giving me a gift. He was doing what we contracted to do for me before we incarnated. He was not a perpetrator; he was simply playing his part in my play of life. He was offering another chapter on abuse for me in my book. I still had more to heal and clear in my life for me to love myself fully. The fact that he did not thank and appreciate all the things I did for him was disrespect. I found out that doing everything in a relationship leads to a feeling of being an indentured servant. Unless there is equality in the relationship there will not be respect.

The disrespect he had shown me was a reflection of the ways that I still disrespected myself. My boundaries needed to be shored up and stronger. There was more work to do.

Two months after Jesse moved out, my oldest son and his girlfriend found themselves without a place to live and moved in with me temporarily. The Universe is always conspiring for me. This gave me the opportunity to strengthen my boundaries on a daily basis. I had always had difficulty being firm and consistent with Adam. This was a wonderful healing opportunity for us both.

I realized in working with my clients that I was not alone in this. Many women I was currently working with were also in relationships where love was withheld. Most women are not aware that this is abuse.

I called Jesse and told him I was filing for divorce at the end of June. It would be uncontested and a self-filing. We had been let out of the contract on our property so we did not have any joint debt. Nor did we have any children. It would be simple, cheap, and no attorneys were required. We met at Jesse's bank to have the documents signed and notarized and we were divorced July 22nd just shy of 13 months after we were married.

We sat side by side in the courtroom before being called into the conference room to go before the presiding judge. We talked comfortably for the 30 minutes we had to wait. Jesse mentioned he hoped that his company van would not be towed as he had parked it on the street.

While we sat together, I told Jesse that there had not been anyone else for me. That I had not begun to date and had not even looked at one Internet dating site. I was comfortable allowing myself the space I needed to readjust to my new life. There would be plenty of time for dating later on.

When the judge asked me if our marriage could be saved, I exhaled deeply and looked at Jesse. I knew if I said yes, he would agree. "No, your honor," I replied. Jesse looked wistfully at me. The judge asked what name I wanted to use. When I replied "Masters," Jesse was surprised. He joked, wasn't I going to use Ana's father's name? I told him I was not and that I had thought long and hard about my decision. We walked out of the judicial center in Atlanta with our arms around each other. There was no hate. There was no resentment. I did not blame Jesse and he did not blame me. It felt to me that Jesse's head was spinning because everything had ended so fast. He seemed a little bewildered about what had really taken place and why we were getting divorced. He did not feel he had done anything wrong.

As we walked out of the cool building onto Pryor Street into the baking Atlanta heat and around the corner to Central Avenue, Jesse expressed his displeasure that his work van had been towed. He had parked it on the street right in front of the judicial center. He whined his familiar whine, making that body movement that little children make when they don't get their way. He was moving his head back and forth as he whined. Even though there were "no parking" signs all over the place I said nothing. I did not judge. I told him I would stay with him and drive him to the impound lot once we found where it was. It took us over an hour to get the required paperwork taken care of.

I waited in the parking lot to be sure Jesse could get his van. As he pulled out of the gate and drove across the street to the place I waited, I got out of my car to say good-bye. I hugged him and he kissed me and that was that. I was divorced. It was officially over.

In the aftermath of our breakup, I have recounted and reassessed every detail of our dating. From the first date, to the day I said I would marry Jesse, until the last day I saw him. I recognize in myself the Pollyanna who sees only the good in people and ignores the negative. I created Jesse to be who I wanted him to be. From believing that because he was a Baptist minister to turning that into my belief that he must therefore be spiritual. That was not true.

When we were dating, I did not have alcohol in my house, so I did not see the evidence of Jesse drinking. He could not keep up the charade any longer. He was not able to hide the truth any longer. I was concerned about his drinking and asked for advice on the subject beforehand. I should have listened to my gut instead. The body never lies. My gut gave me the info I needed and I gave my power away to readers and spiritual mentors that did not have the feeling that I did in my body. Why did I do that? I trust my guidance with every other part of my life. Why when it comes to men do I ignore it? I will tell you why, because I grew to love him and I wanted him. He was very attractive to me; I saw the light in him and not the shadow. We both fell in love with the illusion, not the real person.

We both wanted to believe that this was it. We thought we were perfect for each other. We felt a kinship; a remembrance of what we had had in our past lives together. This familiarity felt like coming home and was what we loved. We embellished the good and excused the waving red flags. We both ignored our rules for dating. Jesse did not want to have a child. Yet he ignored his rule because he wanted me. We moved too fast and did not allow enough time to date and get to know each other before we moved in together and got married. I used the excuse that my daughter was with us and we could not live together to get married.

Jesse cooked me dinner one night when we were dating and I took this to believe that he would cook after we got married. This was faulty thinking on my part. He brought me flowers and a Teavana teapot and tea as a gift while we were dating. He even brought me a necklace from Utah before we were married.

Once we were married the gifts stopped and the romance ended. When my daughter moved in full time, Jesse shut me out. Each time I pushed for more intimacy, Jesse was repelled in the other direction.

All the healing courses, Oneness Blessing training, Deekshas, Global Gatherings and workshops I did propelled me further and further in the opposite direction. Jesse was not interested in spiritual growth. As my vibration was raised he drank more and eventually we were vibrating away from each other, like two opposing magnets.

There was no doubt that we loved each other. However, love is not enough to create a great life together, whether one is married or just in a committed relationship. To have the kind of partnership that I so desired, household duties and tasks must be shared. If one person is performing all the household chores alone, what you have is indentured servitude and disrespect. Jesse did not respect me for who I was. He certainly did not want to share the household duties with me.

As far as the healing and growing together, it seems to me in retrospect that Jesse would have said just about anything to have me and win me over. He also agreed to pay the mortgage and purchase the property with me. Just months later he complained about the payments and that he felt it was too much money.

Although I loved the property and the house, I don't think Jesse felt the same as I did. Especially after he found out what was wrong with it. Not that I kept any of these details from him. I told him everything that I knew to be of an issue before we bought the place. My cup is half full and Jesse's is half empty. It is the difference between us. I am positive and Jesse is negative. These things did not become evident until after we were married. Once we were in a committed relationship all bets were off and Jesse acted like a single guy. I found out that his previous wife was a drinker. I am not sure how to interpret this information. I also found out that almost every member of his family, except his mother was an alcoholic. Background information is paramount when dating. If alcoholism figures prominently, physical or emotional abuse occurred, or one or both parties were sexually molested, unless a tremendous amount of healing work has been done be prepared for serious issues and emotional disconnection.

I was surprised at the depth of my grief at the end of our marriage. Feeling my feelings fully and allowing myself to grieve completely without judgment allowed me to move through the depth of despair I experienced quickly and get to the other side.

LESSONS LEARNED

I had never been fully vested in a relationship before my marriage to Jesse. I had grown considerably from my relationship with Mitch until now. I was all in. I was attracted to Jesse and loved him deeply. There was no doubt about that. I was committed to making our relationship work. I did everything I could think of to get him to be my partner and the other part of the team. Jesse said to me in an affirmative way that I did not need an engagement ring. I should have realized he did not truly value me. The fact that he did not want to spend money on an engagement ring showed me he was stingy. People who are stingy with their money are stingy with their love. I ignored this very strong message.

I realized that you cannot "get" someone to do anything if they don't want to. Jesse had blocks to love and intimacy that surfaced after our wedding. The rejection I felt because he did not want to make love to me was extremely painful. I wanted our marriage to work but I was not prepared to make him my project. I was no longer in the business of "fixing" anyone. His approval or disapproval of me did not matter. I was not prepared to sell my soul to get him to love me. Nor was I willing to change.

I had graduated. As painful as it was for our marriage to end I was in a very different place. I was not a victim. I learned a great deal about myself through this process. It is far better to be on my own and happy with myself, than to be married to someone who does not love and appreciate me as I am. I have my freedom and can do what I want when I want. I no longer need to have someone in my life to be happy.

The biggest lesson I learned through letting go of Jesse was that you don't need to be in pain forever. If you allow yourself to feel your feelings fully and completely you will move through anger and the grieving process to get to the other side of the pain. The gift in this was that I let go of other unconscious programmed and stored emotion by allowing myself to grieve completely. I was feeling joy again. My happiness does not depend on another. My happiness and joy come from my connection with God. I no longer feel empty being alone. I do not feel lonely or sad because I do not have a man in my life or in my bed. I love being with me. I would rather be alone with me than spend a moment being with someone who does not lift me up, love and respect me for whom I am.

Vibration: August 1, 2010:   850

Life Force: 100%

CHAPTER ELEVEN

Awakening

In early August, shortly after my metamorphosis, my son Adam and his girlfriend, Clara, moved out of our house. They became very ill from mold that grew throughout the house.

On August 18, 2010, I heard the unmistakable voice of God, "Get rid of your stuff or we will do it for you!" When I heard the voice I did not argue, I just asked, "If this is to happen could you please make sure that no hurt or harm comes to anyone or any animal?" I immediately thought of a fire. That could be disastrous; all my animals would die trapped inside the house if that happened. I was assured that no deaths would occur. It was an inner knowing.

I had lived in this house on and off for seven years. The house held the energies of two divorces and the death of John within its walls and furnishings. The energies within the house were holding me back. Over the last ten years I had four estate sales and sold furniture, china, crystal and silver. I worked on releasing attachment to the material. It was very difficult for me to do even though I knew on a visceral level that it did not bring me happiness.

On August 20, as Ana and I were getting ready to drive to Diana's, I heard the trees speak to me. I had developed this gift by listening carefully and being aware of my surroundings. I knew that nature and the Universe were conspiring for my greater good to give me signs. I paid close attention and used these signs to help me in my life.

The trees called me seven years ago. They brought me to a different road. I experienced joy every day living there. It was compounded by the natural beauty that surrounded me. This was not from anything material in my world. I could differentiate between my angels, guides and the trees because they felt different. I was tuned in and heard them. They told me to move my pickup truck and my trailer from where it was parked. I did not question what I was told and moved the truck and trailer immediately. When we returned the following day three of the large 100-year-old oak trees had dropped over seven tons of solid oak in the very spot where my truck and trailer had been. The huge limbs narrowly missed the trailer by two feet but hit the house damaging the roof in several places.

When I walked around the back of the house and saw the devastation. I wept when I realized that both Ana and I could have been killed by the impact of the trees. I was so grateful to them for keeping all of us safe. The fact that they fell when we were not in the house was Divine. It was a miracle and I recognized it. I knew it was time for us to leave this beautiful place. The trees sacrificed themselves to send me this powerful message. I felt gratitude for our safety. I experienced sadness for the trees. I realized that everything is transient; nothing is permanent. The message could not have been clearer.

Shortly after the tree incident, it became apparent that the mold was pushing me out the door as well. My ignorance and lack of knowledge of black mold helped to create this situation. Both Clara and Adam had lost weight and were feeling tired and ill. My daughter and I developed asthma. I did not connect all the dots. I passed it off on allergies.

Towards the end of August 2010, I found a suede jacket in the hall closet totally covered with mold; my daughter and I noticed it elsewhere. It covered my wooden furniture and antiques and was inside our dresser drawers. I did research on line and learned just how serious it was. I found a mold remediation company that worked with a law firm. Their testing would be used to prove the there was mold, determine the type and prove landlord negligence.

When the tests came back we found that the house tested positive for Aspergillus mold, which can be deadly. The normal accepted level was anything under one thousand parts of particulates. Our house was four times the legal, healthy limit. I was told that for my daughter's and my health we needed to move immediately and leave everything we owned in the house.

Driving Ana to school one day I saw an "Apartment For Rent" sign in front of a house. I knew that this was an incredible opportunity to unload years of stuff. Soft furnishings are the worst for retaining energy from the past. Leaving everything behind could turn out to be a good thing. I looked at the cute yellow frame house several times before I drove up the driveway. An elderly couple owned the home. Dr. Mallard was a retired Baptist minister. He was 96 and his wife was 90 years old. She was lovely with a beautiful mane of thick white hair. Although she had the beginning of Alzheimer's, she liked Ana instantly and kept smiling at her.

The apartment was quite large. There was a screened in porch for our separate entryway. I knew I would have to find a place for some of our animals. They made concessions for our pets and allowed us one dog and one cat. I was not sure how, but I knew it would work out. I let go of the outcome instead of trying to take care of everything myself. I felt that we were meant to be here. I had to trust.

I knew Mrs. Mallard was not going to be here long. It seemed Divine Design brought us to this place. Being guided to do something that would benefit me was not a surprise. We all felt the hand of God at work.

Now that we had a place to live I considered what options I had for my landscaping equipment and my animals. What I had begun to realize is that God and The Universe can offer us all kinds of different options. We just need to be open to walk through the door that is provided. I asked my neighbor if I could store my mower and trailer on her property. They had over 20 acres and did not mind. I was relieved that another issue was solved easily.

I looked for families that could adopt three of our cats and our beloved Weimaraner, Isabella. When the tree company came to remove the trees I had talked to the owner. He noticed Isabella immediately and shared that he and his wife had several Weimaraners in the past. I heard a voice suggest, "Ask him." I was amazed at how easily it all worked. Ana and I braced ourselves for the event. Karma ran off as we were leaving and did not say good-bye to Isabella.

When we arrived at the street address we were given I could not believe what I saw. This was the exact house that I had adopted Karma from eight years ago. It was a different family but the same house. Again I knew that The Divine was at work orchestrating everything more beautifully than I could have ever dreamed possible.

I called Mitch to let him know about our pending move. He was concerned about the timing of it since Ana had only begun high school two weeks before. He called me back and offered to lend us furniture for our apartment. I was really grateful for the help and the furniture. I realized we had made headway in our relationship. We really worked as a team in Ana's life for her highest and best good, as two parents should. We no longer fought about every issue and detail. Instead, we put aside our differences and were Ana's parents instead of ex's. It took us more than seven years to get here, but we healed our relationship. I had less than I ever had in my life and found myself happier than I had ever been. It was profound. I had truly let go of the past.

We were in the apartment two weeks almost to the day when I flew to Bali for my Akashic Records course. When we arrived in Bali we had to clear customs and immigration. When the agent looked at my passport he asked me to come with him. The cigarette smoke in the shabby office was a cruel assault to my senses after such a long trip. It seemed that my passport had less than six months remaining on it. Typically this was not an issue. However, in Bali it was. I applied for a new green card before my trip. It did not arrive in time to apply for a new Canadian passport. I did not think anything of it when I left the United States. However, in Bali it was a serious matter. I sat at the desk in the immigration office and wondered how I could fly all this way only to be sent back. I was sure God did not want this for me. I silently asked what I could do. I sat in the office for over an hour trying to make sense of the situation. My angels told me to turn on the tears. That was not difficult. I was about to be put back on the next flight to Seoul in less than twenty minutes. The officer kept saying strange things to me that did not make sense. He asked me why he should not send me back. I tried to make sense of what he was getting at. I spent all my money getting there. Then I realized I needed to ask my guides what I could do that would change his mind. My guides told me to slide $200 towards him. Instead I gave him three folded hundred-dollar bills discretely. He looked at the money and slid one bill across the table to me. He said he knew I did not have that much and that he understood I needed to eat while I was there. Next thing I knew I was free to go. I had to realize that it was a gift for me to be here.

I was so appreciative of how everything played out. If it were not for Janice I never would have been able to make the trip. She paid for my ticket and I did healing sessions with some of her family members to repay her. I wanted to kiss the ground in the dirty airport. I put my arm around her and screamed, "We're in Bali!" It was our refrain for the entire two weeks we were there. We appreciated and enjoyed every moment. Even sleeping in the little house without air conditioning and void of screens on the windows was delightful. We loved every minute of it.

Before going to Bali, I received the guidance that Janice and I needed to tone together to purify, balance and clear our chakras. Doing so raised our vibration exponentially. For a month Janice and I spent twenty minutes or so on the phone together every morning and sang different tones to clear our charkas. One morning we sang particularly strong and with high pitches at the end of each tone. On the phone together, we both experienced an incredible awakening that changed us forever. I felt an opening and popping of my chakras and an immediate heightened awareness of all that is. We celebrated the moment for what it was. There was no turning back. We were awake. For me the awakening was a series of events strung together that raised my vibration little by little.

I knew I needed to have more fun in my life. Life does not have to be so difficult and serious. We choose to make it so. I made the commitment to myself to have more playtime acting like a child and enjoying life and nature. I really laughed out loud, being in the moment, instead of constantly monitoring and suppressing my joy and became more spontaneous.

Once we were in Bali we continued the toning practice in the water of the beautiful Indian Ocean. This sacred practice was probably the most wonderful part of our trip. It was wonderfully freeing and purifying out in the warm crystal clear water at sunrise. We played like children enjoying the moment. I remembered missed opportunities that I had in my life when I wished I had done something differently. There would be no more missed opportunities. I was awake and conscious now. I appreciated every minute of my magical world.

Our workshop was held in a large hexagonal room with folding doors on all but two sides. The ocean breeze cooled the air naturally. We sat on cushions on the marble floors and tried to sit up straight for meditation and chanting. Our instructor was a heart-centered Buddhist. He was passionate about the teachings of the Akashic Records. He taught reverence and respect. We learned how to read the Akashic records and channel the Ascended Masters. This course forever changed me. It opened me up to new beings that I had not had access to before. Now I had the Masters to listen to as well as my angels, guides and The Divine. Sometimes there were many voices. I was euphoric for the entire two weeks.

I loved Bali. The beauty of the simple rice fields and the sacred flower rituals done twice a day were so lovely. I felt such peace and serenity there. It reminded me faintly of India. The people seemed so happy and serene. The women dedicated themselves to gathering, cutting and arranging flowers for offerings. Sacred service took up to thirty-five percent of their day.

It was difficult to leave. Janice and I raced to the airport two days early as my son, Matthew, and his fiancé, Andrea, were getting married on Tybee Island October 2. I was happy to return home and hug Ana.

After spending two weeks in a sacred retreat with spiritual people, I was vibrating and radiating love. My son's and daughter-in-law's wedding was held in a beautiful beach house with all the divorced parents and family staying in one house together. We had a fabulous weekend together. Phil, his wife and I all got along beautifully. All the moms spent hours cooking together in the kitchen for the huge crowd staying at the beach house. The weekend was idyllic. Adam was moved to tears when he saw his brother and Andrea standing at the altar looking at one another. All at once he realized, my brother is getting married! Everyone was moved.

After all the years of descent, Phil and I had peace between us and it felt really good. I knew this was good for the boys. I was glad we could all be together and enjoy each other without any negativity or drama. I know it meant a great deal to Matthew and Andrea. I realized that Phil and I came together to have our boys. I learned from our relationship. It had not been a mistake. It was all part of The Divine plan. The space between father and sons had been closed. I was recognizing that my world was a reflection of me. Now that I was emanating peace, it surrounded me. I was no longer angry at the world and life. I had stopped resisting. Instead I was accepting and grateful and appreciative of everything in my life. Instead of being in a state of fear, I was in a state of love. It was evident in my relationship with Phil, his wife and our children.

LESSONS LEARNED

What an amazing and transformational journey it has been. I barely recognize the old me that I have gradually de-created. The past no longer defines me. It is not who I am.

I have let go of avoidance and resistance. I am awake and aware, living in each moment as it happens, living my soul purpose in every breath. I no longer live in a state of worry or fear, coming instead from my heart. I accept what is. I enjoy each moment of my life, expressing my emotions as they come up.

Material goods do not bring me happiness. The fleeting moment of excitement that something new brings is transient. The love and joy expressed through relationships with family and friends and giving and helping others is what fulfills me. I experience spontaneous causeless joy.

The passion that spurred me on to heal my life has become a burning desire to help others on their spiritual path. I have let go of the spiritual baggage of my previous relationship. I am willing to risk my heart again. For only when you step out into the void and risk it all can you find the love that you seek.

I recognize the power of my thoughts. I have created all the events in my life for the purpose of evolving my soul. I am grateful to and honor all my teachers who participated in my soul's evolution. I realize that I am the powerful creator of my own destiny.

Vibration: 900

Life Force: 100%

Adam Ana Mathew And Jennifer

Clara   Adam   Jennifer Ana Mathew Andrea

CHAPTER TWELVE

Victory

When we are children we are open and receptive to all that we come into contact with. All experiences, whether positive or negative in nature, are imprinted in a child's unconscious mind. These imprints become beliefs that affect the person for the rest of their lives.

If we are loved and accepted no matter what, we grow into confident stable adults. We are programmed for success. If, on the other hand, the stimulus and information that enters the child's unconscious mind is negative, critical and demeaning, the child will become an adult with low self-esteem, lacking confidence and the ability to succeed in anything.

Children under five lack the ability to filter out messages that come into their unconscious mind. Whatever the message is, it goes straight into the subconscious. Even after the ability is present, if an event is shocking, the filter disappears and again is directly imprinted on the subconscious. When angry parents sometimes shout at their children the filter is removed and angry or negative messages follow:

"You ungrateful child!" "How could you be so stupid?" "Men only want one thing!" "You'll never amount to anything!" Children learn what they live. When a child is molested the belief is imprinted on their subconscious mind that they are only good for sex, or that sex is love. It is no wonder that when a person is sexually molested as a child that they become promiscuous. It becomes the only way that they feel they can be fulfilled. Sometimes verbal messages are also delivered which go directly into the subconscious mind.

When we resist something it affects us deeply. This suppression creates a shielding in the aura, which is like a wall. If you have ever met someone that is shielded, you feel as if a steel wall surrounds them. They may appear polite on the outside, but you sense that they are guarded. If you are sensitive to energy you will feel it. People sometimes refer to this condition as "defended." Someone who is particularly shielded will appear defensive whenever you make a comment that appears to be critical of them. The self-preservation mechanism of repression and suppression creates stress in the body. The stress or blocked energy is self-defeating in the unconscious mind. The energy from each event that has not been dealt with continues to build up. The more energy that builds in the unconscious mind the more unable a person is to cope with the normal stresses of life. Until a way is found, for example through Spiritual Response Therapy, hypnotherapy or EFT, to release the unconscious blocks this energy will remain in the unconscious creating additional stress and eventually illness. When we are so blocked and shut down we are unable to let emotions out. All it takes is someone to cut us off on the road, or our child to act up in public and we have to explode. When we are suppressing emotions because there is so much that we have stuffed into the recesses of our unconscious we are out of balance. We cannot express ourselves in our natural state. We become wooden and defensive. Energy is not able to go out or come in. We have built a castle with a moat around us and became unreachable.

Our aura and chakras (energy centers) are not static, but move. They are living and expanding. Our aura changes shape and color depending on how we feel at a particular moment. When chakras are operating efficiently they spin. When we are blocked it is like holding our breath, without the natural ebb and flow.

There is more than hope. There is amazing possibility. You don't have to stay like this. There are so many ways to begin to release these blocks and let the energy out. Getting in touch with your pain and feeling it fully is possible with awareness.

The reason we keep attracting people to our lives who hurt us is because they are showing us who we are. We attract people who are at a similar vibration with similar issues. These relationships are providing the mirror for us and our unconscious mind. They are an opportunity for healing. Clearing out unconscious patterns and stuck emotions releases us from these self-defeating patterns. Until we clear our unconscious patterns and attached emotions we will not move forward. It is worth the time and effort to work through this. Stop resisting. Resistance causes suffering. Pray for God's Grace to relieve your suffering at the same time. God's Grace offers a spontaneous healing when it occurs. Once these patterns and emotions have been released we have to begin to change our behavior. As we change our behavior those around us will begin to treat us differently.

Changing codependent behavior is possible. When you love and accept yourself completely as you are, codependency falls away. It happens naturally. Once we are no longer codependent healthy relationships result. Looking at ourselves as the witness from a detached perspective instead of attached to the story disengages the ego. These situations are only being offered for the expansion and growth of your soul. When you are clear of limiting beliefs and patterns we are easily able to manifest great things in our lives. The higher your vibration is the easier it is to manifest. Remember whatever you focus on expands, whether you like it or not.

Being aware of how you are feeling is a start. Noticing your emotions as they come up and naming what you feel helps you recognize what you are feeling. You tend to keep yourself so busy which takes your awareness off what you are really experiencing. When you do not take the time to sit and just be, you really do not have an awareness of your feelings. When emotions come up, experience them. Instead of stifling sadness, let yourself cry. Release it fully. When you feel joy and happiness, express it fully also. Be like a child. It is good for the soul. Staying with your emotions four minutes each day is enough to begin to release the blocks. Honor your experience. When you stifle your tears and sadness you just push it back down and repress it further which increases the blocked energy.

Blocked energy creates illness. Every pain, every illness in your body has an emotional component. If we only look at the physical illness we are not getting to the source and origination of the problem. Taking pharmaceutical medication only treats the symptom not the cause. That is why antidepressants don't work. The underlying cause (anger) is being ignored. The anger needs to be released in a safe environment where no one is harmed.

We are not just a physical being. We are mind, body and spirit. If we do not take time to nurture each part of ourselves we are out of balance and create illness in some area. Take responsibility for your health. Look at what is going on with you emotionally first before popping a pill to attempt to relieve your suffering. At the same time if you have a health issue like high blood pressure or diabetes, this does not mean that you stop taking your medicine. Putting your attention on an issue, recognizing where it began can help to heal the issue. Changing your diet and nurturing yourself by loving you will help to create wellness. It is a fact, happy people are healthier than miserable and negative people.

Being aware means to stop and be still. Listen to your heart. Quiet your mind. Meditate each day. Set aside time for yourself. Nurture and be kind to yourself. Do for yourself some of the things that you do for others. If you are a parent, make time for yourself away from the kids one night a week. Even if it is just for one hour. You are important. Where would your family be without you? Your family will benefit from you returning refreshed and more positive.

When you attempt to quiet your mind you may hear incessant mind chatter and self-defeating ego talk. Being aware of your thoughts is extremely important. Listening to the things that you say to yourself, and making sure that they are always positive is part of awareness. It is within your reach to be positive all the time. When you hear yourself make a negative declaration, stop and rephrase it. Catching your negative thoughts before you send them out into the Universe is important. Positive thoughts and feelings will reap positive results.

When you feel hungry because you are upset are you really hungry? Or is there a void that you are trying to fill that is really emotional in nature?

To have victory over pain and suffering you have to wake up and see what is really going on in your life. Eating to fill an emotional void is "The American Dream" gone bad. We keep ourselves so busy running from the gym to work, to school, and lessons for our children that there is no time for personal reflection and time with God. With two cars in the driveway, huge mortgages and televisions in every room, this lifestyle creates a disassociation with yourself. We stop feeling often eating robotically in front of the television set without sitting down as a family to talk. We will do anything we can to prevent ourselves from feeling pain. Avoiding pain is resistance and creates suffering. Blaming others further reduces us by giving away our power and making us irresponsible.

Trust your guidance. Listen to your body. It will never lie to you. When you wonder if you should do something and you feel uncomfortable in your body, the answer is negative. If you have a question about something and get an uplifting feeling then the answer is positive. Practice with questions that you already know the answers to as a double blind study. Ask what your name is and give the wrong answer. See how this feels in your body. Your angels and guides would never give you guidance to hurt someone else or yourself. If you are getting this type of information it is not from the highest of high. You need your energy cleared. Ask to connect with your high self and hear the voice of God and your angels only.

There have been many books written on the subject of changing your thoughts and changing your world. Wayne Dyer has several good books on the subject. Cleaning up your conscious mind is a step in the right direction. When you become the guardian of your conscious mind your unconscious gets cleaned up in the process. Be protective of your mind. Watch what negative programming you are exposed to. Since 98% of our thoughts are unconscious we are unaware of the self-defeating programs and limiting beliefs that are under the surface. When you hear the phrases that you say about yourself when no one is watching they give you a clue as to what is under the surface. When you say things like, "How could I be so stupid?", "What an idiot I am!" or "I can't do that." you are creating and reinforcing self-defeating programming.

Watching programs with murder and other negativity is not positive for your subconscious mind either. The news seldom is filled with sunshine and rainbows. Why allow that to enter your unconscious mind?

When you are positive your health will improve, you will attract positive situations and outcomes into your life. Notice the parking space available right in front of the grocery store.

Be grateful. When good things happen say thank you. When you appreciate the good in your life and are grateful more good will flow to you. It is a natural state of being open and receptive. When you are ungrateful you are closed to what God can offer you. Say a prayer of gratitude for your health, your family and your job. If you don't have a job say thank you for the right and perfect job God is sending you. When you say thank you to God for something, it is already done. You have to ask, and immediately say thank you. It may not come in your timing, but it will come in God's. The thing you need to remember is that when your prayers are answered they are for the good of all, not just you. Some things take a little longer to orchestrate. Have faith and trust.

Surround yourself with positive people. Write down your goals and what you want to accomplish. The written word is more powerful than the spoken word. Create victory in your life by writing positive creating statements each day. I call this PCS. Writing these creating statements each morning before you begin your day sets the tone for the unfoldment of good for the day.

Our words and thoughts are amazingly powerful. Write it down and it will be done. While writing this book I used these each morning to create a powerful healing work that would help others. I also used these statements to bring people to my estate sales. I had a record number of people attend and made thousands of dollars with only two days of advertising. When you create win-win statements you will be victorious. We are not alone in this world. When we help others we help ourselves.

Use affirmations immediately upon awakening and when you can put your mind in neutral. Affirmations need to be stated in a positive manner and as simply as possible. Sometimes we are unconscious when we are driving. We find ourselves at our destination and don't even remember getting there. We are in our unconscious state then. Sometimes performing a task that we have done thousands of times before like shaving in front of the mirror, showering or peeling vegetables in the kitchen are done in a state of unconsciousness. I like to call it being in neutral. It is that place where the mind has been disengaged. This is a really good time to use affirmations because they enter your unconscious mind. Posting a note on the mirror in the bathroom is a great idea. Each time you stand in front of the mirror and put on your make-up or shave you are reminded of your affirmation.

Remember those who trigger you and cause you to have emotional reactions are not the cause. The issue is with you. As angry as this statement might make you, as it did me, it is true. When you have a reaction you are the one with the issue. When you point your finger at another, remember there are four pointing back at you. Honor those that are your biggest teachers. Sometimes they are perceived as enemies. Those people are your biggest teachers and like a huge spiritual two-x-four across the head. They are a big catalyst for change. We usually have our biggest growth while dealing with someone who really seems to be a pain in our behind.

Letting go of the outcome and allowing things to unfold naturally increases ease and ends suffering in your life. Being able to let go and "let God" will create victory for you. When you try to control the outcome and push for results or completion, you get in the way. We sometimes create more issues than we would if we took our hands off the rudder and let God take charge. We think we are causing all the events in our lives to unfold when they really happen automatically.

Everything that happens in your life occurs for a reason. You may not be aware of the reason at the time, but you can be sure it is for your soul's growth. Whoever shows up in your life is the one; if only for a time. No one is a mistake. Nothing you do is a mistake. All these events are lessons in your life. Somewhere in the lesson there is a silver lining. All you have to do is look for it. Be victorious instead of feeling like a victim. Once something ends it is over. You can be sure that when something ends that it is for your highest and best good. Your soul grew from the experience. People change. You have changed. That is what we are here to do.

As you grow and expand experiences will come your way that *feel* similar to something from the past. Be open to new experiences and do not judge them by someone else's perceptions and filters or from your own past. Go slowly without fear. Rather than turning and running in the other direction. Remember if you do not step out into the void of the unknown and risk being vulnerable again, you are shutting yourself off from wondrous opportunities that may be offered.

When we change ourselves we change the world. Instead of complaining about others and what they are doing to you, take responsibility for you and be the change. Create victory in your life. The only one we have the power to change is ourselves. Do not waste your energy trying to change another. This is codependent and egotistical. Who do you think you are that you have the power to change anyone else? Nothing will be the same in the presence of awareness.

The world and our lives are our classroom. To have victory in your life is to realize that everyone in your life is your teacher, even and especially your children. We are all in this together learning from one another. Some days you may be the teacher and other days I might be the teacher. But in the end we all walk on the path of life together. If you look carefully we are all holding hands. Even in the dark we all find our way.

To your personal victory!

Vibration: 900

Life Force: 100%

Ego: 0%

ACKNOWLEDGMENTS

To my daughter, Ana, for allowing me to complete this book in my own timing, thank you. I love and appreciate you just the way you are. You have been my light during the times of darkness and an amazing teacher for me. You are one beautiful young lady. Never forget your purpose. Know that being different is not a bad thing but a wondrous gift. So many would give anything to be who you are.

Thank you to my sons, Adam, and Matthew, for your love, support and assistance with some of the time line reconstruction. I thank you for your acceptance and love of me and of my efforts to write about some of the most challenging times in our lives. Thank you for sharing your experiences with me and reliving the past for this book. I love you both.

To Andrea, I am so glad you decided to join our clan. You are perfect for Matthew. I love you. You have helped me to see how to be like a child again. Thank you for this gift. To Clara, you are such a wonderful addition to our family. I love and appreciate you. The gift that you have been to Adam and our family is appreciated. To both you beautiful, loving women, thank you.

To my mother and father for giving me the courage to face another day. I love you. I appreciate the sacrifices you both made for me. I appreciate you being there for me when I needed you, Mom, and all the help you have given me for my many moves.

I have tremendous gratitude to the Ascended Masters and my teachers, guides and angels on the other side who never steer me wrong. I love and appreciate your guidance. You have helped me to have a deeper understanding of love and acceptance. To Susan Cowan and John Armbruster, thank you for your assistance and love. It is nice to know I have friends in high places!

To Jane Brown, my beloved editor. It was truly an honor to work with you these past few months. I appreciate the long and tireless hours you put in. Your acceptance of my quirks and me is appreciated. You made it all so easy. I am so glad that you accepted when I asked. I could not have found a better person to work with. I love you.

To all of my wonderful and dedicated teachers in this lifetime. Thank you for the journey. It was tough but it did not kill me. It was long, but you made it interesting.

ODYSSEY - VICTIM TO VICTORY

To William Dargin, for your spiritual support and friendship and offering me the spiritual two x four to me so sweetly. Paybacks are not really hell. I appreciate you loving me enough to break my driver.

To Alan Barr, my friend and also family member, thank you for your undying love and support of my work and me. I appreciate your friendship and you most of all. Thank you for your beautiful work on the photographs for this book.

Thanks also to Diana Davis and Joanne Butler my sisters in SRT. I am so glad to have you both in my life. The light that you two generate is amazing. Gomati and Vasistha, I love you and I thank you for your guidance and friendship over the past several years. Panache and Jan Desai I thank you for your contribution to my life I love you both. Linda Porter and Patrick Bishop, I thank you for your love and support.

To all my clients, I am grateful to you. I wish you love and causeless joy.

To Karma, Percy, Lydia and Chloe, I'm back! Thank you for your patience and unconditional love. To Isabella and Toby for understanding the process, we continue to love and miss you.

RESOURCES

WORKSHOPS

Jennifer facilitates three day workshops for soul clearing and deep emotional integration. These workshops are transformational and uplifting. They offer opportunities to experience feelings fully in safety. Participants learn how to experience emotions and work with their feelings as they move into higher states of consciousness and empowerment. Training is provided that offers life-changing resources through experiential group work. Participants return to their world empowered with increased awareness of all that is. Contact Jennifer through www.JenniferElizabethMasters.com

PERSONAL SESSIONS

Getting to know your Inner Radiance is what sessions with Jennifer are all about. Clearing negativity, patterns and limiting beliefs immediately raise your vibration and allow increased mental clarity and inner peace. Telephone sessions are available Tuesday through Thursday from 9:00 a.m. - 3:00 p.m. Contact Jennifer through her website.

PRACTITIONER CERTIFICATION

Jennifer provides two certification classes each year. These classes are designed for professional healers and therapists.

www.JenniferElizabethMasters.com	Jennifer's website
www.Ascendingtooneness.com	Ascension Meditation
www.Innersourcetools.com	Meditation Tools For Business People
www.Panachedesai.com	Panache Desai

SUGGESTED READING

First Thunder	MSI
Excuses Begone	Wayne Dyer
The Power Of Intention	Wayne Dyer
The Spontaneous Healing of Belief	Greg Braden
The God Code	Greg Braden
The Energy Connection	Joyce Rennolds
If The Buddha Dated	Charlotte Kasl
If The Buddha Married	Charlotte Kasl
The Four Agreements	Don Miguel Ruiz
The Akashic Records	Ernesto Ortiz
Messages From Water	Dr. Masuro Emoto

I have used the book below for the last 20 years. It has helped me to become victorious!

Heal Your Life	Louise Hay

ABOUT THE AUTHOR

Jennifer was born in Toronto, Ontario. She worked as a flight attendant with Air Canada where she discovered a love of travel. She has lived in Montreal, London, England, Gaithersburg, Maryland and Atlanta, Georgia.

Jennifer became a certified hypnotherapist in 1998. In 2001 she started a landscaping company, For Heaven Scapes, Ltd. She has owned and operated this company since that time.

Through her own journey of self-discovery she found a profound desire to help people evolve and grow. This became her life purpose in 2007. Jennifer works with clients that are committed to growing spiritually. She uses Spiritual Response Therapy and Hypnotherapy as well as a Soul Clearing that she has developed since her trip to Bali, Indonesia.

Jennifer is a Certified Life Coach, hypnotherapist, Spiritual Response Therapy practitioner and an ordained minister. She also works with the Ascended Masters and does Akashic Records consultations by appointment.

Send Inquiries to:

Jennifer Elizabeth Masters
12850 Highway 9 North
Alpharetta, Georgia 30004

www.selfloveguru.com